Birding
Rocky Mountain National Park

Birding

Rocky Mountain
National Park

Scott Roederer

Johnson Books: Boulder

Spring Creek Press: Estes Park

Published by Johnson Books, a division of Johnson Publishing Company, 1880 South 57th Court, Boulder, Colorado 80301. E-mail: books@jpcolorado.com

9 8 7 6 5 4 3 2 1

Cover design by Debra B. Topping
Cover painting "Blues in the Rockies" and text illustrations by Scott Rashid

Library of Congress Cataloging-in-Publication Data
Roederer, Scott.
    Birding Rocky Mountain National Park / Scott L. Roederer.
        p. cm.
Includes bibliographical references (p.   ).
    ISBN 1-55566-318-4 (alk. paper)
    1. Bird watching—Colorado—Rocky Mountain National
Park—Guidebooks. 2. Rocky Mountain National Park
(Colo.)—Guidebooks. 1. Title.
    QL684.C6 R64 2002
    598'.07'23478869—dc21

2002000660

Printed in the United States by
Johnson Printing
1880 South 57th Court
Boulder, Colorado 80301

To all the birders of Rocky Mountain National Park who have gone before me, especially Allegra Collister, Ted and Lois Matthews, Warner and Ruth Reeser, Dr. Walter Collins, Dr. Richard Beidleman, and Dr. Ronald Ryder.

Contents

Acknowledgments

MANY PEOPLE HAVE helped with this book. My wife, Julie, has been at my side on many birding trips, providing her eagle eyes, sit-down-and-wait patience, and the carrying capacity for more field guides.

Members of the Estes Park Bird Club, including Susan Ward, Jerry Zaninelli, Dick Coe, Jim Thompson, and others, have given generously of their immeasurable knowledge of birds and have kept me posted on the new sightings. Warner and Ruth Reeser have answered innumerable questions and given freely of what more than twenty-five years of local birding experience can provide.

Special thanks to Scott Rashid for sharing his expertise on birding the YMCA grounds and for his great illustrations on the cover and throughout this book.

Staff members at RMNP have helped with data and ideas. They include Jeff Connor and Jeff Maugans, both of whom gave generously of their time and expertise to read my manuscript and make comments.

To all of them I give my thanks and wishes for the next new Park record.

Introduction

THERE'S NO PLACE on earth quite like Rocky Mountain National Park (RMNP). But the allure goes past the scenery. There's the wildlife, too, and the bird life is certainly an important part of that for those of us who will slam on the brakes for a Northern Goshawk while we may only slow down for an elk.

If you brake for birds, this book is written for you, in hopes that I can help you make the most of your birding time in RMNP and the surrounding area. Rocky itself is entirely a mountainous habitat, extending above timberline, and the birds you've probably come to see are those endemic to the high country of aspen, pine, spruce, and tundra.

Specialty species for those visiting Rocky Mountain National Park include **White-tailed Ptarmigan, Blue Grouse, Gray Jay, Clark's Nutcracker, Williamson's Sapsucker, Three-toed Woodpecker, Mountain Chickadee, Pygmy Nuthatch, American Dipper, Western Tanager, Pine Grosbeak, Red Crossbill, Townsend's Solitaire, Wilson's, MacGillivray's,** and **Virginia's warblers, Brown-capped Rosy Finch, Black Swift, Northern Pygmy-Owl,** and others.

Covering elevations from 7,700 feet to 14,255 feet and an area of 264,354 acres, Rocky contains three life zones: montane, subalpine, and alpine. Numerous trails and the highest contiguous paved roadway in the United States, Trail Ridge Road, give unequaled access to the land and its birds. In short, there's no better, more accessible area I know of to find the birds of the Rocky Mountains. In 2000 Rocky Mountain National Park was added to the national list of Important Bird Areas. IBA designation recognizes the vital role of RMNP in the perpetuation of bird species.

THIS IS AN INTIMATE, detailed guide to the best places to find birds in Rocky Mountain National Park. I wrote it as if I were there with you as your birding guide, and there are specific directions that will take you just where you need to go to find birds. My hope is that those directions will require little pondering on your part as to what they mean, but taking you through the woods on paper is a challenge. Please remember that fact if you're ever ready to throw the book into the bushes, and let me know how to improve those directions. I've used landmarks that I think will not change over the years, but they won't be perfect. Trees fall, streams change course. Even parking lots migrate!

For the automobile part of finding birds, I've given mileages. **Look for boldface instructions to reset your trip odometer to zero.** Most of the sites described are near a road, incidentally, but almost all require some walking or hiking.

When I mention a specific species of bird, such as **White-tailed Ptarmigan**, it will be given in boldface to help you pick it out when you're scanning the pages or working from the index.

Organization of the Book

In the first two sections of the book, I describe the best birding spots in Rocky and talk about the species you may see there. All the major locales discussed are on the east side of Rocky Mountain National Park. The west side of the Park is not as accessible, although there is good birding at turnouts and trails along the twenty miles of Trail Ridge Road from Milner Pass to the Grand Lake Entrance Station. I cover those sites in Chapter 4.

On the west side you're not likely to find different birds from those on the east side. The converse is not true. Unusual migrants are definitely more likely on the east side, and there is more diversity of habitat. If you bird the west side, you'll find many birds, but there isn't a single species on our specialties list that you *need* to go there to see. The majority of people come first to the east side and spend most of their time there. I wrote the book with this in mind.

The third section covers birding areas in the mountain park in which Estes Park is located. Mountain parks are high-elevation basins or valleys with significant grasslands. Surrounded by mountains, they often act as migrant traps and funnels for returning breeding birds. The Estes Valley, as locals call our mountain park, is a particularly exciting area to bird in the spring and fall. In this section you'll find out where the local birders hang out in spring, a hot spot with over 220 species recorded, many of them rare to Colorado.

In the fourth section, I've added an important chapter, one on trip planning. Too many people arrive in Rocky in July unprepared for snow on Trail Ridge Road. Too many people spend time watching for rattlesnakes when they should be watching for the next new bird. (I've never seen a rattler in the Park; it's too high in elevation.) I'll set you straight on all that. Also in this section is a species-by-species guide to the birds of Rocky Mountain National Park. Using the resources of Park records, local birders, and my own experience, I've tried to give you the best shot at finding the birds you want most to see.

You'll also find two appendices, one with the checklist of birds for RMNP and the other with a checklist for that Estes Valley hot spot I mentioned earlier. A bibliography of helpful publications follows.

The Seasons of Rocky Mountain National Park

Some people like to say there are only two seasons up here, winter and July. Warm-blooded people say the two seasons are winter and the Fourth of July. Of course, it has snowed in Estes Park on the Fourth of July…

I hate bird books and checklists that don't define seasons. When it's spring in Georgia and the peach trees are in bloom, we're still in our winter parkas. So much depends on latitude and elevation that seasonal terms must be specifically identified, and I'll do that in the next few paragraphs. For more information on the weather and the best time to come for birds, see Chapter 11.

When I speak of spring in the text, I'll generally be referring to the period of April 1 to June 1. Some birds, such as **Mountain Bluebirds**, arrive each year the first week in March but that month cannot be described as "spring." Less hardy (or more sensible) mountain breeders arrive in April and May. Shorebirds stop at area lakes in April. The peak of warbler migration, including many vagrants, is generally the third week of May.

Weather in April and May is very erratic. Average highs in April are in the low fifties, in May the low sixties. Lows average mid-twenties in April and mid-thirties in May. What those averages really mean is that we have some very nice days and some very nasty, snowy days.

Summer is June 1 through September 1 in terms of this book. By June 1, the resident mountain birds have generally reestablished themselves in habitat at their preferred breeding elevation, and the summer-only birds, such as **Western Tanagers**, have returned. Average highs are in the seventies with lows in the mid-forties. A typical summer day sees blue skies and sunshine in the morning with an afternoon thunderstorm always possible.

The migrant birders have returned, too, so most of the text of this book is geared toward the summer season. As a birder, that's when you'll want to be here. For more specific details on what to expect for birding through the summer months, see Chapter 11.

We start looking for fall migrants, such as **Townsend's Warbler**, as early as mid-August, but fall covers the period of September 1 through November 1. Summer-only species disperse from their nesting territories in early August and begin to leave by late August. By November 1, most of the migration of land birds is over. In fall, the weather is generally clear and the air crisp. Highs are in the seventies and sixties, lows in the thirties. It's a great time to visit RMNP, even though every day more birds are heading south or moving down in elevation.

In terms of birding and weather, winter *is* long, stretching from November 1 to April 1. During this time, we generally have only our resident mountain birds—chickadees, nuthatches, jays, and others. A few winter visitors, such as **Gray-crowned** and **Black rosy finches** and **Northern Shrikes**, join the residents. Christmas Bird Counts usually come in with around forty-five to fifty species, with only 107 or so on the cumulative list from over sixty counts. As you might expect, the weather is cold and windy. January is the coldest month with average highs in the high thirties and lows in the teens.

In a nutshell, here are the seasonal terms used in the text and checklists. Remember, these are the seasons of Rocky's birdlife and sometimes have little to do with weather:

- spring—April 1 to June 1
- summer—June 1 to September 1
- fall—September 1 to November 1
- winter—November 1 to April 1

The Lay of the Land

Rocky Mountain National Park rises from 7,700 feet in elevation on its eastern boundary to 14,255 feet at the top of Longs Peak. Although it's all mountainous country, there are remarkable differences in the habitats you'll find, differences the birds certainly understand and that you should, too, if you want to find them.

The lowest elevations of Rocky are largely open ponderosa-pine forests of the montane zone, interspersed with grasslands, meadows, and some deciduous growth, including aspens and balsam poplars. Ponderosa forests are interspersed with firs, spruces, and other pines as you move higher in the montane zone. At about 9,000 feet, Douglas firs, lodgepole and limber pines, and Englemann spruce become dominant as you enter the subalpine zone. Here you'll find denser forests, making access sometimes difficult except by road or trail. Riparian willows, aspen groves, and the occasional mountain meadow provide habitat diversity. The subalpine forests thin as you move toward timberline at 11,400 feet, where the krummholz and tundra of the alpine areas of the park begin.

Entering at the Beaver Meadows Entrance to RMNP and traveling west on Trail Ridge Road, you'll pass through the three life zones in a matter of forty-five minutes. Following Trail Ridge Road over the mountains takes you to the west side of the park, where the base elevation is about 8,700 feet.

It's difficult for a newcomer to know where to stop for birds in the immensity of Rocky Mountain National Park. Indeed, many areas you'll walk through may seem devoid of bird life. Tramping through a lodgepole forest, for instance, can often be about as exciting as downtown Denver for birds. Here are some general hints to help you know where to look for birds beyond the areas I'll mention later in the book.

Birdy Areas

The key habitat characteristic to seek out, in Rocky and anywhere you bird, is diversity. You'll find more birds in areas where habitats are intermixed— the edge of a meadow, along a stream, where ponderosa pines mix with aspen. Spotting these habitats in the mountains is no different from finding them at home, except they may not stand out quite so much. Here are a few things to watch for:

• Look for aspen groves. They represent a diverse habitat wherever they occur. Aspen is a pioneer plant, often growing where a fire has burned pines and spruces. Aspen also often indicate wet ground, too wet for evergreens, but just right for **Blue Grouse.** Aspen of eight or nine inches in diameter and larger provide nesting cavities for an amazing variety of birds.

• Follow streams, especially at lower elevations. Most streams in the area have been worked by beaver at one time or another. The damming of a stream spreads it out, destroying the trees that the beaver haven't already downed. After the beaver move on and the dams wash out, willows grow and meadows are created. As you drive the Bear Lake Road along Glacier Creek, you'll see the riparian willows and grassy areas left for you and for the **Wilson's Warblers** by beavers.

• Check out large areas of standing dead trees. Whether caused by insect or fire damage, these areas attract woodpeckers, as you know, and they also create an opening for sunlight to nourish lower-story shrubs and grasses attractive to other species. **Three-toed Woodpeckers,** in particular, are attracted to these areas.

A good topo map can help to improve your planning. Look for non-green areas. Most of the time, they indicate meadows. I recommend the National Geographic/Trails Illustrated map of Rocky Mountain National Park, available at bookstores and outdoor shops in Estes Park. It's not as detailed as the quads you could buy, but then you won't have to carry around sixteen maps. Waterproof, tear-proof, and shaded to help you find the meadows—you can't beat it. You should also carry a compass, not only to help with maps but to follow the directions in this book more easily.

The Birds of Rocky

I won't bore you with a written-out version of a checklist. Instead, this section concentrates on *mountain* birds, those closely associated with the elevations and habitats found in the Park in summer. If you're headed for Rocky to bird, these are probably the birds you've got on your wish list.

There are many birds you can count on seeing in their proper habitat: **Broad-tailed Hummingbirds** where wildflowers are in bloom, **Steller's Jays** and **Pygmy Nuthatches** in the ponderosa forests, **Clark's Nutcrackers** in cone-bearing pines, **American Pipits** on the tundra, **Red-naped Sapsuckers** and **Warbling Vireos** in aspen groves, **Mountain Chickadees** and **Yellow-rumped Warblers** in the spruce/fir forests, **Mountain Bluebirds** in meadows, **American Dippers** along streams, and **Dark-eyed Juncos** nearly everywhere.

Other species require some work and maybe some luck, as well as the proper habitat. They're fairly common, but they're not present in great numbers or they're difficult to find. You should still see many of these birds in a week's worth of outings. **Dusky, Hammond's,** and **Cordilleran flycatchers** and **Western Tanagers,** in ponderosa and spruce/fir forests, **Prairie Falcons** in open areas near rock cliffs, **Wilson's** and **MacGillivray's warblers** in riparian areas, **Red Crossbills** in spruce/fir forests, and **Williamson's Sapsuckers** in aspen groves.

Other birds are not at all common. They are here only in limited numbers or in limited habitat. Some of these you can get simply by working at them or by spending a lot of time in the right kinds of places. Others may require some luck or a lot of luck. They include: **Blue Grouse** in wet meadows, **White-tailed Ptarmigans** and **Brown-capped Rosy Finches** on the tundra, **Northern Goshawks** in dense forest, **Northern Pygmy-** and **Northern Saw-whet owls** in aspen groves interspersed in pine forests, **Black Swifts** overhead in river drainages with nesting populations, **Brewer's Sparrows** in open mountain parks, and **Pine Grosbeaks** in higher-elevation forests.

Finally, there are those wonderfully maddening birds, the true rarities. Some of these are still on *my* wish list. All these birds are known to live in or visit Rocky Mountain National Park, but they are all difficult to find. It's also almost impossible to tell someone where to go for them. (More on that in Chapter 12.) Rare birds include: **Boreal Owls** in high-elevation spruce/fir forests, **Flammulated Owls** in ponderosa forests, and **Three-toed Woodpeckers** in stands of dead trees.

NOW MY SYMPATHETIC DISCLAIMER. I've birded across the country. I've got lots of books just like this one. They drive me nuts when they promise birds. I'm not doing that in this section or anywhere else. I'll do my best to lead you to some hot spots for birds, and they are the best spots I've found. If I get too enthusiastic and it sounds like I'm promising you a **Three-toed Woodpecker** in Upper Beaver Meadows, I am not. I'm only promising you that it's one of the more reliable places in the Park to find one at the time of this writing.

ONE FINAL WORD. Remember that you've come to Rocky to enjoy, to relax, to get away from the rush. Don't let your search for birds drive you to distraction. Don't let your vacation be as exhausting as your work routine.

In the years that I guided flyfishers, I realized that part of my job was to get them to relax, to get out of the productivity mode so they could once again feel the childlike wonder of wading in a stream. Every time I go birding with my wife, I relearn the value of enjoying nature, of sitting still in an aspen grove and letting a **Blue Grouse** come to us, of remembering to smell the alpine forget-me-nots, of napping next to a whispering stream. We see our share of birds, too.

And don't just do the trails and roads I've mentioned in the book. Take a hike that sounds inviting or pull over at an unmarked parking area and try your luck. If you find the next great birding spot, let me know.

With that in mind, let's talk about those places that are best for birds. We'll start with four areas I consider the best places in Rocky Mountain National Park to find a wide diversity of mountain birds. In the second section, we'll visit four other productive areas.

I wish you good weather, singing birds, and arms weary from holding up those binocs.

Birding
Rocky Mountain National Park

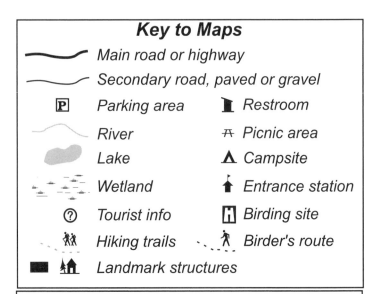

Key to Maps

⌒ Main road or highway

⌒ Secondary road, paved or gravel

P Parking area   🚻 Restroom

River   ⚘ Picnic area

Lake   ▲ Campsite

Wetland   ⬆ Entrance station

? Tourist info   🄷 Birding site

🚶🚶 Hiking trails   🚶 Birder's route

🏠 Landmark structures

Driving instructions to most birding sites within Rocky Mountain National Park start at the entrance stations.

To Reach Beaver Meadows Entrance: From the intersection of Highways 34 and 36, east of Estes Park, take Elkhorn Ave. through downtown Estes Park. Turn left on Moraine Avenue and continue to the entrance station.

To Reach the Fall River Entrance: From the intersection of Highways 34 and 36, take the Highway 34 Bypass past the Stanley Hotel and continue to the entrance station.

Directions to the other RMNP sites and locations in the Estes Valley begin at the intersection of Highways 34 and 36.

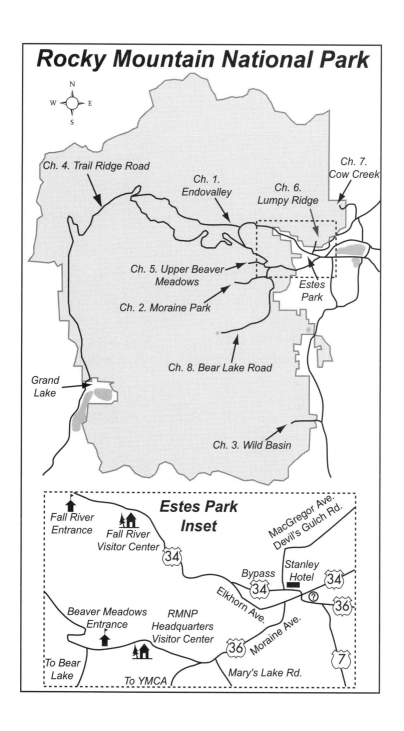

Rocky Mountain National Park

N
W—E
S

Ch. 4. Trail Ridge Road

Ch. 1. Endovalley

Ch. 6. Lumpy Ridge

Ch. 7. Cow Creek

Ch. 5. Upper Beaver Meadows

Ch. 2. Moraine Park

Estes Park

Ch. 8. Bear Lake Road

Grand Lake

Ch. 3. Wild Basin

Estes Park Inset

Fall River Entrance

Fall River Visitor Center

MacGregor Ave.
Devil's Gulch Rd.

34

Bypass
34

Stanley Hotel

34

Elkhorn Ave.

?

36

Beaver Meadows Entrance

RMNP Headquarters Visitor Center

36

Moraine Ave.

7

To Bear Lake

To YMCA

Mary's Lake Rd.

Birding the Best of Rocky

1

Endovalley

DIVERSITY IS THE KEY WORD in describing Endovalley, one of Rocky Mountain National Park's premier birding spots. Here you'll find a mature spruce and fir forest interspersed with ponderosa pine and aspen, seeps and brooks, a small lake surrounded by willows and aspen, a stream and its riparian habitat, wet and dry meadows, and a rock-strewn slope. In short, just about every mountain-bird habitat, except alpine tundra, is found in Endovalley.

In summer, Endovalley's everyday bird life includes chickadees, kinglets, nuthatches, flycatchers, vireos, woodpeckers, and solitaires, and many other mountain birds. You'll find dippers, warblers, and sparrows in streamside areas and wrens, sparrows, bluebirds, and snipe in meadows. Established aspen groves here are invaluable nesting sites. Recently Endovalley has been one of the best locations for **Three-toed Woodpeckers**, one of Rocky's specialties. They've nested within thirty feet of the road.

In addition, Endovalley is perhaps the best area in the Park for spring migrants. It's not unusual, for instance, to stumble across a **Black-crowned Night-Heron** along the stream or near the lake in May. Eastern warblers, such as **Blackburnian Warbler**, **Chestnut-sided Warbler**, **Ovenbird**, and **Northern Waterthrush**, have also been spotted in the area. Geographically, Endovalley represents a natural funnel to the high-country tundra, and birds such as **American Pipits** can be found here, waiting for the weather to allow them to continue their upward journey.

All of Endovalley is accessible from the road, making it a good starting place for those still acclimating to Rocky's high elevation and a great spot when you only have an hour or two for birding. I'll cover four areas

3

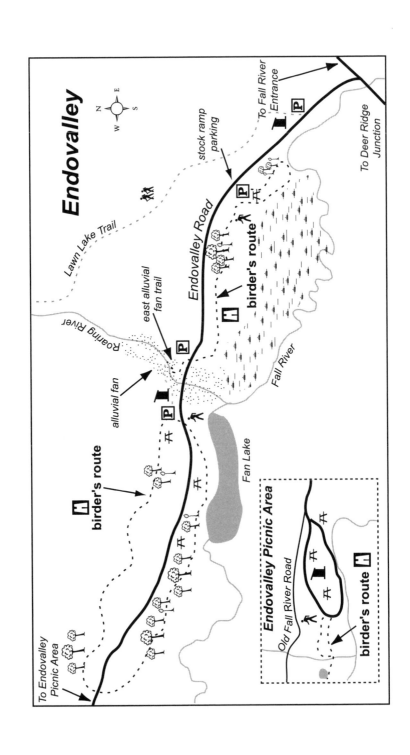

Endovalley

N E W S

Lawn Lake Trail

Roaring River

alluvial fan

east alluvial
fan trail

stock ramp
parking

P

To Fall River
Entrance

To Deer Ridge
Junction

Endovalley Road

P

Fall River

H birder's route

P

H birder's route

Fan Lake

P

To Endovalley
Picnic Area

Endovalley Picnic Area

Old Fall River Road

birder's route **H**

in this chapter—Endovalley proper, Old Fall River Road, Little Horseshoe Park, and Upper Aspenglen.

To Reach Endovalley

Enter the Park at the Fall River Entrance. **Reset your trip odometer to zero here.** Continue west to where the road curves sharply left (0.3). Note the small turnouts on both sides of the road just before the curve that provide parking for the Upper Aspenglen birding site, described later. After rounding the curve, you'll enter the open meadows of Horseshoe Park, where you may see bighorn sheep along the road.

It may be worth your while to stop at the west end of the sheep-viewing parking lot on the left side of the road (1.7) in spring and early summer to check out Sheep Lakes for waterfowl, such as **Canada Goose, Mallard, Ring-necked Duck, Green-winged, Cinnamon,** and **Blue-winged teal,** and waders, such as **Spotted Sandpiper, Killdeer,** and occasionally **White-faced Ibis.** The lakes are kettle lakes—water collected in depressions left by receding glaciers. They depend on melt water and groundwater and can be dry or nearly so in years of drought. Bighorn sheep and other mammals are attracted to them by mineral deposits they lick for nutritional value.

This vantage point over Horseshoe Park can also be good for raptors, and **Prairie** and **Peregrine falcons** have been seen here, as well as accipiters. **Red-tailed Hawks** are fairly common. You may get lucky enough to spot the uncommon **Northern Harrier** cruising over the meadows in late summer or a **Golden Eagle** overhead anytime.

After you have checked out Sheep Lakes for birds (and hopefully seen some bighorns), continue west until the road curves south. Take a right turn at the sign for Endovalley (2.1).

What You'll Find—Endovalley

Your first stop will be past the Lawn Lake trailhead, which is on the right shortly after you turn on the Endovalley Road. Park in a smaller parking lot on the left with a stock ramp (2.5), being careful not to block the ramp. **Three-toed Woodpeckers** recently nested in the aspen grove immediately west of this parking area. A year after the Three-toeds nested there, a pair nested in a tree easily visible from the east alluvial fan trail, a short distance west. Another pair nested at the west end of the Endovalley Picnic Area at the end of the road that same year.

Even so, **Three-toed Woodpeckers** are not very reliable from year to year in terms of location. A walk through the aspen grove west of the stock ramp parking lot will at least help show you the typical nesting habitat they prefer. During breeding season, the best way to locate the woodpeckers is to check likely aspen stands or scattered individual aspen trees for active nests. Nesting season is from about May 15 through July 15. Inclement spring weather can set both of those dates back by two to three weeks.

Most of the **Three-toed Woodpecker** nests I've seen have been in aspen, from seven to thirty feet above the ground. Sometimes the nest is in a small grove of aspen. Just as often, it's in a tree in a scattered group of aspen within a pine or spruce forest. The aspen tree is typically alive and well, but dead or dying trees are sometimes used. The host tree needs to be a minimum of about eight or nine inches in diameter.

A key habitat requirement is ready access to dead or dying pines and spruces. There is apparently a short period, perhaps two or three years after they die, when these trees provide the best forage for the woodies. This may account for the unreliability of nesting sites from year to year. Favorite nearby feeding trees are often heavily debarked by a nesting pair.

Freshly excavated nests have bright wood around the entrance hole, rather than weathered, gray wood, and in aspens show the traffic underneath the hole where the birds' tail feathers have worn off the white on the bark, leaving it cleaner and greener. This "tail scrub" beneath the hole is more extensive than it is with the sapsuckers that nest in the same areas. Although I don't have vast experience with Three-toed nests, many I've found have a series of test drillings near the final entrance hole.

When you find an active nest, sit down fifty or sixty feet away and watch. Use a scope for close-up views. Once a nest site becomes known, incidentally, it gets a lot of attention. Be sure not to disturb the nest of these birds by remaining in an area too long or observing at too close a

Three-toed Woodpecker

distance. Trying to look in the nest or even approaching it too closely can result in abandonment. In the past, the Park has had to close areas near nests because of aggressive birders. These birds are uncommon in RMNP. Protect them—and the interests of other birders—by being careful not to disturb their nesting and by being careful whom you tell! One more note on **Three-toed Woodpeckers**. In the field, the subspecies in this area (*dorsalis*) can be mistaken for a scruffy **Hairy Woodpecker**. Don't miss an opportunity for a lifer by assuming you've seen a Hairy.

FROM THE STOCK-RAMP PARKING LOT, follow a path leading up the rise to the east. Continue over the hill and down toward Fall River. As you near the stream, find a small aspen grove on the left and check the trees for active nest holes. I call this the Aspen Apartments, and it often houses an amazing variety of birds in June and July. During a recent breeding season, one tree had **Tree Swallows**, **Violet-green Swallows**, **Mountain Bluebirds**, and **Red-naped Sapsuckers** all nesting in it at the same time! **House Wrens** also use these trees, as well as **Northern Flickers** (**Red-shafted**) and **European Starlings**. This is one of the few areas you'll find starlings in the Park.

Continue east along the river about fifty yards and check out the riparian willows across the stream. **Wilson's Warblers** are found here; this is just about the lowest nesting elevation for them. You may also wish to cross the road from here and explore the forest edge in the area near the Lawn Lake trailhead. **Pygmy Nuthatches** and **Williamson's** and **Red-naped sapsuckers** frequent this area, and **Western Tanagers** have nested near the parking area. This is also a good place to listen on spring and early summer evenings for **Northern Saw-whet Owls**. They are heard regularly near the Lawn Lake trailhead.

Bird the willows to the south, as you work your way back toward your car. **Song**, **White-crowned**, and **Lincoln's sparrows** can be found here. **Wilson's Warblers** are found near wet areas, and you should listen for the "ha, ha, ha—he, he, he" of a **MacGillivray's Warbler**. **Broad-tailed Hummingbirds** are common. The males choose an exposed branch from which to defend their territory and like to use the open areas near the willows for breeding displays. Listen for the metallic trill of their wings in flight. **Vesper Sparrows** are sometimes heard in this area, but they're usually on the other side of the stream in drier grasslands.

There are often two or more families of **Black-billed Magpies** in this area, numbering up to a dozen birds. They nest in the bulky bundles of sticks you may see in the willows and alders throughout the area. Magpies nest relatively early, and by the end of June, the short-tailed immatures can put on quite a noisy show.

Once you work your way back to the parking area, continue walking west through the aspen grove where the Three-toeds nested. This area usually has two or three pairs of nesting **Red-naped Sapsuckers**, along with good opportunities to hear and see **Lincoln's Sparrows** in the wetter meadows to the south. **Warbling Vireos** are often found in the aspen. **Hairy Woodpeckers** sometimes nest here, also. Continue through the aspen, bearing gradually to your right, until you reach the road, where you'll see a parking area on the other side. Before crossing the road, you may want to work the area of dead trees south of the road, sampling its bird life while trying to keep your feet dry.

The trees were killed as a result of the Lawn Lake flood. In the early morning hours of a summer day in 1982, the aging man-made dam at Lawn Lake failed, sending an immense cascade of water down the narrow canyon of Roaring River to the north of where you're standing. The scarred trough that resulted is clearly visible here and from Trail Ridge Road. The flood water carried huge boulders and other debris down the mountainside as it came, creating the alluvial fan you'll be walking through. The fan blocked the flow of Fall River, forming Fan Lake. The lake was more picturesque before the Park Service lowered its level in 1996 to prevent a failure of the "dam" created by the alluvial fan.

To give you an idea of the immensity of the flood, consider that Horseshoe Park, through which you traveled to get to Endovalley, was generally underwater. Flood waters as deep as six feet filled downtown Estes Park that day. Three people lost their lives in the flood, and the property damage was in the millions.

The alluvial fan, with its boulders and dead trees, is good bird habitat. Swallows, nuthatches, and woodpeckers (especially **Northern Flickers**) use the dead trees for foraging and nesting, and **Mountain Bluebirds** often nest here. A **Red-headed Woodpecker** is seen in the area almost every spring. **Common Snipe** like the wet areas. Bird this area, if you wish, letting the birds determine your route, and return to the road.

CROSS THE ROAD and walk to the west end of the parking area. Bird the east alluvial fan trail which starts from there. All of this area is excellent for birds. Watch on the left in the willows for **MacGillivray's Warbler**. They nest here and in the area north of the trail. Stop along the trail for views to the right into this excellent habitat. **Cassin's Finches** may occur, as well as **Western Wood-Pewees**, **Ruby-crowned Kinglets**, **Townsend's Solitaires**, and other mountain birds. **Three-toed Woodpeckers** have nested in the area. **Western Tanagers** make regular appearances, and one June I was surprised by an **Ash-throated Flycatcher**.

The trail continues to a bridge over the stream, where you may find an **American Dipper**. Just sit down beside the stream, enjoy the scenery, and wait. An ouzel will likely be along in a few minutes. Watch for it to come zipping along the stream, close to the water—dippers don't fly *over* bridges. This stream is pretty small to support dippers, but its proximity to the bigger Fall River and the availability of nesting sites among the rocks exposed by the flood makes it a good place to see one. Dippers like whitewater and rocks in their home water, so this is excellent habitat for them. Many people see their life bird here.

Amid the boulders in the alluvial fan, you will likely find, appropriately, a **Rock Wren**, a bird that's making a bit of a comeback in the Estes Valley and Rocky Mountain National Park but is still considered uncommon. They are more numerous across the stream, on the west side of the alluvial fan.

AT THIS POINT, return to your car and drive west over the alluvial fan. Park at the lot on the right side of the road just west of the fan (2.9). The area on both sides of the road west of the parking lot is where you should plan to spend a good share of your time. As you'll see, there is a great deal of different habitat in the space of about a half mile.

Bird the picnic area near the parking lot. **Black-billed Magpies** and **Steller's Jays** like to make an appearance here, in search of leftovers, and a **Clark's Nutcracker** or two will often keep the watch, too. (Remember that feeding wildlife is illegal.) **Pygmy, White-breasted,** and **Red-breasted nuthatches, Western Wood-Pewees,** and **Mountain Chickadees** can also be found. **Red-naped Sapsuckers** sometimes nest in the aspens in the middle of the parking circle.

Cross the road and walk among the aspen groves and the willows near the lake as you work your way west. **House Wrens** are common here, and you'll see **Tree** and **Violet-green swallows.** If you missed the **Song, White-crowned,** or **Lincoln's sparrows** mentioned earlier, bird the meadows and willows near the lake for them. **Vesper Sparrows** are also possible in the drier grasslands, as are **Brewer's Blackbirds. Broad-tailed Hummingbirds** frequent this area once the flowers bloom.

On Fan Lake, you will likely find a variety of waterfowl in April and May. By June, all that's left may be **Mallards** and **Ring-necked Ducks,** but **Blue-winged, Green-winged,** and **Cinnamon teal** are possible. The ubiquitous **Canada Goose** has recently started hanging out here and is now a nester some years. **Spotted Sandpipers** are often present on the sandy eastern beach and where the stream enters the lake, and **Killdeer** are here some years. Rarely you'll find a **Great Blue Heron** or **California Gull** in summer. The gulls favor mountain lakes and are often found on Lake Estes and Grand Lake/Shadow Mountain Reservoir in summer. Fan Lake is a bit small for their liking, but you may get lucky.

Throughout your bird walk in this area, check out any woodpecker sounds and be on the lookout for active nest cavities. **Three-toed Woodpeckers** have been spotted several times a little farther west on the north side of the road and also closer to the alluvial fan, again on the north side. A **Williamson's Sapsucker** pair has nested in aspen trees along the road, and they are present nearly every year someplace in the area.

If you continue west, you'll eventually come to an extensive willow carr on the left. **Wilson's Warblers** may be found here, along with the wetland sparrows. A **Belted Kingfisher** sometimes works the beaver ponds. **Red-winged Blackbirds** may be seen here, too, as they can throughout the areas you've just walked, and occasionally **Yellow-headed Blackbirds** have wandered here in spring.

Work your way west as far as you wish; I usually stop when I get near the rock wall of an obvious road cut on Endovalley Road, a half-mile by car from where you're parked. Then cross the road to the north side, walking uphill as far as you wish, and work your way back to your car along the hillside. Let the birds show you where to go through this area rich in diverse plant life. It's an especially good area for **Hammond's Flycatchers** and a good place to see **Western Tanagers**, but that species is never predictable. **Warbling Vireos** can be heard, if not seen, especially in aspens intermixed with evergreens. **Williamson's** and **Red-naped sapsuckers**, **Hairy Woodpeckers**, and **Northern Flickers** nest in the area. Check out any fresh nest holes for **Three-toed Woodpeckers**, especially farther uphill in aspens near the stands of dead trees.

AFTER RETURNING TO your car, drive west to the end of Endovalley (4.0) where there's a picnic area frequented by quite tame **Steller's Jays**, **Mountain Chickadees**, occasional **Clark's Nutcrackers**, and the infrequent **Gray Jay** (winter, spring, and fall). Park at any spot and walk the loop road. In the spring and early summer, this is a reliable area for **Golden-crowned Kinglets**. **Ruby-crowned Kinglets** are common all summer. Both are best found in May and early June when they're singing. Without their calls to guide you, they're nearly impossible to locate; even when they are singing, they can be tough. You'll find them in the tall spruces and firs, although you can occasionally spot them lower as they forage near or on the ground.

While you're watching for kinglets in those tall trees, check for the uncommon **Pine Grosbeak**, which can be seen sitting or foraging near the tree tops. **Red Crossbills** sometimes do a fly-over, so be alert for their "tu-tu" calls.

For many years, the picnic area has been the best place to find a **Fox Sparrow** (*schistacea* subspecies). They typically nest in the willows near the entrance to the picnic ground. Begin looking and listening at the start of the one-way loop and work your way along the road east to the beginning of the dirt road up Fall River Pass. Best located during nesting season (mid-June to mid-July) when the male is singing from a perch, they are generally found on or near the ground in the willows along the road. This is a popular area for birders, and you should be careful not to disturb the sparrows. Stay on the road; don't pursue them into the willows.

Many people get their **MacGillivray's Warbler** while looking for the **Fox Sparrow**. The warblers are found on both sides of the road in this same area, as well as farther south in the willows along the picnic-ground road. **Wilson's Warblers** are also found in this habitat.

As you bird the picnic area, you'll find a gated dirt road at the west end. Walk along it for a short distance, passing a well house on the right and crossing a wooden bridge over a small side stream, to a lovely bog pond where **Wilson's Warblers** (May and early June), **Warbling Vireos**, and **Song Sparrows** may be found. **Golden-crowned Kinglets** are often easier to spot here than in the picnic area. During spring migration in May and early June, **Northern Waterthrushes** have been found here, along with even rarer eastern warblers, such as **Ovenbird** and **Blackburnian**. The stream along the path and the pond itself can have **American Dippers**, but this pond may be dry by mid-July.

Three-toed Woodpeckers recently nested along this road, just before you cross the side stream. If you wish, you may follow an indistinct trail uphill near the well house to another outbuilding. This leads to an area of dead trees along the stream and allows access to the aspen grove up the hill, where Three-toeds have also nested. You'll find an informal trail leading east that you can follow back to the picnic area if you wish. It provides great views of Endovalley.

What You'll Find—Old Fall River Road

You can make a long day of it by starting your birding early in Endovalley, stopping for a snack or lunch at the picnic area, then turning up the one-way dirt road over Fall River Pass. Be sure your stop in the picnic area includes a restroom break. There are no restrooms until you reach the top. (A guide to the road is available at Park visitor centers and at the start of the road.)

Old Fall River Road is open from late June or early July through early September, depending on the snow pack. It was the original route up to the alpine areas of the Park, and photos of Model-Ts and Stanley Steamers between snow banks higher than the cars remind us how easy we have it today and how adventuresome drivers of old were. The nine-mile road ends at the Alpine Visitor Center on Trail Ridge Road, and you can finish your day with a sunset trip back down to Estes Park, if you like. If you have enough time, you should take a separate day and go early to see more birds and to miss the almost constant traffic on the road after 9 A.M.

When I bird the road, I roll along with windows open and stop at turnouts when I see or hear birds. Between the sounds of Fall River and the traffic noise, hearing birds can be difficult. Deadfall makes pursuing birds off-road time-consuming and arduous in many areas. I guess I'm trying to say that, in general, you should take the road for the experience and scenery more than for the birds.

The Old Fall River Road begins at the entrance to Endovalley Picnic Area. It's a winding, steep, one-lane road with lots of switchbacks, but it's perfectly safe for cars and RVs less than twenty-five feet long. Trailers are prohibited.

At the beginning of the road, reset your odometer to zero. I'll mark some good spots to watch birds, but you should stop anytime you see or hear birds of interest. Any of the many small turnouts on the road may provide you the opportunity to find that difficult higher-elevation species you've missed. **Western Tanagers**, **Red Crossbills**, **Pine Grosbeaks**, **Clark's Nutcrackers**, and **Ruby-crowned** and **Golden-crowned kinglets** tend to favor the wetter habitats and denser spruce/fir forests found along this road.

Just past the Chasm Falls Trail parking, find a small turnout on the right (1.4). There's an aspen grove on the right with an informal trail leading into it. Here I often find **Mountain Chickadees**, **Red-breasted Nuthatches**, and other regulars. Recently a **Williamson's Sapsucker** nested in the aspen. Continuing west on the road you'll come to a generally birdy section (1.8–2.7). You should stop at a couple of the turnouts in this stretch and walk the road. You may hear **Ruby-crowned Kinglets**, **Brown Creepers**, and **Warbling Vireos**. **Red Crossbills** are possible anywhere in this section, and you're likely to hear, if not see, **Hermit Thrushes**. Check the ridge line to the north for raptors, such as **Red-tailed** and **Cooper's hawks** and **Golden Eagles**. I especially recommend a turnout on the left (2.2) next to a small slough. It's the only straight-in parking spot on the road, so you should have little difficulty finding it.

Farther along the road, you'll see open meadows on the left. Park at a small turnout on the left (5.8) where a trail will take you to the eastern edge of Willow Park, about 10,400 feet in elevation. There are two other parking areas, often full at lunch time, just up the road if this one is busy. If you haven't found a **Wilson's Warbler** yet, this will likely be the spot—they nest in the scrubby willows.

You may also find **White-crowned Sparrows** here, another high-elevation bird, and **Lincoln's Sparrows**. Early in the day or later in the evening, you may find a skulking **Fox Sparrow** singing in this habitat, although the willow habitat is being overgrazed by elk here and may not be high and dense enough for them now. The surrounding spruce/fir forest is good for **Cassin's Finches**, **Yellow-rumped Warblers**, and **Ruby-crowned Kinglets**. The clearing presents an opportunity to see raptors, including a **Northern Goshawk**. Many other birds are possible, so you may want to spend some time in the meadows and along the forest edges.

Chapin Pass trailhead (6.9) provides hiking access to the tundra. **White-tailed Ptarmigan** have been seen along the trail, but more accessible ptarmigan sites are listed in Chapter 4. Farther along the road, you enter the krummholz, the stunted forest of the timberline margin. I suggest you take one of the turnouts along this stretch of the road. Look for **Cassin's Finches** and **Lincoln's** and **White-crowned sparrows**. As you continue up to the alpine tundra, expect **Horned Larks** and **American Pipits**. The area along the road appears to be suitable habitat for **White-tailed Ptarmigan** and it's only about a mile from one of the best areas in the Park to see them, Medicine Bow Curve, but we've never been able to find one here. That shouldn't keep you from getting out of the car and looking. At the least, you'll enjoy the fine views north to Wyoming. Remember that you are at high elevation. Do not overexert—it can kill you. Take your time, catch your breath, and monitor your heart rate, especially while you're becoming acclimated.

Your drive will end at 11,796 feet in the parking lot of the Alpine Visitor Center (8.9). See Chapter 4 for more information on birding on the way back to Estes Park.

Driving the Old Fall River Road is a good way to cover a lot of prime high-elevation habitat. And, of course, it's a great drive with outstanding scenery. Take your time; there's no point in hurrying. You'll really like the switchbacks!

What You'll Find—Little Horseshoe Park

Another area near Endovalley that you may want to try is Little Horseshoe Park, a small mountain park where **Williamson's Sapsuckers** and **Three-toed Woodpeckers** have been found and where **Northern Goshawks** and **Clark's Nutcrackers** are highlight species. Several other species will be found in this quiet, out-of-the-way birding spot. To reach the area, return on Endovalley Road to its intersection with the Park entrance road and turn right (south). **Reset your trip odometer to zero here.**

You'll cross the bridge over Fall River and go past a large parking lot on the left (0.3). After the road begins climbing toward Deer Ridge Junction, you'll see a paved overlook parking area on the left (0.9). Just uphill from this overlook, park in an informal turnout on the right (1.0). Cross the road and walk uphill to a gated dirt road (1.1); do not park at the gate. If you miss the first parking area, watch for a stream tumbling down on the right and park immediately beyond it (1.2). Cross the road and walk downhill from there to the gated road.

This gated dirt road leads to Little Horseshoe Park. As you walk down it, you'll cross Hidden Valley Creek and then pass through an extensive area of standing dead trees, a good place to watch for **Three-toed Woodpeckers.** Continue through a campsite and past a building used by educational groups at the end of the road and follow a path into Little Horseshoe Park. Bird your way around the edge of the meadow to the right, concentrating on the aspen groves to the south and east. As you circle the meadow, you'll find a trail in the northeast corner that you can use to return to the road, keeping left at the trail junction near where you pick up the trail.

In the aspen groves and along the edges of the meadow, watch for **Mountain Bluebirds** during nesting season. **Chipping Sparrows, House Wrens**, and **Western Wood-Pewees** are fairly common. I've also found **Williamson's Sapsuckers** most years, nesting in or near the aspens. **Pygmy, Red-breasted**, and **White-breasted nuthatches** and **Western Tanagers** can be found in the spruces and firs. **Clark's Nutcrackers** frequent the hillside to the south and fly over the meadow frequently.

I regularly see a **Northern Goshawk** in Little Horseshoe Park—it's where I send people for whom this is a target species. Only the YMCA (Chapter 9) and Cub Lake Trail (Chapter 2) have as many regular sightings of this elusive raptor. Be sharp and know your field marks, because seeing a perched goshawk is rare. With the surrounding forest and open meadow, this is ideal habitat. I've seen the birds as I work the forest margins, but I've also seen them fly from one edge to the other. If that happens to you, count yourself lucky to have had an amazingly long look at a bird that is typically seen briefly going full bore through the trees.

What You'll Find—Upper Aspenglen

Another out-of-the-way birding spot is Upper Aspenglen. As described in the directions to reach Endovalley, park at turnouts on either side of the road near the first curve, 0.3 miles west of the Fall River Entrance. Follow an indistinct path up the small valley to the west, just at the start of the curve. You'll find a meadow and an open ponderosa forest bordered by spruce and fir with a few aspen intermixed. This is diverse habitat but limited in size. You're not likely to see a lot of birds, but there are two species of interest that are fairly reliable here, at least during the nesting season.

One is **Western Tanager**, a bird that is sometimes difficult to find. They nest in the area and can be found regularly in June and early July. The other is **Cassin's Finch**, another problem bird in terms of reliable locations. Again, June through mid-July is prime time to try for one. Both species may be seen later in the year but are not found as reliably. The lower half of the meadow is generally where you'll spot both species, if they're around. They favor the ponderosas there.

Mountain Chickadees and **Red-breasted** and **Pygmy nuthatches** are fairly common. You may find **Green-tailed Towhees** in the meadows, as well as **Chipping Sparrows**. **Great Horned Owls** probably nest up this quiet valley, since I've seen one nearly every year. Recently someone reported seeing a **Sharp-shinned Hawk** chasing a Great Horned Owl here. **Townsend's Solitaires** are seen regularly. **Golden-crowned** and **Ruby-crowned kinglets** are here during nesting season. **Dusky** and **Cordilleran flycatchers**, along with the more common **Western Wood-Pewees**, hunt insects from exposed perches.

Work your way up the first meadow and continue to higher ones if the birding is good. Although there aren't as many species here as there are in other places in the Endovalley area, I think you'll be pleased by the ones you find. It's worth a stop for an hour or so, especially in early summer and especially if you've come up short on the two target species I've mentioned.

ALL-IN-ALL, Endovalley and the related areas described here are places you won't want to miss. Endovalley is a great place to start your Rocky Mountain National Park birding adventure. Visiting it more than once is definitely recommended.

2

Moraine Park

MORAINE PARK, a mountain park formed by a glacier, is one of the top birding spots in Rocky Mountain National Park. The North Lateral Moraine, a narrow ridge running east and west, and the complementary moraine on the south are the rubble piles created as the glacier pushed its way down. Dramatic geology went on to create one of the Park's most scenic areas accessible by car and one of its best birding areas.

I'll be concentrating on three areas in Moraine Park: the Cub Lake Trail, the Fern Lake Trail, and the open meadows and riparian habitat of the mountain park.

The Cub Lake Trail follows the trees along the west edge of the park. **Steller's Jays, Pygmy Nuthatches,** and **Mountain** and **Black-capped chickadees,** as well as other mountain species, are found here. **Hammond's, Dusky,** and **Cordilleran flycatchers** are also fairly common, and the lucky birder may see species such as **Northern Goshawk, Northern Pygmy-Owl, Red Crossbill, Western Tanager,** and **Pine Grosbeak.** I found **Eastern Bluebirds** near the trailhead one summer and a **Black-and-White Warbler** near the trail another summer, so oddities are definitely possible.

Cub Lake Trail is one of the locations where ranger-led walks concentrate on birding, and you may wish to join one of these walks. Check the Park newspaper you'll be given at the entrance station for days and times.

The Fern Lake trailhead is a **Blue Grouse** site, and the Fern Lake Trail offers opportunities for specialties such as **MacGillivray's** and **Virginia's warblers** and **American Dipper.**

19

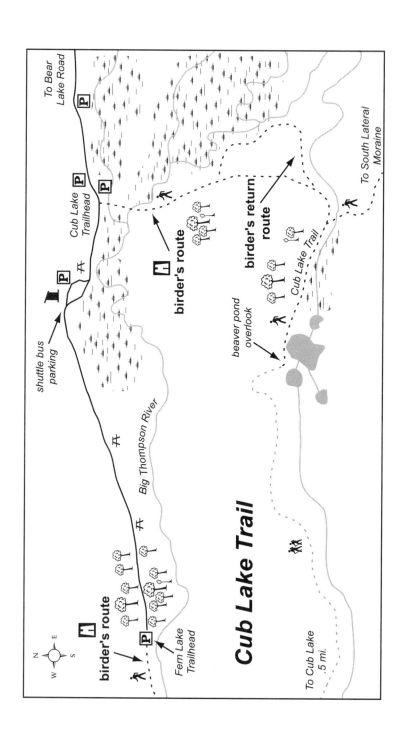

Cub Lake Trail

To Bear
Lake Road

To South Lateral
Moraine

Cub Lake
Trailhead

shuttle bus
parking

Big Thompson River

birder's route

birder's route

birder's return
route

Cub Lake Trail

beaver pond
overlook

Fern Lake
Trailhead

To Cub Lake
.5 mi.

N
E
S
W

The open meadows of Moraine Park host **House Wrens**, **Song** and **Brewer's sparrows**, and **Tree, Violet-green**, and **Barn swallows**. **Common Snipe, Willow Flycatchers, Wilson's Warblers**, and **Vesper** and **Lincoln's sparrows** are found in the wetter areas along the streams. **Mountain Bluebirds** can be seen feeding in the meadows.

Anywhere in Moraine Park, you may be lucky enough to see **Black Swifts** overhead. Three river drainages on the east side of Rocky Mountain National Park have swifts: Glacier Creek (farther along the Bear Lake Road, Chapter 8); North St. Vrain Creek (in Wild Basin, Chapter 3); and the Big Thompson River, which runs through Moraine Park. In any of these drainages, feeding swifts range down from their high-elevation nests and may be seen at any time of the day, if you're lucky. They tend to be seen at lower elevations more commonly after mid-July or on overcast days, but they may be found any summer day.

With **Black Swifts, Blue Grouse**, and other specialties, birding in Moraine Park is exciting. It's another area of varied habitat and easy access, and you may see many of the mountain birds you're hoping for right here. The three areas I'll guide you to are some of the better birding spots in Moraine Park, but the more time you spend exploring, the more birds you'll discover.

To Reach Moraine Park

Enter RMNP at the Beaver Meadows Entrance. **Reset your trip odometer to zero here.** Take the left turn for Bear Lake Road (0.2). You'll drive over the North Lateral Moraine, and as you enter Moraine Park, you'll see a turn on the left to the Moraine Park Museum (1.4), where you'll find interpretative displays and ranger talks about the area and its wildlife. A few yards past this, turn right to Moraine Park Campground and the Cub Lake and Fern Lake trailheads. This is where we'll begin our birding.

What You'll Find—Cub Lake Trail

Turn left just before the campground (2.0), following signs to the Cub Lake trailhead. After the turn, the road drops down and follows a branch of the Big Thompson River to the Cub Lake trailhead (3.2). Parking is limited both here and at the Fern Lake trailhead at the end of the road. It's best to arrive early for parking and birding. The light is better early, the people fewer. The Fern Lake trailhead, in particular, fills up by 9:00 A.M. in summer, earlier on weekends. If the Cub Lake parking areas are full, proceed a quarter mile to another parking area.

The trail leads 2.3 miles to Cub Lake, a lily-covered seep pond, but the best birding is in the first mile-and-a-half or so. You'll be walking along the edge of a forest of ponderosa pines mixed with aspen, junipers, firs, and spruces. The trail overlooks the meadows and riparian willows of Moraine Park to the east. It's this mixture of habitats that should keep you busy with the common mountain birds while giving you the opportunity to find several tough ones.

From the parking area, cross the first wooden bridge and continue to the bigger bridge over the Big Thompson River. If you're lucky, you'll see an **American Dipper** here, but don't wait too long or you'll lose your edge on getting an early start. Dippers are active all day, so do your waiting when you return. **Spotted Sandpipers** also nest along the stream and fly up and down making their rounds. You should see **Violet-green** and **Tree swallows**, and a group of **American Crows** love the spruce trees to the east. **Red-tailed Hawks** are overhead frequently, and you should start watching for **Black Swifts**.

I have some sensible advice about finding **Black Swifts**, and I'll share it with you now and remind you later in the book at other swift sites. To find Black Swifts, you only need to be in an area you know to have them and then look up. That's right. We don't usually look up when we're birding unless we notice a bird overhead, and it usually takes one the size of a raptor to make us notice. Instead, I want you to take time to scan the sky overhead regularly. Watch for swallows and you'll sometimes find swifts with them. Mostly, stop often and look up! Of course, a little help from the swifts is important, too.

Your chances of seeing a **Black Swift** in Moraine Park are not as good as they are in Wild Basin or Glacier Gorge, but people see them regularly here. I know of a visiting birder who claims he *always* gets his swift in Moraine Park. Every year. If so, he gets his bird by taking the time to look up.

Cross the bridge and check out the open area on the west for **Lincoln's** and **Song sparrows**, **Black-billed Magpies**, and the occasional **Wilson's Warbler**. Circle through the willows and rejoin the trail just as it enters the trees. **Cooper's Hawk** and **Prairie Falcon** are uncommon sightings above open areas such as this meadow.

The trail now becomes an undulating path along the western edge of Moraine Park. You should begin to pick up an assortment of the common mountain birds listed earlier in this chapter. Add **Pine Siskins, Warbling Vireos, Broad-tailed Hummingbirds, Red-naped Sapsuckers** … the list of possibilities is long! Some of the more difficult-to-find species include **Brown Creeper, Common Nighthawk, Williamson's Sapsucker, Western Tanager**, and **Red Crossbill**. One June, a **White-eyed Vireo** was caught in a banding net in Moraine Park, so anything is possible!

Just as you begin this part of the trail, you'll find a small side canyon to the west. This canyon and other areas off the main trail can produce excellent birding, but remember that Cub Lake Trail is a high-use area. Most off-trail areas have a game trail or informal path; stick to those established trails. Take the time in this area to listen for the common **Ruby-crowned Kinglet** and the uncommon **Virginia's Warbler**. Outside of Wild Basin, Cub Lake Trail probably provides your best chance to see this western warbler. They're tough to find, even when they're calling. Patience and pishing are necessary to see one in the heavy shrubbery they prefer.

As you continue on the trail, be alert to other calls. The chatter of a flock of **Red Crossbills** can signal a brief flyover. The **Western Tanager's** robin-like song is easily overlooked in the excitement of all the birds. A **Northern Goshawk** is regularly seen, too, and it may be the warning calls of other birds that tips you off to its presence.

One of the main attractions of this part of the trail is the possibility of finding three of the four *Empidonax* flycatchers regular to the National Park: **Dusky, Hammond's**, and **Cordilleran flycatchers**. (If you don't own a copy of Kenn Kaufman's *Advanced Birding,* better pick one up before you hit the Cub Lake Trail.) Throw in **Western Wood-Pewees** and maybe an **Olive-sided Flycatcher** just to take your mind off the *Empidonax*, and you'll see why this is flycatcher-watcher's heaven.

Dusky Flycatchers are often seen along the first half-mile of the trail, before it turns west and climbs out of Moraine Park. They're found in the ponderosas mixed with aspen and alder. **Hammond's Flycatchers** are less common. Both species arrive in May and continue singing into July. Their songs are similar, so listen to your tapes before you hit the trail. *(Note: Use of recordings to attract any wildlife is not allowed in RMNP.)* Once you've studied both birds and become familiar with them, you'll notice differences in song, length of primary-feather extension, eye-ring appearance, and bill size, shape, and color. I'll leave it up to Kenn's book to help you with the first identification, however.

Although this isn't the best place to find a **Cordilleran Flycatcher**, you may hear their distinctive call anywhere along the trail. I've found them near the beginning of the trail, farther along after the trail turns west, and in a grove of aspen mixed with spruce and fir on the trail above Cub Lake.

Continuing along the wooded section of the trail, you'll walk through a small opening surrounded on the west by dense, tall shrubbery, mostly chokecherry and juniper. This is good habitat for **Virginia's** and **MacGillivray's warblers**, although you may have a tough time luring either into view. And don't forget to look up for **Black Swifts**.

At the point where the trail curves west, listen for **Green-tailed Towhees** in the moist meadows on the left. The walk from the parking area to this point, about a half-mile, will probably be your best birding, but you should continue up the trail for at least some distance after it turns west and leaves Moraine Park proper. It will take you alongside beaver-pond meadows, good habitat for several species, including **MacGillivray's Warbler**, a difficult bird to find after it quits singing in July.

You may also find a fourth *Empidonax* flycatcher. **Willow Flycatchers** are found in the riparian willow habitat along this part of the trail. The song and call are quite different from that of the **Dusky** and **Hammond's**, but your main starting point is habitat. You may also find a Willow Flycatcher in the streamside willows along the Big Thompson River. Taking the side trip for **Brewer's Sparrows**, described later in this section, may help you locate this uncommon flycatcher.

I usually continue west past several small ponds to a larger one next to the trail. Continuing just a few yards past it takes you to a nice overlook of the bogs and ponds. In dry years these ponds may be reduced in size. Look for waterfowl, including summer resident **Mallards** and **Ring-necked Ducks** and the less common **Cinnamon, Green-winged,** and **Blue-winged teal.** You may be fortunate to hear **Virginia Rails** or **Soras** or even see one. They nest in this area. And don't forget to check for **Black Swifts** overhead.

IF YOU'RE ON THE TRAIL just for the sake of birding, you may wish to turn back when you reach the big pond described above or farther along at the first long, steep climb. Most of the elevation gain to Cub Lake is in the last mile. The birding higher on the trail is more routine, with **Mountain Chickadees, Ruby-crowned Kinglets,** and the occasional **Hairy Woodpecker,** but there are a couple of reasons for a birder to continue to the lake.

If you continue up, you'll pass through a beautiful aspen grove with a forest floor of ferns. This wet forest was the site of a rare bird find one June when a group identified a **Black-throated Blue Warbler** (while my wife and I were away in Michigan trying to find one). It's an area worth investigating while you rest from the steep climb.

At Cub Lake, you have a chance at a **Blue Grouse,** although other sites, including the Fern Lake trailhead covered later in this chapter, are more reliable. On several occasions, we've seen one along the shore of the lake, sitting on a rock in plain view. Blue Grouse seem curious about people, and the picnickers here amuse them, I think. Walk the lower trail as you get to the lake, taking it all the way to its west end. You may see **Ring-necked Ducks** among the **Mallards** on the lake, and **Spotted Sandpipers** sometimes nest here.

For the more adventuresome, the trail continues over the saddle to the west and down to The Pool on the Fern Lake Trail. See my recommendations on birding from the Fern Lake trailhead to The Pool later in this section. If you take this hike to return to your car, you will (excuse the expression) kill two birds with one stone by doing two trails, but you'll also add considerably to your day hike. The hike to Cub Lake and back is

Blue Grouse

4.6 miles. The hike from the Fern Lake trailhead to The Pool and back is 3.2 miles. If you take the trail from Cub Lake to The Pool, down to Fern Lake trailhead, and *then* down to your car at the Cub Lake trailhead, the trip will be over six miles, considerably longer than either individual hike.

IF YOU DECIDE to go back the way you came and haven't seen all the birds on your wish list, especially the flycatchers, you can return to the place where the trail turns west and take a branch trail that leads to the right, along the South Lateral Moraine. The sign to Cub Lake is at this trail junction. This trail offers the same kind of habitat as the first part of the Cub Lake Trail, but the views of the riparian area are more open. The stream is more visible here, too, and you may see **Spotted Sandpipers** and **American Dippers**. This spur is one of the more reliable areas for **Dusky Flycatchers**.

Return to the main trail. Just east of the spur, the trail drops to the edge of the meadow before re-entering the trees on the way back to the parking area. You may want to take the opportunity here to get a closer look at the grasslands and riparian willows in this part of Moraine Park. Walk directly east toward the whitened skeletons of willows along a dry creek bed, 200 yards or so away. When **Brewer's Sparrows** are nesting in the meadow, you're likely to see them among these dead willows.

After checking for the sparrows, you can return to the trail or work your way back toward the parking area through the meadow, letting the birds determine your path. **Mountain Bluebirds** and **Black-billed Magpies** are common, and as you approach riparian willows, check for **Willow Flycatchers**, **Brewer's** and **Red-winged blackbirds**, **Song Sparrows**, and **Wilson's Warblers**. **MacGillivray's Warblers** and **Lincoln's Sparrows** are occasionally seen in these areas, too.

Wet riparian areas are good places to spook up a **Common Snipe**. (The question is who is more spooked, the birder or the bird?) Snipe can be heard winnowing in Moraine Park on evenings in spring and early summer. Some years, you may also see **Common Nighthawks** in the late afternoon.

Return to your car. If you have the time and energy, you may want to combine your Cub Lake birding with the walk into the Moraine Park meadows described later in this chapter. The Fern Lake Trail birding described next is really better done on a separate day, so that you can get a very early start in hopes of finding **Blue Grouse**.

What You'll Find—Fern Lake Trailhead

To reach the Fern Lake trailhead, drive west from the Cub Lake trailhead. After you pass a parking area and shuttle-bus loading zone (3.5), the road goes through a mixed forest that is very good for birds. Watch for two turnouts on the left (3.9, 4.1) where you can park if you want to bird this area on the way back. At both turnouts, informal trails lead through the meadows and aspen. Bird the road and as much of the meadows leading over to the stream as you can. You may find some of the birds you missed on the Cub Lake Trail.

The Fern Lake trailhead is at the end of the road (4.2). The parking area is usually full by 8:00 A.M. or 9:00 A.M., but if you're serious about the main target bird for this area, **Blue Grouse**, you'll be there long before it fills.

I only have a few places in RMNP where I send people to see **Blue Grouse** with real hope they'll see one on any given day. Grouse are definitely tough. But I've seen a number of grouse here. I've had to stop for them in the road. I've spooked them while walking along the stream. They are here. On several occasions I've seen them right in the Fern Lake trailhead parking area, and that's where I suggest you start first thing in the morning.

It's been said that the **Blue Grouse** is a bird you shouldn't intentionally look for. But it is a bird you should position yourself for—you have to spend time in its habitat. That almost always means meadows and grasses in or near wetter habitats, such as aspen groves and riparian areas. The road from the shuttle-bus parking to the Fern Lake trailhead leads through prime Blue Grouse habitat.

Here's my best advice if you need a **Blue Grouse**. Get yourself parked at the Fern Lake trailhead in the very early morning or the late afternoon/evening. Get out and walk the road, walk the area between the road and the river, and hang out in the parking lot. Watch birds but don't even think about Blue Grouse. Sooner or later, they'll come to you. They're not shy, and they don't try to hide.

Don't mistake what I'm saying. You could spend a week or more in this area and never see one, but if you're going to find a **Blue Grouse** in Rocky, it will probably be here or in similar habitat.

One July we hiked the loop to Cub Lake and around to The Pool with some friends. We had two cars, so we drove to the Fern Lake trailhead to drop one off. Near the trailhead, we had to stop for a **Blue Grouse** crossing the road. When we got to Cub Lake, there was a Blue Grouse sitting on a rock by the lake. A two-grouse day! It's the kind of story you love to tell people for whom this is a nemesis bird. If you're one of them, I hope the nemesis ends at the Fern Lake trailhead.

AFTER YOU'VE BIRDED the roadside areas near the Fern Lake trailhead, you may want to take the fairly easy 1.6-mile hike to The Pool. This hike will lead you through denser growth where you may find **Western Tanagers**, **Townsend's Solitaires**, **Black-capped Chickadees**, **Warbling Vireos**, and **Golden-crowned Kinglets**. The steep slopes near the beginning of the trail provide habitat for **MacGillivray's** and **Virginia's warblers**, always good finds.

I'd recommend a stop along the river any place you have a good view up and down the water. When the insects are hatching from the river, you'll often see several species of birds flycatching above the water. These may include **Yellow-rumped Warblers**, **Cedar Waxwings**, and **Western Tanagers**, as well as "real" flycatchers. An **American Dipper** is very likely to fly by if you give it time.

To look for an **American Dipper**, take your lunch over to the river. Sit down and keep an eye on the water—it's a good tactic for finding one. Dippers don't have anything better to do than fly up and down a stream looking for their own lunch, which is comprised of aquatic insects and the occasional hapless baby trout. They almost never leave the watercourse, and they have definite territories set up in summer. It's just that those territories are linear, following the stream. If you're in a dipper's territory, sooner or later it will fly by. It may even land nearby and put on its underwater flying show for you. The birds are very trusting and allow relatively close approach. You should have a good opportunity to see one anywhere along the trail to The Pool.

What You'll Find—Moraine Park Meadows

If you have extra time, you may want to take a walk across the open meadows of Moraine Park. Before you just stop someplace and start walking, be warned that Moraine Park is cut by the braided channels of the Big Thompson River, and many are hidden from view until you've almost stepped into them. It's not a simple task to walk across the park unless you have hip boots!

For an introductory walk through the grasslands, I'd recommend the horse trail, reached from the road on your way out. Drive back past the Cub Lake trailhead. When the road curves left and begins to climb toward the campground entrance road, find a turnout adjacent to a private driveway halfway up the hill on the west side of the road. Park here or at a nearby turnout on the right. Walk east along an old gravel road toward a prominent grove of balsam poplars to find the horse trail.

As you walk across the meadow, you may see some of the sparrows that prefer drier habitats. **Vesper, Savannah,** and the less-common **Brewer's sparrows** may be here, and in late April and early May, you may see **Clay-colored Sparrows.** Watch for sparrows in areas where taller bushes grow; they often nest in or near them. If you're looking for a Brewer's, pish at every bush until you rouse one; otherwise you'll walk past most of these skulkers. They will come up to investigate, however, and give you enough identification time if you know what you're looking for.

Mountain Bluebirds can also be seen feeding in the meadows, as can **Brewer's Blackbirds** and **Black-billed Magpies.** Look for the bluebirds on exposed perches or isolated errant rocks left by the glacier. **Common Ravens** and **American Crows** are regulars, and raptors may fly over.

In the balsam poplars, **Hairy Woodpeckers** and the less common **Williamson's Sapsuckers,** as well as *Empidonax* flycatchers, may be seen. **House Wrens** like the understory cover, and you may find a **Green-tailed Towhee** along the margins of the grove. **Yellow-rumped Warblers** and **Warbling Vireos** are possible, and poplar stands like this one are popular with **Yellow Warblers**, especially during migration. **Pine Siskins** are found in the thistles nearby when they bloom in July and August. In August and September, **Northern Harriers** are sometimes seen over the meadows.

Like Endovalley, Moraine Park is attractive to vagrants during migration. It's not as reliable for unusual birds because of the mountainous terrain to the east, but I have found **Eastern** and **Western kingbirds** and **Western Meadowlarks** in the open grassland at the east end of Moraine Park. One late-May morning, I found a **Blue Grosbeak** in bushes near the poplar grove. If the birding at the poplar grove is good, you may want to continue on the trail as it crosses the meadow going east.

IF YOU'RE CAMPING, Moraine Park Campground is probably the best one on the east side of RMNP for birders. (You'll need reservations for this campground in summer. See Chapter 11.) There should be lots of birds right in camp, including uncommon species such as **Williamson's Sapsucker**, and if you're road weary, you can spend a full day hiking from camp to the excellent birding areas described in this chapter. There's nothing quite like a whole day spent outside the car when you're on a road trip!

Whether you're camping in Moraine Park or just birding, I hope you'll find many memorable birds here. You can't find a more beautiful place to pursue your favorite sport.

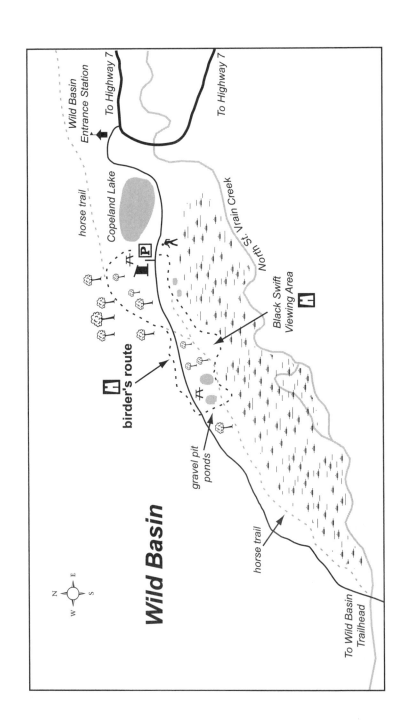

Wild Basin

To Highway 7

Wild Basin
Entrance Station

horse trail

Copeland Lake

North St. Vrain Creek

Black Swift
Viewing Area

birder's route

gravel pit
ponds

horse trail

To Wild Basin
Trailhead

To Highway 7

3

Wild Basin

TRAVELING SOUTH FROM the Estes Valley on the Peak-to-Peak Highway (Highway 7) toward Allenspark takes you 1,000 feet up to the flanks of Longs Peak and to another part of Rocky Mountain National Park that's definitely worth exploring for its birds.

There are four major access points to Rocky along the highway between Estes Park and Allenspark: Lily Lake, Twin Sisters trailhead across from Lily Lake, Longs Peak trailhead and campground, and Wild Basin. The Twin Sisters and Longs Peak trailheads provide access to popular climbs, but they're not particularly noteworthy for birds, unless you want to find **White-tailed Ptarmigan** the hard way—by climbing Longs Peak. Both Lily Lake and Wild Basin provide good birding opportunities, and I'll concentrate on those two areas in this section.

Lily Lake offers good waterfowl watching and has a wetland where **Soras** and other unusual water birds can be found. It's really at its best during spring and fall migrations, but I think it's worth a stop anytime during the summer. It only takes thirty minutes to an hour to check out the area, and you may find something very unusual.

Wild Basin, as its name suggests, is a beautiful area. The basin itself is a wide riparian park with numerous beaver ponds and the North St. Vrain Creek running through it. And it is certainly still wild—its willows almost impenetrable except for the area of the river corridor. The mountains to the west are a great place for a hike, and you're likely to find all the typical mountain birds and maybe some hard-to-find ones in Wild Basin and along the trails that start there. The area is still "rustic" and a bit out of the way, by Park standards, and it's one of my favorite places to bird.

Currently Wild Basin is the best place in Rocky Mountain National Park to find **Black Swifts**. Most of my recent sightings come from here, and there is an accessible nesting site you may want to visit. It's also the best site for **Virginia's Warblers**, and many other hard-to-find species show up here. The hike I'll recommend includes the chance to see **Blue Grouse**, **Northern Pygmy-Owl**, **Pine Grosbeak**, and other exciting birds.

To Reach Lily Lake and Wild Basin

You can access the start of this trip from two areas. *From the west side of Estes Park,* take Mary's Lake Road from Moraine Avenue (Highway 36). Drive past the lake to the intersection with Highway 7. **Reset your trip odometer to zero at the intersection** and turn right.

From the east side of Estes Park, find the intersection of Highways 36 and 7 near the power plant on Lake Estes. Turn south on Highway 7, the Peak-to-Peak Highway, and travel 3.4 miles to Mary's Lake Road on the right. Do not turn here, but **reset your trip odometer to zero.**

From this point, drive south on Highway 7 to Baker's Curve (0.4), where you'll see signs for Cheley Camp and the turn for Fish Creek Road, part of the Estes Valley loop drive described in Chapter 9. From here, the highway climbs up out of the Estes Valley.

You'll gain about 900 feet in elevation and trade the ponderosa pines for lodgepole pines, Douglas firs, and spruces. The views across the Estes Valley from the road are outstanding but are better enjoyed from turnouts on your way down. And they are better *not* viewed by the driver except from a turnout. Several cars have tumbled down the hillside here over the years, and the result is never pleasant.

From Lily Lake (2.9), you'll continue on Highway 7 to Wild Basin (9.4). Details of the drive are covered in the section below on Wild Basin. *(Note: Although I'll cover the birding sites in the order you come to them, you should proceed directly to the Wild Basin trailhead if you intend to do the Ouzel Falls Trail, due to limited parking at the trailhead. You can catch the other areas on the way back or on another day.)*

What You'll Find—Lily Lake

Just as the highway levels out after the climb, you'll see a turn on the left for the historic Baldpate Inn, made famous by the mystery novel and movie, *Seven Keys to Baldpate*. Baldpate is a good place to have lunch, view the collection of keys, and observe the hummingbird feeders outside the dining room windows.

Our first official stop is Lily Lake (2.9), acquired in 1989 from private ownership through the efforts of several conservation funds. Turn right into the parking lot next to the lake. The Park stocked this lake with native greenback cutthroat trout, and they've done well here. Hence, the lake parking lot is often full of anglers' cars. You should be able to find a spot at the visitor center across the highway if that's the case. (Recent proposals call for the parking lot at Lily Lake to be moved a short distance south to a planned new trailhead. Signs should direct you to the new parking area if that comes to be.)

From the parking lot, go left around the lake. The handicapped-accessible trail goes all the way around the lake, but the best birding is at the small wetland along the south shore and then in the mixed grassland, fir, and aspen habitat south of there. First check out the lake for waterfowl resistant to flyfishers' float tubes. There are often **Mallards** and **Ring-necked Ducks** year-round, but early and late in the season you may find **Redhead**, **Lesser Scaup**, and **Blue-winged**, **Green-winged**, and the occasional **Cinnamon teal**. **American Coots** migrate through and were breeders on the lake in the past. Lily Lake has an historic sighting from August 1939 of a pair of **Common Gallinules**, a rare straggler to Colorado and the only Park record, so it is attractive to any migrating waterfowl looking for a resting spot. **Spotted Sandpipers** can also be found on the shoreline, although they usually move on during breeding season to less crowded places.

Continue walking toward the south end of the lake. This is a good area to pick up your **Brewer's Blackbird**, and **Red-winged Blackbirds** nest here. After the trail curves right and you cross a prominent wooden footbridge, watch for standing water to the left of the trail. Natural springs in this area have created a small wetland used by ducks, shorebirds, and rails. The lake's only source of water is from springs, both the ones you see here and others located under the surface of the water. The springs produce enough water in this wetland that it was used in the past to rear fish to be released into the lake for anglers staying at Baldpate Inn and the lodge that was located at the southwest corner of the lake.

Walk slowly along this part of the trail. It's better *not* to walk over toward the wetland. It will disturb the birds, perhaps ending your birding opportunity. If you are patient, the birds in the wetland will eventually show themselves. It's better to visit the area early in the day, before the influx of visitors disturbs the birds enough to drive them deep into the reeds, but the wetland is sheltered by the tall grasses, so you can sometimes find birds even at midday.

This wetland can have an amazing assortment of birds during migration. One September, I found six **Solitary Sandpipers**, a very unusual bird for the mountains. With them were **Soras**, another uncommon species that nests here. **Blue-winged Teal** skulked around in the reeds, adding to the variety. One May I found a **White-faced Ibis**, and the following May, a **Virginia Rail**, an even more uncommon bird than the **Sora**, was calling, so many species might be found here, at least during migration. **Common Snipe** nest here, as do land birds, such as **Song Sparrows**.

Watch between the openings in the grasses and reeds for glimpses of birds from the lakeside trail. Continue working the area in this way until you reach the west end of the wetland. Here you'll find a spur trail heading south along a dry hillside. From the vantage of the hillside, you can survey more of the water. Check the willows for **Wilson's Warblers** and **Lincoln's Sparrows**.

After birding the wetland, you can continue around the lake, if you wish. The birding isn't often noteworthy in itself, but it's a beautiful, pleasant walk. There's a chance for **Pine Grosbeaks**, as well as **Western Tanagers**, **Clark's Nutcrackers**, and **Common Ravens**, but mostly you should go just for the stroll.

To continue birding from the hillside along the wetland, work your way south near the willows, then east toward the highway, letting the birds (and dry land) determine your route. **Cordilleran Flycatchers** can be found here, as well as **Yellow-rumped Warblers**. In the willows and bushes, watch for **White-crowned, Lincoln's, and Song sparrows**. The edges of the forest may have **Chipping Sparrows** and **Brown Creepers**, and flyovers by **Red Crossbills** and **Band-tailed Pigeons** can make for some furious birding. **Flammulated Owls** have been heard, if not seen, in the Lily Lake area more than once. These owls reportedly arrive late in the year and depart early, so the true summer months of June, July, and August would be the best opportunity to find them.

It was in the "true summer month" of June when I was birding this area in a snowstorm with five inches of snow already on the ground. I heard what sounded like a weak **Northern Flicker** call, but the only tree in the vicinity of the call was a dense, thirty-foot-high spruce, hardly the kind of tree you'd expect flickers to use. Finally, I was able to approach the tree close enough to pinpoint the source of the call. Sitting on a clump of snow at the very top was a **Common Snipe**, its bill opening and closing to the rhythm of the "flicker call." Strange things happen to birds and birders in June snowstorms!

Work your way toward the highway and follow the trail you'll find back to the parking area and your car. From here we'll continue south to Wild Basin.

What You'll Find—Wild Basin

From the Lily Lake parking lot, turn south onto the highway (right from the lakeside parking area or left from the visitor center lot). In the next mile, the road goes through a trademark lodgepole pine forest, one of the least productive habitats for birds. Soon the view will open up on your right. A turnout with a sign for Longs Peak (4.8) provides one great view of Longs Peak, well worth stopping for. The summit of Longs is just to the right of the prominent notch.

If you've always wanted to climb the mountain, the view may inspire you (or forever convince you that this is one big brute and you'd rather spend your mountain time birding). Put your scope on the East Face and see if you can spot climbers. Binocs are sufficient to see climbers who've reached the top in the early afternoon. The meadow in front of you is home to **Black-billed Magpies, American Crows, Common Ravens, Mountain Bluebirds**, and **Red-tailed Hawks**. In the winter, watch for **Northern Shrikes**.

Across the road to the east, you'll see the entrance to the Enos Mills cabin. Mills was almost solely responsible for the creation of Rocky Mountain National Park in 1915. He lived here in the Tahosa Valley until his death in 1922. His daughter, Enda, who's a birder, maintains the cabin as an historical museum dedicated to the work of her father, and you should visit it if you're interested in the history of the area.

Farther along the highway, a turn on the right leads to the Longs Peak trailhead and campground (5.5). This is a crowded area and not particularly birdy, although **Gray Jays** and **Clark's Nutcrackers** hang out in the parking area and campground. Continue south on Highway 7. Watch for St. Catherine's Chapel on the right (7.3), built in 1936 of granite from the area and trimmed with sandstone from the quarries in Lyons, at the base of the foothills. The St. Malo Retreat and Conference Center was one of the Pope's stops on his trip to America a few years ago. I don't think he was here to bird, however. Too bad.

A short distance beyond the chapel is a forest service campground (7.6), one of the two in the area. (The other is about a mile past the turn to Wild Basin.) Meeker Park Lodge, another historic building, is on the left, less than a mile past the campground. About a mile past that, you'll find the turn to the Wild Basin Area on the right (9.4). Take the turn and continue on the paved road to a right turn on a dirt road to Copeland Lake and Wild Basin (9.7).

Enter RMNP here at the Wild Basin Entrance Station and drive about 100 yards to Copeland Lake, a man-enhanced bathtub of a pond that's seldom very productive for water birds. Continue around the lake to a picnic area on the right (10.1), the main stop if you want to bird the basin itself. *(Note: The parking area at the trailhead ahead fills early in summer, about 8:30 A.M. and earlier on weekends, so you should proceed and bird the basin trail later or on another day, if you're doing the Ouzel Falls hike described below.)*

In the picnic area itself, you may find **Western Tanagers, Steller's Jays, Mountain Chickadees, House Wrens, Pygmy, Red-breasted**, and

White-breasted nuthatches, Western Wood-Pewees, and Green-tailed Towhees. Red-naped Sapsuckers and Northern Flickers nest nearby and may also make an appearance. A Dusky Flycatcher often nests in the picnic area, and Hammond's Flycatchers are sometimes here, too. Northern Pygmy-Owls have been seen occasionally.

After birding the picnic ground, cross the road and go left around the end of the pole fence. (Only a dude tries to cross a fence like this when he can go around it!) Follow an informal path south for about fifty yards until you find a well-defined trail, where you'll turn right (west).

Beginning here, you should start routinely scanning the sky for Black Swifts. This area and the Ouzel Falls Trail described later in this chapter are the most reliable places in RMNP to find them. During a recent July and August, I went three-for-three finding swifts, once on the Ouzel Falls Trail and twice on the basin trail. I've also found them regularly in June. On all these occasions, I saw the birds midday. I actually believe my own theory—to find Black Swifts, look up. Sounds simple, but we birders don't usually focus our attention overhead.

Check especially any swallows you see. Swifts are sometimes seen in their company, although they may be flying higher. When I first saw Black Swifts on the basin trail, it was because I stopped to watch Violet-green Swallows overhead. A swift was among them!

Review your field marks if you're not familiar with swifts. Compare the flight silhouette of swallows and swifts. Swallows have much broader wings, particularly where they meet the body. Swallows have a slower wingbeat and soar more than swifts. (Roederer's Second Rule of Swift Watching is: If you're not sure it's a swift, it's a swallow.) In addition to separating Black Swifts from the swallows you'll see, you must also know the field marks for White-throated Swifts, which are seen here on rare occasions.

FOLLOW THE MAIN TRAIL WEST. Soon you'll come to a series of small, shallow, gravel-pit ponds to the left of the trail. Much of the land you'll be walking through has seen the workings of man from the years before this area was added to the National Park. Gravel from these ponds is likely helping dam up Copeland Lake. The first pond may be dry by midsummer, but the second almost always has water.

Black Swift

You may find **Spotted Sandpipers**, **Mallards**, or even **Ring-necked Ducks** on the ponds. Land birds are also attracted to water; watch for **Broad-tailed Hummingbirds**, **Mountain Chickadees**, **Red-breasted**, **White-breasted**, and **Pygmy nuthatches**, **Western Tanagers**, **Warbling Vireos**, and **Ruby-crowned Kinglets**. **Black-capped Chickadees** are sometimes seen here. **Yellow-rumped Warblers** (**Audubon's**) should be easy to find early in summer. **MacGillivray's Warblers** are less common, but they're also here.

Continue west past the last couple of gravel pits, which generally have little or no water in them. The trail enters an open ponderosa forest mixed with aspen and some spruce. I like to walk the edge of the ridge south of the trail in the section after the last gravel pit. You'll still be in the ponderosas, but aspen and alder on the left provide a more diversified habitat. **Dark-eyed Juncos** (**Gray-headed**) are found here, and you may find **Lincoln's Sparrows** and **Wilson's Warblers** working along the willows at the edge of basin. Many other species are typically found in this section of the route.

Avoid side trails that lead into the willow carr to the left; they lead only to misery. They're mostly game trails and anglers' trails and often peter out in the worst places, leaving you with wet feet and only one sensible option, backtracking. Walking through this riparian area, even after a life bird, is *not* recommended. The beaver have done a thorough job of excavating hip-deep holes (known to anglers as "ankle breakers"), and there are plenty of bungee sticks left from their gnawing to pierce your body should you fall. Have I convinced you?

You will soon find a man-made irrigation ditch, which feeds Copeland Lake. If it's full and you find it difficult to cross, follow it toward the road. There's a bridge where the main trail crosses it. After crossing the ditch, rejoin the main trail, now wider due to horse traffic. Continue about 100 yards or so to a pronounced dip in the trail where it drops four or five feet in elevation. At the mid-point of this dip, find an informal path to the left (south) and follow it to an open meadow that overlooks the basin's riparian habitat. (If you miss the dip for some reason—probably good birds—you'll see where an old roadbed crosses the trail; follow it to the meadow.)

The forest margin on the way to the meadow usually provides great birding. Expect the mountain species mentioned before, but look also for **Cassin's Finches, Brown Creepers, Black-headed Grosbeaks,** and other unusual birds. **Dusky Flycatchers** like the pine trees along the margin, and the aspen grove to the east can be good for **Hairy** and **Downy woodpeckers,** as well as **Western Wood-Pewee.**

The meadow is my best **Black Swift** viewing platform. It gives you the opportunity to see lots of sky. **Tree** and **Violet-green swallows** will likely be overhead, and that should encourage you. A cloudy day is best for viewing, both because it's easier to pick out the birds and because a low ceiling forces the birds down, but you can find swifts without that advantage. Be patient. **Black Swifts** are uncommon and are erratic in their feeding patterns.

As you walk the edge of the basin, you might also hope for the uncommon **Willow Flycatcher** in the willows, as well as **Wilson's Warblers. MacGillivray's Warblers** are often heard and seldom seen in the impenetrable brush. Try pishing or whistling a pygmy-owl call. On spring and early summer evenings, you may hear **Common Snipe** winnowing above the wetlands. **Red-winged Blackbirds** and **Mallards** can be seen flying over the wetlands, and a **Red-tailed Hawk** may be overhead. **Common Nighthawks** are occasionally seen later in summer.

As you work your way along the edge, notice two prominent dead trees to the west along the edge of the willow carr. (It's possible, of course, that they may have blown down by the time you read this.) Check them out carefully for flycatchers and woodpeckers. Near the base of the closer tree, notice an abandoned beaver lodge. The snag farther away is better for birds, and you'll get a closer view of it as you proceed along the trail.

Return to the trail and continue west. The first of two small ponds will be on your right. Both ponds have more vegetation around them than the ponds at the start of this walk and are good for **Dusky Flycatchers, Ruby-crowned Kinglets, Yellow-rumped Warblers,** and **Warbling Vireos. House Wrens** should be easy to come by, and **Hermit Thrushes** are found here, especially in early summer. I've located **Brown Creepers** several times in this area by paying attention to their high-pitched calls and following the sound to these fascinating birds. Listen, too, for

Townsend's Solitaires. **Red-naped** and **Williamson's sapsuckers** frequent this area, and I've seen a **Three-toed Woodpecker** nearby. There are also occasional reports of **Northern Pygmy-Owls** from this location.

WHEN YOU'VE REACHED these ponds, which are located near the road and a parking area with picnic tables (10.6), you've covered the birdiest part of the trail. I usually follow the trail a little farther to where it overlooks a beaver pond close on the left. **Song Sparrows** and the wetland warblers mentioned earlier are possible here. There's an informal path to the north that follows the west side of the second pond back to the road, but if the birding is good, you may wish to continue west on the trail. In another half mile, you'll come to the road and the bridge over North St. Vrain Creek.

If you decide to return to your car from the ponds, it's about a half mile back. You can return the way you came, but I usually take a different way back, walking near the road. A short distance east of the ponds, I cross to the north side of the road, checking out the damper areas at the base of the cliffs where aspen grow. I've occasionally found **Blue Grouse** in the deep grasses and ferns.

As you return along the road, you'll see where the horse trail crosses the road, just before the place where the ditch also crosses the road. Take the horse trail uphill to the north and east. It will lead to the hillside above the picnic area where your car is parked. You'll see the picnic area's wood fence from the trail. This trail provides a good opportunity to see **Green-tailed Towhees**, and there are usually **Virginia's Warblers** on the hillside above the trail during breeding season. They are fond of dense shrubs, six to ten feet tall, often associated with aspen. Some uphill scrambling may be required if you hear them singing and want a good look. This is currently the most reliable spot in RMNP to see them. **Three-toed Woodpeckers** have also been reported from this trail. Return to your car after birding the trail.

What You'll Find—Ouzel Falls Trail

If you're up for a bird hike, continue past the Copeland Lake picnic area to the end of the road. I don't recommend too many hikes in this book, but I do like the hike to Ouzel Falls. If you know that ouzel is another name for **American Dipper**, you'll even find its name inviting.

Drive west across the bridge over the river (11.1). In the next mile or so, you'll see several turnouts on the right along the very narrow road. *(Note: I hope you'll drive this part of the road at birding speed for safety's sake—I once met a Grayline bus coming down this road at a good clip!)* Many of these turnouts have picnic tables, and this is a great place to watch for **American Dippers**. If you don't see one in the time it takes to eat a snack, I'll be surprised. It was on this stream that I watched a dipper emerge from the water with a three-inch trout in its beak. Down went the trout, heron-style. Most of the dipper's diet consists of aquatic insects, and if you have the opportunity to see one "flying" underwater, you'll notice it using its beak to dislodge small rocks in hopes of finding a mayfly nymph or caddis larva. Reach into the water and pull out a rock or two to see what's living on its bottom side. That's dipper dinner.

You'll pass the Finch Lake trailhead (11.7) on your way to the Wild Basin trailhead (12.0), which is often full by 8:00 or 8:30 A.M. on weekdays in summer, earlier on weekends. If you find it's full, you may wish to leave your car at one of the turnouts along the river and walk to the trailhead.

There are three major destinations from the trails that begin in this area. One goes to Finch Lake and Pear Reservoir from the trailhead you've driven past. The Finch Lake Trail goes through dense forest for most of its length and is not as scenic or birdy as the name suggests. A second destination is Thunder Lake, accessible from the Ouzel Falls Trail. A spur leaves the main trail about 1.5 miles in, and the lake is another 2.7 miles. I haven't birded this trail, but you're unlikely to find anything unusual here (except good fishing at Thunder Lake). The trail goes through heavy timber most of the way.

I recommend the third, and main, destination—Ouzel Falls, 2.7 miles from the trailhead. Follow the trail from the parking lot at the end of the road to Copeland Falls, less than a half mile in. This is another **American Dipper** stop. Then continue to Calypso Cascades, 1.8 miles from the trailhead.

This first part of the trail is difficult birding. In spite of interspersed aspen, the spruce/fir forest is dense and the constant sound of rushing water makes birding by ear difficult. Birds are few and difficult to find, but you may see **Hairy Woodpeckers**, the less common **Williamson's Sapsucker**, **Townsend's Solitaires**, **Swainson's** and **Hermit thrushes**, **Mountain** and **Black-capped chickadees**, **Red-breasted** and **White-breasted nuthatches**, **Yellow-rumped Warblers**, **Warbling Vireos**, and **Dark-eyed Juncos**. **Broad-tailed Hummingbirds** can be seen in the infrequent openings.

The trail goes through excellent **Blue Grouse** habitat, and they can be seen near the trail, especially from mid-July through September, when grouse families are on the move. Watch for them in grassy areas, especially those areas interspersed with ferns. The presence of ferns and aspen trees indicate the kind of wet grassland grouse often prefer. When the families are out and about, they can be anywhere along the trail.

At Calypso Cascades, look for **Hermit Thrushes** feeding babies in late July and August. The stream here may occasionally have an **American Dipper**. Relax for a few minutes to enjoy the falls, and you may see one. From Calypso, continue another 0.9 miles to Ouzel Falls. The best birding on the trail is a few minutes beyond the Cascades when you start across part of the burn from a 1978 fire. You should spend some time in this still-regenerating meadow. Many of the birds you'll see can be expected: **Yellow-rumped Warblers**, **Dark-eyed Juncos**, **Pine Siskins**, and **Steller's Jays**. But there can be some real surprises and some very good birds here.

On a hike here one July, my wife and I found an **Olive-sided Flycatcher** perched at the top of one of the burned snags. While we were working on that bird, two birds flew across the meadow, and we had the hard-to-find **Pine Grosbeak** on our day list. As we proceeded, we saw a pair of **Brown Creepers** feeding young in a nest under the loose bark of a burned tree. Another lucky find. Other birders have reported **Band-tailed Pigeons** in the burn.

A surprise for us, at that time, was a pair of **Black Swifts**. I was glassing Longs Peak when they flew across my view. Our luck continued on the way back through the area after visiting Ouzel Falls; we added **Northern Flicker** and **Cassin's Finch** to our burn list. On another trip, we found **Black Swifts** again—I've come to expect them there now—and a **Northern Pygmy-Owl** hunting the burn from a high perch in one of the dead trees. It's just the kind of area that often keeps you going from one bird to another without let-up.

Continue to Ouzel Falls after you bird the burn. **Black Swifts** nest behind the waterfall. To have a chance to see them at the falls, you should start as early as possible, but no later than 5:30 A.M. in mid-summer. If you make good time (i.e., no birding on the way), you may be able to reach the falls before 7 A.M. and that *may* be early enough to see them, especially if it's overcast. The earlier, the better. Even when they're feeding young, swifts may only be in the nesting area in the early morning and very late evening, so it's still chancy. An evening trip would require staying almost until dark, and the light will be poor for viewing swifts and even poorer for the walk out. I don't recommend it.

Whether or not you catch the swifts, you may see the falls' namesake here. A pair of **American Dippers** (a.k.a. ouzel, water wren) usually nests at the falls. For the hardy, the trail continues to Ouzel Lake, 4.9 miles from the trailhead. Above the falls, the trail again goes through burned areas, and you may find some more of those "good" birds. The elevation gain for Ouzel Falls is 950 feet; for Ouzel Lake, it's a stout 1,510 feet.

Beyond Ouzel Lake is Chickadee Pond, Bluebird Lake, Junco Lake, Pipit Lake, and Lark Pond, just in case you're into bagging geographical locations with the names of birds. If you head up to Thunder Lake, don't miss Eagle Lake and Falcon Lake, and don't forget to hit Finch Lake, mentioned earlier, on your way out. You may find ouzels at Ouzel Falls and chickadees at Chickadee Pond, but I wonder about a bluebird at Bluebird Lake. It's above timberline.

PERHAPS ALL THE lakes and falls named for birds should give us a clue. Wild Basin is a great place to be and a great place to bird. Spend the morning on the Ouzel Falls Trail and return to the basin trail for the afternoon. Then stop at Lily Lake for the evening—maybe you'll find a **Flammulated Owl**. I can't think of a more pleasant way to spend a birding day in Rocky Mountain National Park. Just remember to take your eyes off the great scenery long enough to look up. The swifts are there!

4

Trail Ridge Road

TRAIL RIDGE ROAD and the chance to see **White-tailed Ptarmigan** and **Brown-capped Rosy Finches** might be reason enough for a birder to come to Rocky Mountain National Park. Actually, just the trip over Trail Ridge Road would be reason enough for *anyone* to come to Rocky! Nowhere else in the United States can you travel on a higher paved road that goes someplace. And nowhere else, anywhere, will you likely find a highway with any better views. Let me know if you do.

Trail Ridge Road is closed in winter, but it's almost always open by Memorial Day weekend, often a week or two earlier. It may close for the season as early as mid-September, but the typical closing is mid-October. The road may be closed temporarily due to snow or ice at any time. Although the road is paved, there are frost heaves, narrow sections with good "exposure" (as they say in mountaineering circles), and lots of summer traffic. You should expect the going to be fairly slow, especially after 9 A.M. Grand Lake is only fifty miles from Estes Park over Trail Ridge, but it usually takes over two hours, even if you don't stop for the scenery or the birds.

The weather is unpredictable up top, and you should be prepared for cold temperatures and wind, even on the Fourth of July. Afternoon thunderstorms can be dramatic, fast-moving, and life-threatening. Hypothermia can happen any time of the year to someone ill-prepared for the weather, and it can happen at surprisingly mild air temperatures if you get wet or are exposed to high winds. In short, as soon as you leave your car in the alpine tundra, you'd better have your act together: dress properly, watch the weather, and hike sensibly. Remember to drink plenty of water and take it easy.

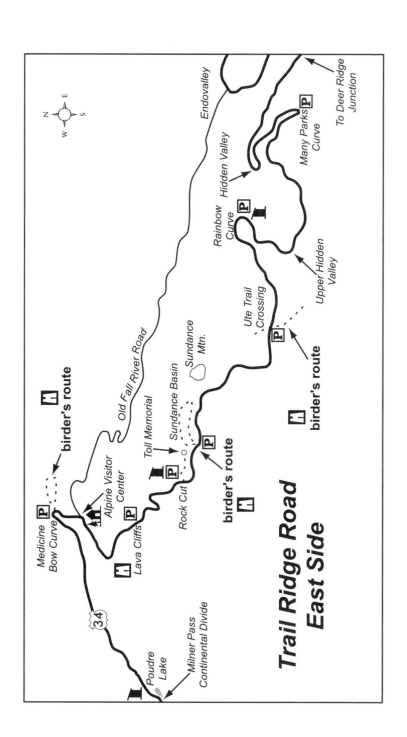

Trail Ridge Road
East Side

Having said that and hoping it will keep you from being one of those men in sleeveless T-shirts, shorts, and Tevas or women in—believe it—high heels and silk blouses, whom locals like to shake their heads at, a day on Trail Ridge Road is an adventure waiting to happen. Take your macro lens to photograph the tiny alpine flowers. Walk to the highest ridge and be on top of the world. Have a snowball fight in July. Gaze at Gorge Lakes across Forest Canyon and wonder how long it would take to hike there and how big the trout are. Find a life bird. Find two life birds!

To Reach Trail Ridge Road

For our purposes, Trail Ridge Road begins at Deer Ridge Junction where Highways 34 and 36 meet in the National Park. From the Fall River Entrance, travel approximately four miles to Deer Ridge Junction and turn right on Trail Ridge Road. From the Beaver Meadows Entrance, drive 3.1 miles to Deer Ridge Junction and the beginning of Trail Ridge Road. **Reset your trip odometer to zero here.**

What You'll Find

For the best chance at **White-tailed Ptarmigan**, you should start this trip early. Get up at first light and get going. Not only will you beat the crowds, but the birds and other wildlife will be much more active and nearer the road. If your main objective is ptarmigan, you should drive more or less directly to the recommended sites, so that you'll be there soon after sunrise, about 6:30 A.M. in mid-summer. There is a very good reason for this. Early in the morning, the wind doesn't *usually* blow. By 9:00 A.M., there is typically a heady wind that increases as the day progresses, and it affects the birding in two ways.

First, it drops your comfort level dramatically. You'll likely be spending a lot of time up top looking for the bird—there is nothing to substitute for time afoot in the right places in the tundra if you want to find a ptarmigan. The early morning temperature will be in the upper 30s or lower 40s with a warming sun. Dress warm and keep active and you'll be comfortable. The temperature later in the day may be in the 50s or even the 60s, but with a stiff wind, your comfort will be dramatically re-duced. Some summer days, the wind is bad enough that only with a parka and wind pants will you be willing to spend the necessary time looking for ptarmigan.

Second, the lack of wind (and traffic noise) in early morning allows you to hear the male ptarmigan calling or, in July and August, the female ptarmigan admonishing her young with clucks. Early morning can be fantastic for viewing other wildlife, too. Last time I was up there early, I had to stop twice for bighorn sheep *in the road*. Then I stopped to watch a bull elk, still in velvet, browsing right beside the road. In the early morning light, with the backdrop of shadowed Forest Canyon, this was a calendar shot. Best of all, I was alone on the road, and I could just stop and watch. *(Note: Please don't stop in the middle of the road unless there is no traffic. It's bad manners and dangerous, and I'll honk at you!)*

If such an early start doesn't work for you or if you can't resist doing a lot of birding along the way, go anyway. In July and early August, many days are pleasant enough that only the threat of afternoon thunder-storms may curtail your birding.

ENOUGH ADVICE. On your first trip up, you may just decide to follow the route as outlined here. If you don't find ptarmigan, you will have scouted out the areas and you can devote a special, early-morning trip to finding the bird. If you go to Medicine Bow Curve, the best site for the bird, you can note the locations I'll mention and hit them after you've found your ptarmigan.

From Deer Ridge Junction (elevation 8,937 feet), travel west 1.5 miles to a dirt road on the right. This leads to a picnic ground next to Hidden Valley Creek (9,100 feet). Farther along the road is Hidden Valley (2.5). Don't stop at either spot on your way up for ptarmigan, but you should note their locations. If you're coming back late in the evening, you may want to stop at these areas and check for **Northern Pygmy-Owls** and **Northern Saw-whet Owls**. We've heard pygmy owls here, and our local owl expert says there are saw-whets throughout this area.

Hidden Valley is also the only location I'm aware of in the Park where **Boreal Owls** have been found. They call January through March and are nearly impossible to find if they're not calling. However, there are reports of boreals calling occasionally in mid-summer at other locations in Colorado, and they may do so in Rocky, too. Much remains to be learned about Boreal Owls in Rocky Mountain National Park.

Hidden Valley, the site of a ski area for many years, is currently being restored to a more natural state. In fact, the cleared areas of the former ski runs—and the access they provide to the high-elevation spruce/fir forest—offer the best birding. It was near the bottom of those runs that **Boreal Owls** were discovered one winter. At this writing, you must park near Trail Ridge Road and walk about a half mile to the old ski hill. A picnic area with restrooms and trails is planned for the future.

PAST HIDDEN VALLEY, you'll be in the subalpine zone, and by the time you reach Many Parks Curve (4.1) at 9,620 feet, you'll be passing through a dense spruce/fir forest. I recommend you stop here and at other turnouts before you reach Rainbow Curve (8.1) at 10,829 feet. These stops represent great roadside access to the birds of the high forest.

I hadn't really thought about suggesting these stops until a visitor whom I'd directed to the ptarmigan locations told me he'd had great birding at Many Parks Curve and other stops on the way up. He'd seen a **Three-toed Woodpecker**, a **Hermit Thrush**, **Pine Grosbeaks**, and **Band-tailed Pigeons**, all lifers for him. These stops have become regular birding areas for me since that report.

Stopping at the turnouts will be most productive early in the day. At any of them, expect to see **Clark's Nutcrackers**. The Park is trying hard to discourage hand-feeding of these birds and the chipmunks and ground squirrels, but changing habits—both those of humans and birds—is a long-term effort. You may also see **Gray Jays**, but they're less common. Finding the other subalpine birds is more a matter of being in the right place at the right time. You may see **Red Crossbills**, and a **Swainson's Thrush** may serenade you. **Steller's Jays**, **Dark-eyed Juncos**, **Townsend's Solitaires**, **Yellow-rumped Warblers**, **Pine Siskins**, and **Mountain Chickadees** are more common.

You may want to stop at the small turnout less than a half-mile past Many Parks Curve. This is the Mummy Range Overlook (4.4). It will give you an astounding view of the alluvial fan and the destructive power of the Lawn Lake flood in the canyon of Roaring River above Endovalley, where you may have already birded.

Try the unmarked turnout at 5.9 miles and at Upper Hidden Valley (6.9), also unmarked. At both stops you can admire the mature spruce and fir trees and check again for birds, including **Band-tailed Pigeons**. Between Upper Hidden Valley and Rainbow Curve (8.1), you'll pass a sign marking 10,560 feet in elevation, two miles above sea level. At Rainbow Curve, you'll almost certainly find **Clark's Nutcrackers**. A very lucky find would be a **Blue Grouse**. I've seen one there among the rocks below the parking area, and a birding tour company finds them there regularly.

After Rainbow Curve, continue along the Knife Edge where you'll be entering the alpine zone and traveling through a burn that occurred in the 1800s. Taller trees with branches on the leeward side only are called banner trees and demonstrate the harshness of the winter winds. The low-slung trees farther along that look a bit like bonsai trees are known as krummholz. They're the last trees you'll see for a while, since you're nearing timberline, about 11,400 feet in Rocky. Note the low willows growing near the road—they're the primary food source for **White-tailed Ptarmigan**.

At the Ute Trail Crossing (10.1), you'll be in the tundra (11,440 feet). I don't recommend this stop on the way up, but you should take note of the small parking area on the left (south). If you don't find a ptarmigan at one of the more reliable sites, this area offers another chance to find one on the way back. Either side of the road may have ptarmigan, but I've had several reports of ptarmigan seen along the Ute Trail on the way down to Upper Beaver Meadows, especially in late summer.

Now that you've arrived at the top of the world, here are the birds you can watch for at turnouts and as you walk the tundra. **American Pipits** nest on the tundra. They should be fairly easy to find. They are commonly seen flying straight up, then hovering as they give their flight song. **Horned Larks** also nest here. Watch for a **Prairie Falcon**, the most common raptor of the tundra despite its name. Although it's the most common raptor, you'll have to be lucky to see one. Less common, but more easily seen when present, are **Red-tailed Hawks** and **Golden Eagles**.

White-crowned Sparrows nest in the more extensive stands of willows and in the krummholz, and **Cassin's Finches** can occasionally be found in that habitat, also. **Brown-capped Rosy Finches** are found close to cliffs, where they nest, and near snowfields, where they feed.

Violet-green and **Tree swallows** are possible, as are **American Robins**. **Common Ravens** can be found most days. **Rock Wrens** are uncommon but apparently increasing. Any other bird you find on the tundra, except **White-tailed Ptarmigan**, is unusual in this habitat, if not in the Park. During migration, you might be surprised by an uncommon raptor, and more than one person has been stunned by the sight of **American White Pelicans** riding the thermals over the tundra!

As you might expect, the bird life in the tundra is limited. But there are two species that attract a lot of attention. They are, of course, **White-tailed Ptarmigan** and **Brown-capped Rosy Finches**. The ptarmigan is seldom seen below timberline, although there are historical records of a flock seen in the winter near Grand Lake and a more recent winter report of one near the YMCA west of Estes Park. The finches do come down in elevation during the winter and can be much easier to find at that time of year at feeders in Estes Park and sometimes at feeders in Boulder, Fort Collins, and other Front Range cities. In the winter, they are usually joined by **Gray-crowned Rosy Finches** and often a few **Black Rosy Finches**, neither of which are reported as nesting in the National Park.

LET'S SEE IF WE can find a ptarmigan and give you a shot at the erratic rosy finches, which can be more difficult to find. Continue west and watch for a small turnout on the left (12.4) at 11,920 feet. Looking east-northeast, you'll see Sundance Mountain. More directly north you should see the top of the rocky outcrop of the Toll Memorial (also reached by trail from the Rock Cut turnout ahead).

This has been a good **White-tailed Ptarmigan** spot, but should probably be left for the way back. If you don't find a ptarmigan at Medicine Bow Curve ahead, return here and work your way up toward Toll Memorial. (You'll see people standing on the rocks there on any summer day.) Thoroughly bird the area right at the base of the rock outcropping, where **Brown-capped Rosy Finches** have also been reported. Here you'll find

White-tailed Ptarmigan

lots of rocks the size and color of summer ptarmigan. Bird slowly and stop often to watch for movement. This area has been the second most reliable place for ptarmigan for me, especially after mid-July when the family groups are out and about. I've seen as many as a dozen birds here in late August and early September. Bird the basin toward Sundance Mountain if you don't find ptarmigan near Toll Memorial.

Continue on to Rock Cut (13.2). You'll pass through the dramatic namesake of this parking area (12,110 feet) just before you get there. Besides **Clark's Nutcrackers**, there are solar restrooms here. The effects of the change in altitude often make them a welcome sight. **White-tailed Ptarmigan** are occasionally seen along the Toll Memorial Trail. If you're there before the crowds, it might be worth the walk. It's such a heavily used area that the trail is paved. Hiking off the trail sets a bad example and invites justified criticism from those who stick to the trail. So, you'll have to get lucky and find a bird close to the trail. You can also reach the Sundance Basin birding area described above by following the trail to Toll Memorial, then working your way around the base of the rock outcropping. You should see **American Pipits** and **Horned Larks** along the trail, as well as pika and marmot.

Just a half mile west of Rock Cut is another, smaller parking lot. A boardwalk leads over a snowfield, which shrinks throughout the summer but usually doesn't melt entirely. If you're up early enough that nobody else is around, you should stop. **Brown-capped Rosy Finches** like to hang out at the edge of snowfields watching for insects on the snow. The bugs are easy to find that way, you see. You should check each snowfield you come to or can hike to easily. The less disturbed they are, the better your chances.

Continue to the large parking area on the right for Lava Cliffs (15.3), an exposed rock face that is a nesting area for a number of birds, including **Brown-capped Rosy Finches**. Check also for **Violet-green Swallows**, **American Pipits**, **Horned Larks**, and **Common Ravens**, all of which frequent the cliffside. **Prairie Falcons** have nested here in recent years. There is an extensive snowfield in this glacier-carved cirque. You should study its margins, watching for movement. A scope would definitely help you identify a rosy finch here. **White-tailed Ptarmigan** are sometimes found in this area, also.

It's best to make at least a brief stop at Lava Cliffs on the way up, to check for rosy finches while it's still early, and then another when you return, if necessary. Realistically, you have to be fortunate to find **Brown-capped Rosy Finches** in summer. I haven't found them to occur as regularly in recent years, but other people seem to have more luck than I do on this particular bird, especially at Lava Cliffs.

Return to your car and continue west. By the time you reach the Alpine Visitor Center (17.3), you will have traveled over Trail Ridge Road's highest point at 12,183 feet. Take a deep breath of the rarefied air. Soon you'll be out in it looking for **White-tailed Ptarmigan**. Speaking of which, they have been seen from the windows of the Visitor Center, which overlooks the top of Fall River canyon. Add to that the possibility of seeing **Brown-capped Rosy Finches**, **Horned Larks**, and **Clark's Nutcrackers** from the shelter of the Visitor Center, and you have a very good excuse to stop on the way back. You'll find displays inside and restrooms. You can even trot over to the gift shop/snack bar, have chili dogs for lunch, and get out of the cold if the weather's bad.

But don't stop now. Continue just about a half mile more to Medicine Bow Curve (17.7), named for the view of Wyoming's Medicine Bow Mountains on the northern horizon. Park your car—you're in **White-tailed Ptarmigan** country. Walk to the northeast corner of the overlook proper and look for a trail east. Follow that trail and keep to it as much as possible. It becomes less distinct and finally disappears a couple of hundred yards east.

You will want to work the areas above and below the line of the trail. Tundra is delicate and care must be taken to limit your impact. In areas of high traffic, such as the first part of the path off Medicine Bow Curve, stay on trails. Where tundra is damaged, such as some of the old road beds, it can take a hundred years or more to mend. Since the earth itself is not readily replenished at this elevation, deep scars that reach below vegetation are virtually permanent.

However, tundra is also tough stuff. If you take care to step on rocky areas where possible, replacing bigger rocks if they become dislodged, and avoid aggressive, Vibram-soled footwear, you'll go a long way toward protecting the tundra. In a group, it's better, I think, to spread out, both for the sake of the tundra and to cover more ground in search of ptarmigan.

Medicine Bow Curve has had hard usage over the years. I don't think the beaten-down path is caused just by birders—general-use tourists, butterfly watchers, alpine flower fanciers, and wildlife researchers have all been down the path. The impact of concentrated use at the beginning of the trail will be obvious. The naturalness of the tundra once you've gone past that area will also impress you. It means the people using it are being respectful. Help keep it that way.

Although Medicine Bow Curve has been the most reliable area recently for **White-tailed Ptarmigan**, it's not always easy to find them along Trail Ridge Road these days. Current popular thought lays the blame on elk; their population has increased dramatically in RMNP and the Estes Valley. Studies have shown that one of their primary sources of food in alpine areas is the willows ptarmigan depend on. But ptarmigan populations in RMNP are also thought to be cyclical, with a period of seven to ten years. We may just have been in one of the low points, and in fact there have been many more sightings of ptarmigan recently than there were in the past few years.

In any case, there will probably always be **White-tailed Ptarmigan**, here at Medicine Bow and throughout the alpine tundra of Rocky. It's just that with fewer birds, they're even more difficult to find. I've almost booted a ptarmigan in a group of birds without seeing it, and I watch for them. So, this will take every bit of your birding concentration and observation skills.

First, it really does help to be at Medicine Bow Curve just as the sun is high enough to give you good light and some warmth. There will likely be little wind, which will help you hear a male calling in early season or hens fussing after chicks later in summer. If you're first on the hill, the birds will not have been disturbed and will be more active. If you're really lucky, you'll just walk 100 yards east and find one.

Chances are that you'll have to work the area more thoroughly than that. The birds can be anywhere from the top of the ridge down to the krummholz, although they seem to favor the area downhill from the general line of the trail. If there are two or more of you, spread out. You can't appreciate how camouflaged they are until you find a ptarmigan. You can easily walk right past one. The best tactic is to walk a ways and then stop for a while. The stops are essential. The birds often freeze when you approach them, but if you stop long enough, they'll move. I don't know if they get too nervous to sit still or just have a short attention span and relax. Ptarmigan may simply get curious about you.

Stopping also makes you stationary, allowing you to better detect movement. Scan the tundra *slowly*, watching for movement, any movement. Look close by and then use your binocs for greater distances. When a rock moves, especially a rock with a beady black eye, you've got your bird. And listen. I doubt that you'll have trouble distinguishing the ptarmigan's call from those of the **American Pipits** and **Horned Larks** you may also hear, but it might help to listen to a tape before going afield, especially early in the summer.

Remember that the use of tapes to attract wildlife within the Park is illegal. This is a high-traffic area for birding, anyway, and I would hope you'd forego any thought of using tapes even if it were legal to do so. A tape will likely only distress both males and females, and use of tapes might eventually cause them to move off this most reliable breeding spot. If it makes you feel better, tapes would probably only work well for a short time early in the breeding season anyway, generally before the road opens.

This is a big area, and it will likely take you two hours or more to cover it. During a recent American Birding Association convention, birders hadn't even unloaded from the bus when someone spotted a ptarmigan next to the road. Don't even think you'll be that lucky!

We all understand birder's luck and nemesis birds. The **White-tailed Ptarmigan** is definitely a nemesis species for many people. I recently took a wildlife photographer to Medicine Bow Curve. Ptarmigan was one of his target birds, although he had it on his life list, and he'd been having a difficult time finding one. We walked in a short distance, and he spotted a male right away. Sitting farther along the trail, near the ptarmigan, was an older couple. They had binoculars, and we suspected they were looking for ptarmigan in a time-honored fashion, the sit-down stake-out.

As we walked up to them on our way for a closer look at the ptarmigan, the woman asked if we'd seen any. The man was almost indignant when we told him there was one just thirty yards in front of them. I think he thought we were playing a cruel joke on him, and it took him a little while to come to the realization that he was actually looking at one. Later we found out why. He'd been after this nemesis bird for forty years! This was his eighth trip to Rocky, mainly to look for **White-tailed Ptarmigan**. We all got lucky that day.

I hope you don't have to wait forty years, but don't be surprised if you can't find one right away and maybe not at all on your first trip to the tundra. If you do see a ptarmigan along Trail Ridge Road, you'll find most of the birds have colored bands on their legs as part of ongoing research projects. Unfortunately, the bright bands don't make the birds any easier to find!

After birding Medicine Bow Curve, you can return to some of the other birdy spots mentioned earlier or proceed west on Trail Ridge Road. If you decide to return to Estes Park, stop at the Alpine Visitor Center to check out the displays and look for **Brown-capped Rosy Finches**. (Don't forget the chili dogs!) Try Lava Cliffs again. If you didn't find **White-tailed Ptarmigan** at Medicine Bow, try Sundance Basin and Toll Memorial or the Ute Trail Crossing mentioned earlier.

Heading west as far as Farview Curve, about six miles, will give you the opportunity to pick up some of the uncommon, high-elevation birds, such as **Gray Jays**, **Pine Grosbeaks**, and **Red Crossbills**. Be warned that the view from Farview Curve may entice you to explore the entire west side of the Park.

IF YOU CONTINUE WEST, stop first at a small, forested turnout on the right (20.5). **Pine Grosbeaks** and **Gray Jays** have been seen here regularly. You may want to check out Poudre Lake and the willows surrounding it by stopping at a turnout just before the lake or at Milner Pass (21.6). **White-crowned** and **Lincoln's sparrows** nest in this habitat. **Spotted Sandpipers** should be seen around the shoreline. Once past Milner Pass, you're officially on the west side of Rocky.

Continue to Lake Irene (22.2) and have lunch, with **Gray Jays** and **Clark's Nutcrackers** for company. **Townsend's Solitaires**, **Pine Siskins**,

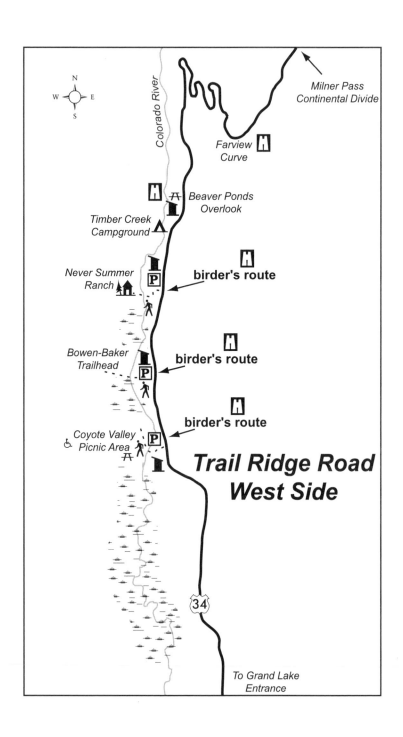

Milner Pass
Continental Divide

Colorado River

Farview
Curve

Beaver Ponds
Overlook

Timber Creek
Campground

Never Summer
Ranch

birder's route

Bowen-Baker
Trailhead

birder's route

birder's route

Coyote Valley
Picnic Area

*Trail Ridge Road
West Side*

34

To Grand Lake
Entrance

Mountain Chickadees, Ruby-crowned Kinglets, and other birds of the high country can be found here as well. **Pine Grosbeaks** are seen occasionally, as are **Red Crossbills.** After lunch, walk west to Lake Irene and follow the trail around the lake.

Farview Curve (23.8) has a great view of the beautiful Kawuneeche Valley and the Never Summer Range. **Clark's Nutcrackers** and **Gray Jays** may be found here. There are several turnouts ahead that provide birding opportunities in the meadows and riparian areas of the valley below, and I'll introduce you to them in the next few pages. The west side of Rocky is quite different from the east side in appearance and vegetation, due in part to the greater precipitation it receives, particularly in winter. However, the west-side bird life is not as varied as the east side's, because of its higher elevation and less diversified habitat.

To bird the rest of the west side, continue past Farview Curve, down the switchbacks to the Kawuneeche Valley. The Beaver Pond Overlook picnic area (29.1) gives you a close-up view of the predominant habitat of the northern part of the valley. **Mallards** and other waterfowl are here, as well as **Lincoln's Sparrows, Wilson's Warblers,** and other wetland birds. You may see a **Great Blue Heron** on the ponds or flying overhead. Here and at the other sites I'll mention, watch for moose. They favor the riparian areas along the river.

A site more typical of the west side is Never Summer Ranch (30.2), where the Park has a regular bird walk. Head west on the trail to the ranch. In the meadow, watch for **Savannah** and **Lincoln's sparrows** and **Red-winged Blackbirds.** The trail takes a hard left, paralleling the stream to the west. Before it makes a hard right, look for an informal but well-used path toward the spruce and firs next to the stream. If you don't find this path, access the riparian area from the bridge ahead, following fishermen's trails. You should see **Wilson's Warblers** and **Song** and **White-crowned sparrows** in the willows near the stream. **Red-naped Sapsuckers** like the combination of evergreens and willows. **Spotted Sandpipers** nest along the stream in this area.

Return to the trail and continue toward the ranch buildings. You'll see a stand of aspen on the right. There are many nest holes used by **Red-naped Sapsuckers, Violet-green Swallows,** and other species. **Williamson's**

Sapsuckers are seen regularly on the west side and may also be present here. Around the buildings, check for **Cordilleran Flycatchers, Western Wood-Pewees, Broad-tailed Hummingbirds**, and **Yellow-rumped Warblers**. Volunteers are usually on hand to give you a tour of the ranch. Return to your car and drive to the Bowen-Baker trailhead (31.5), an access point to National Forest land across the meadow. Start by checking for **Cliff Swallows**, which usually nest on the back side of the restroom. **Savannah Sparrows** and other grassland species should be present in the meadow. Bird the trees and the riparian area where you park and on the other side of the Colorado River—they're more productive than the lodgepole forest on the west side of the meadow. Check for **Ruby-crowned Kinglets, Pine Siskins**, and **Williamson's Sapsuckers**, in addition to the species noted for the Never Summer Ranch.

Coyote Valley Picnic Ground (32.1) has a handicapped-accessible nature trail that will take you through grasslands along the stream and provide opportunities to see species you may have missed at the other locations. The dead snags in the parking lot have many nest holes and should be checked through mid-July.

If you continue toward Grand Lake, you'll exit Rocky Mountain National Park at the Grand Lake Entrance Station (39.7). Beyond it a half mile on the left is the Kawuneeche Visitor Center. A few miles ahead you'll find the left turn to the village of Grand Lake. The main birding attraction in this area is the waters of Grand Lake and Shadow Mountain Reservoir. Although outside the Park's boundaries, both are great places to find **Bald Eagles, California Gulls**, and **Ospreys**.

You can access Grand Lake within the village at several places. Try the road over the inlet between Grand Lake and Shadow Mountain. There's a boat launch and picnic area at the end of the road. A side trip south on Highway 34 along the shore of Shadow Mountain Reservoir can also be productive. Try the Pine Beach access and the Green Ridge Campground road that crosses the dam. Both are about four miles from the turn to the town of Grand Lake.

If you decided to explore the west side, there's nothing quite like the sunset trip back to Estes Park over Trail Ridge Road, with a stop or two to listen for owls. If good birding makes you too late for the sunset, be sure to stop near the top of Trail Ridge Road for the greatest star show you've likely seen.

I TRULY HOPE you find a **White-tailed Ptarmigan**, for it is certainly Rocky Mountain National Park's trademark bird. And nobody should have to look at as many lichen-covered rocks as you will without finding one with beady eyes and a pleasant disposition. Most of all, let's hope it doesn't take you forty years to find one!

PART TWO

Birding the
Rest of Rocky

5

Upper Beaver Meadows

THE BEAVER MEADOWS ENTRANCE to Rocky Mountain National Park is the entryway for most visitors, and you don't have to travel far beyond it to find two good birding areas: Upper Beaver Meadows, found at the end of a dirt road that leaves Highway 36 about a mile from the entrance station, and Beaver Meadows, the lower end of the same meadow, found less than a half mile in, just off the Bear Lake Road.

The Upper Beaver Meadows birding area is a pretty little valley of meadows and aspen bordered by ponderosa and spruce/fir forests. There are two good reasons for a birder to visit this spot. First, for several years this has been the most reliable place for **Williamson's Sapsuckers**; and second, **Three-toed Woodpeckers** have recently taken up residence near a burn in the area.

Like many of the other places featured in this book, the valley following Beaver Brook up from Upper Beaver Meadows offers a diversified habitat in which you have the chance to see several different species. Unlike many of the other places, this one is out of the way, so you may want to save Upper Beaver Meadows for a weekend or any time you need a half-day away from the crowds.

The second site described in this chapter is Beaver Meadows (although it might be more accurately called Lower Upper Beaver Meadows). The Holt guide to Colorado birding refers to it as Upper Beaver Meadows and describes it as one of the premier birding spots in Rocky. Although that's a bit of an overstatement, this relatively small area does have a good concentration of mountain birds. Again, it's a diverse habitat with dense pines on the confining slope to the south and a wet meadow with

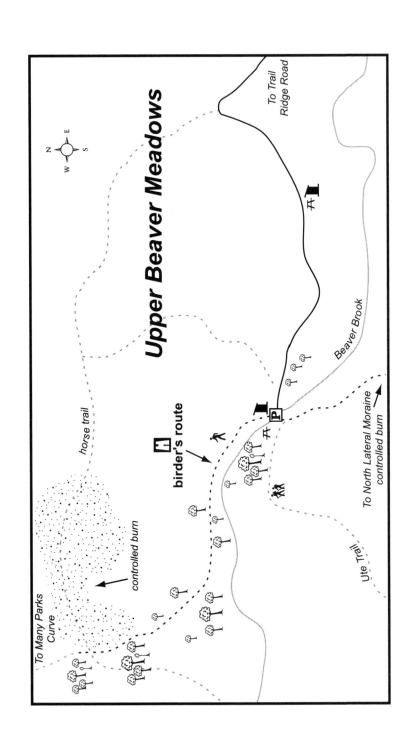

Upper Beaver Meadows

To Trail
Ridge Road

Beaver Brook

To North Lateral Moraine
controlled burn

Ute Trail

birder's route

horse trail

controlled burn

To Many Parks
Curve

N
W E
S

aspen and associated riparian habitat. By whatever name it may be called, this section of Beaver Meadows is convenient to the Park entrance, seldom crowded, and productive when other areas aren't. It's a great stop when you only have an hour or when you're looking for midday birding.

To Reach Upper Beaver Meadows

Enter the Park at the Beaver Meadows Entrance. **Reset your trip odometer to zero.** To reach Upper Beaver Meadows, continue west past the Bear Lake turn (0.2) to where the road makes a hairpin curve to the right. The turn to Upper Beaver Meadows (0.7) is on your left just past the apex of the curve. A sign marks the turn. Follow the dirt road 1.4 miles, going past the helipad and then a picnic area to the end of the road, where you'll find a second picnic area with a restroom.

What You'll Find—Upper Beaver Meadows

Birding in the dry grasslands along Upper Beaver Meadows road can be good for **Vesper Sparrows, Black-billed Magpies, Green-tailed Towhees**, and other species, so don't hesitate to stop if you see something interesting. A **Red-headed Woodpecker** made an appearance here early one summer. You may want to walk parts of the road or of the trail (described later) that skirts the grasslands on the south side of the meadows.

As you drive past the first picnic area, notice the fenced area where Park biologists are studying the effects of grazing by elk and deer. Note that if you live in Estes Park and want to have a garden, this is how tall your fence must be! Another fenced area is located at the end of the road.

From the parking lot at the end of the road, you'll be heading west/northwest up a valley with a small creek in it. A dry ridge defines the north boundary of the valley, and a pine-and-fir forest marks the south boundary. As you leave the parking area, walk west past the outhouse. Follow the edge of the aspen grove, keeping the tiny creek on your left, and then head uphill to a trail on the right side of the valley.

Stay on the trail as much as possible. You can follow this little valley all the way up to Many Parks Curve on Trail Ridge Road, which you'll see at various points if you look up the mountain.

You may find **Mountain Bluebirds**; they nest in cavities in the aspen trees along the trail. It's perfect habitat for **House Wrens** and a good place to finally spot a **Warbling Vireo** in the aspens. They're common here, and because you can walk around trees to get a vantage spot and can often climb a slope beside a tree, you have a good chance to get an identifying look at a bird that's often maddeningly difficult to see. There has been some speculation that the western Warbling Vireo will be split from the eastern version, making this a potential lifer of the future if you're from the eastern or midwestern states. Note the song, which is quite different from that of the eastern bird.

Dusky Flycatchers can sometimes be found in the alders along the forest margin, and **Hammond's Flycatchers** may be seen in spruce and fir farther along the trail. Other flycatchers, such as **Western Wood-Pewees**, may be seen up the slope in the ponderosas. Listen for **Cordilleran Flycatchers**, especially toward the top end of the valley. Along the forest margin you'll likely hear **Ruby-crowned Kinglets** in spring and early summer. Once you're acquainted with their song, their numbers may surprise you, here and in the Park in general.

The woodies are here, too. Look for **Northern Flicker, Hairy** and **Downy woodpeckers,** and occasionally **Red-naped Sapsuckers**. A pair of **Williamson's Sapsuckers** has nested here for the past several years, making Upper Beaver Meadows one of the most reliable spots for this sought-after species. Start looking for them when the valley widens to a grassy meadow a few hundred yards up the trail. They nest in aspens and range widely throughout the meadow when feeding young. There is almost always a pair in the lower part of this meadow. Recently a pair nested in an aspen just five feet from the path!

If you're in need of a **Williamson's Sapsucker**, spend some time here checking out the aspens or just sitting quietly and waiting for one to find you. Remember that the female looks rather like a petite **Northern Flicker**—nothing at all like the male. In fact, early biologists thought they were two separate species.

Williamson's Sapsucker

The brush along the creek is a favorite place for **Dark-eyed Juncos,** **Lincoln's Sparrows,** and **White-crowned Sparrows** (early and late in summer). **Chipping Sparrows** are common throughout the area. **Swainson's** and **Hermit thrushes** are possibilities in the valley and at the forest edges, especially as they migrate through. **Cassin's Finches** are sometimes seen in the valley, and the irruptive **Red Crossbill** and uncommon **Pine Grosbeak** can occasionally be found. This is one of the few areas where I have hope of regularly finding a **Western Tanager.**

Although I haven't yet seen one here, I think **Blue Grouse** are possible, too. The moist bottomland and associated aspen groves certainly are similar to other places I've found them, and they are seen regularly on Deer Mountain, the mountain to the north, where they are heard drumming in May. A **Northern Saw-whet Owl** nested in an aspen tree in another part of Upper Beaver Meadows, so they may also be in this valley.

You can continue up the valley, staying among the aspen or following the informal trail, for as long as you want, until it finally climbs toward Many Parks Curve above. About a half-mile up the valley proper, you'll cross a trail where you'll find a hitch rack. This is another nesting area for **Williamson's Sapsuckers.** If I haven't seen one on my way up the valley, I'll often sit down near the hitch rack and wait. If a pair is nesting in the area, it isn't long before one of them will make its rounds nearby. The open ponderosa forest mixed with aspens that you'll find near the hitch rack is ideal for Williamson's.

Following the horse trail uphill to the north leads you through a controlled-burn area. **Three-toed Woodpeckers** have moved in here in recent years. I've seen them as I make my way up to the horse trail in burned trees along the path, and there are reports of them from the area of the trail as it climbs the north ridge. All the other woodpeckers mentioned above may also be found here, along with **Pygmy** and **White-breasted nuthatches. Western Tanagers** are also drawn to burned areas.

In a small aspen grove adjacent to the controlled burn, I recently noted nine species nesting: **Downy, Hairy,** and **Three-toed woodpeckers, Northern Flickers, Williamson's Sapsuckers, Mountain Chickadees, Pygmy Nuthatches,** and **Violet-green** and **Tree swallows.**

You may be tempted to take the horse trail south back to the parking area, but I can't recommend it for the birds, and it's considerably longer. Better to follow the horse trail north through the burn for a while and then bushwhack back to your car or head back down the way you came and hope that the **Red Crossbill** you've been looking for has flown in.

IF YOU WANT TO TRY another place for the **Three-toed Woodpecker**, return to the parking lot, cross the creek on the wooden bridge, and take the trail that heads south. However, this side trip is a long shot if the Three-toed is all you're going for, and your time is probably better spent in the Upper Beaver Meadows burn area, Endovalley (Chapter 1), or Cow Creek (Chapter 7).

In about thirty yards, the Ute Trail heads off to the right on its way up to Trail Ridge, but you should continue straight ahead. In a quarter mile or so, just inside the trees, you'll reach a junction. Continue south, following the trail signs to Moraine Park, as the main trail climbs the moraine. Another, older, controlled burn is evident as you near the top, and the trail follows the edge of it for another quarter mile.

There may be **Hairy** and **Downy woodpeckers** in the area, so be sure of your identifying field marks. You may be lucky enough to see a **Northern Goshawk** and are likely to see **Western Wood-Pewees** and other flycatchers, nuthatches, and chickadees in the burn.

To extend this walk and bird the meadows you drove through on your way in, return to the bottom of the moraine and take the trail to the right, marked Upper Beaver Meadows. Follow it along the edge of the meadow. Check for **Vesper**, **Savannah** (May), and **Chipping sparrows**. **Green-tailed Towhees** are likely to be here, and **Black-billed Magpies** are common. **Willow Flycatchers** are sometimes found along the stream.

After about three quarters of a mile, you'll find a trail leading north toward the road. You could take this trail and walk back along the road to your car if you've found the birding productive, but you've probably already had a representative sample of the bird life you'd find. Taking this whole loop will extend your hike by well over an hour, so you may want to bird the meadows for a short distance and return to your car.

I HOPE YOU ENJOY this lovely, out-of-the-way area. The only company you're likely to have when you walk up the valley is other birders who have read this book. Take care of the habitat, minimize your impact by staying on the informal trails you find as much as you can, and enjoy a few hours away from the rush.

To Reach Beaver Meadows

To reach Beaver Meadows from the Beaver Meadows Entrance Station, turn left on the Bear Lake Road (0.2). Cross the meadow and find a parking area on the right just as the road enters the trees, about 100 yards from the turn. There should be a picnic table on the right to indicate that you've found the place. Since there's only room for two cars at the picnic area parking, you might have to park at the turnout closer to the entrance road or travel to a safe place to turn around and then park on the opposite side of the road. Be sure you're able to pull completely off the road or expect a ticket when you return. Even if there are picnickers present, you should stop, since you'll be working your way west to bird.

What You'll Find—Beaver Meadows

From the picnic table, walk along the indistinct trail leading west that follows the bottom of the wooded hillside on your left. Beaver Brook runs through the wet meadow on your right. Riparian habitat and scattered aspen are the features of this area, along with the pines and firs of the hillside.

In the pines, watch for **Western Wood-Pewees**, **Townsend's Solitaires**, **White-breasted** and **Pygmy nuthatches**, **Ruby-crowned Kinglets**, and **Yellow-rumped Warblers (Audubon's)**. You should find the gray-headed race of **Dark-eyed Juncos**, too. I've seen **Great Horned Owls** in this forest, and you may get lucky and find **Red Crossbills** feeding on cones near the treetops. This is one of the better places for **Townsend's Solitaire**, a species that can be difficult to find in mid-summer when the birds are generally quiet. Watch for one high in the pines.

In the aspen groves, check nesting holes for **Hairy** and **Downy woodpeckers**, **Red-naped Sapsuckers**, **Northern Flickers**, **House Wrens**, and **Violet-green** and **Tree swallows**. There is usually a pair or two of **Mountain Bluebirds** and occasionally a pair of **Western Bluebirds** nesting in the aspens, too. Check streamside areas for **Lincoln's Sparrows**. Stay on high ground as much as possible, avoiding any crossing of the meadow to the north, which is very mucky.

Along the edge of the forest and in the riparian/aspen areas, check for **Hammond's** and **Dusky flycatchers**. You may also find a **Cordilleran Flycatcher** here. **Mourning Doves**, not a common species within the Park boundaries, are also present some years. **Steller's Jays** and **Chipping Sparrows** are fairly common in both habitats, as are **Warbling Vireos**. When you've birded this area to your satisfaction, return the way you came.

I've also had good luck crossing Bear Lake Road and birding to the east. In the more open areas here, you may spot **Red-tailed Hawks** in the sky above and **Green-tailed Towhees** near the shrubby vegetation in the grassy areas. **Broad-tailed Hummingbirds** are more common in the open meadow, also, and if you've been living right, you may find a **Western Tanager**.

AS YOU CAN TELL, there is good birding to be had in this small area. It should keep you busy for an hour or two, working your way west as far as the birds warrant and then returning to cross Bear Lake Road and bird the lower meadow. This is a good place for lunch and midday birding, since the birds seem to be active here all day.

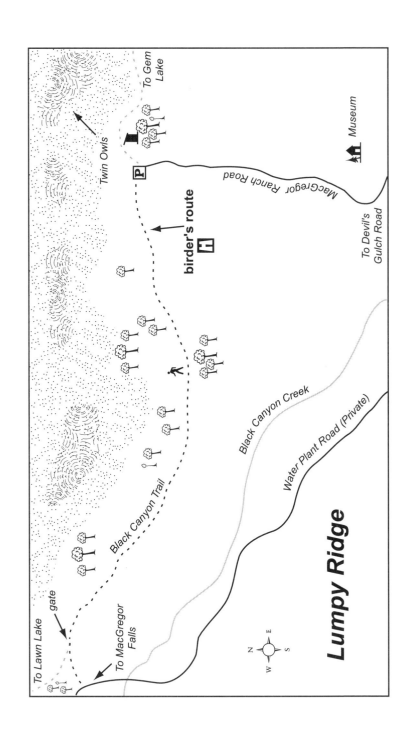

To Gem Lake

Twin Owls

Museum

MacGregor Ranch Road

birder's route

To Devil's Gulch Road

Black Canyon Creek

Black Canyon Trail

Water Plant Road (Private)

To Lawn Lake

gate

To MacGregor Falls

N
E
W
S

Lumpy Ridge

6

Lumpy Ridge

THAT WONDERFUL exposed-granite ridge that forms the north boundary of the Estes Valley is Lumpy Ridge. Aptly named, the rock formations here are the home of **White-throated Swifts**, **Prairie Falcons**, and **Red-tailed Hawks**, and the playground of serious rock climbers. The most prominent feature of Lumpy Ridge and the one most intriguing to birders is Twin Owls. See if you can spot the enormous rock owls from Devil's Gulch Road or, for that matter, nearly anywhere in the Estes Valley.

Not only will swifts and raptors be of special interest, you may see some species that are difficult to find in other areas of the Park. Extensive grasslands, plenty of exposed rock cliffs, and a hay meadow make the habitat of Lumpy Ridge quite different from most of the rest of Rocky Mountain National Park, and the bird life reflects that. There are interesting birds here and even more interesting possibilities, and that's why Lumpy Ridge is one of the sites in the Park where naturalists regularly lead bird walks.

To Reach Lumpy Ridge

There are two main access points to Lumpy Ridge—MacGregor Ranch and the Gem Lake trailhead, which I'll mention later. To find both, start at the intersection of Highways 34 and 36 in Estes Park. **Reset your trip odometer to zero here.** Take the Highway 34 Bypass west past the Stanley Hotel to the turn to Devil's Gulch on MacGregor Avenue (0.4). Turn right and follow the road to where it curves east (to the right). The entrance to MacGregor Ranch is on the left at the curve (1.1). Follow the paved road north past the ranch headquarters and the museum to the trailhead parking area (1.9).

This small parking lot is not suitable for RVs or oversized vehicles, and there is no adequate turnaround at the end, so scope out where the open spots are as you approach the lot. No roadside parking is permitted. To be assured a parking spot, you should be there by 7 A.M. on weekends. Later may be okay on weekdays. You're in competition with the rock climbers, and they like an early start to avoid the afternoon thunderstorms. There is a flip-up sign at the entrance that supposedly tells you whether the lot is full, but I've found it to be unreliable. The location of the Lumpy Ridge parking area is almost constantly being reevaluated by the National Park and may, by the time you read this, actually be relocated to another spot in the neighborhood. Signs should indicate a change, if there is one.

MacGregor Ranch, an historic cattle ranch, is managed as an educational site now and, as such, is still maintained as a working ranch. Ranch hands use only non-mechanized equipment to make hay, and the Percheron draft horses you may see on the way to the trailhead earn their keep under harness. During the late summer cutting season, you may see them working in the fields. The ranch hands still drive cattle along roads (and I'm not talking about a truck and trailer) to and from summer pasture. If you're interested in this part of the area's history, there is a museum at the Ranch (open in summer) that you may enjoy visiting.

If you don't find a parking spot at MacGregor Ranch, your choices are to park along Devil's Gulch Road and walk in, which adds about 0.8 miles, or to use the Gem Lake Trail, which will add about a mile-and-a-quarter to your walk. To find the Gem Lake trailhead, continue on Devil's Gulch Road past the MacGregor Ranch turn less than a mile to a small parking lot on the left. Like the MacGregor parking area, this one fills up early in summer and on weekends in spring and fall. No additional parking is available nearby.

The Gem Lake Trail takes you into a mixed ponderosa forest, and all the birds of that habitat may be seen there. The trail is noted for outstanding views of the Estes Valley. At the trail junction about three-quarters of a mile in, take the left branch to Twin Owls and the parking lot at MacGregor Ranch.

What You'll Find

After you get over the initial wow of the close-up you'll have of Twin Owls from the parking lot, use your binocs to scan the rock walls and the sky around the top of the formation. The view is deceiving. It seems that you're close enough to be able to see birds with the naked eye, but they're a long way up. You'll be standing at an elevation of about 7,950 feet. The top of Twin Owls is 8,789 feet, over 800 feet higher.

White-throated Swifts nest on the rock formations, and you should see them near the top of Twin Owls and neighboring rocks. They are almost always present in summer but may range away from the cliffs during parts of the day. If you miss them when you start your walk, check again before you leave. **Violet-green Swallows** may also be in your field of view, so remember my second rule of swift watching: If you have to wonder whether it's a swift or a swallow, it's a swallow. (My first rule, which you'll remember from previous chapters, is to look up in swift country, and you're already doing that!)

Although **White-throated Swifts** are sometimes seen at higher elevations, even on the tundra in some areas of Colorado, Lumpy Ridge is the best place in Rocky for them. I have seen them once in Wild Basin and once on the Cub Lake Trail, places where **Black Swifts** are more common. They also occur just on the other side of the ridge in the Cow Creek drainage, and I've seen them very occasionally in Endovalley. But I've found them at Lumpy Ridge nearly every day I've visited the area in summer.

If you have a scope, you should bring it on this walk. Just from your experience in the parking lot, I think you'll agree that a scope could make the difference in identifying a raptor perched on the rocks above. There's good sparrow viewing on the trail, too, and a scope will enhance your enjoyment of them.

After checking for swifts, walk to the west end of the trailhead parking lot, where you'll find an information sign. Here you'll see a map showing the thirty-one named climbing areas. During raptor breeding season, you'll also find a poster delineating areas closed to climbing to protect the nests of **Prairie** and **Peregrine falcons**. **Red-tailed Hawks** also nest in the area, as do **Golden Eagles**. In addition to these, watch for the three accipiters, **Cooper's** and **Sharp-shinned hawks** and **Northern Goshawks**, all of which can occur along the trail. You may even be fortunate enough to see an **American Kestrel**, a bird that is common on the plains but uncommon at higher elevations.

During spring migration, you may get really lucky and spot a **Swainson's Hawk** or even a **Broad-winged Hawk**, and during fall and early winter, check out any buteos for a **Ferruginous Hawk**, rare to the mountains but seen here before. In short, if you like raptors, this is a great area.

Scan the rock formations here and along the trail for the telltale whitewashes that indicate raptor nests or roosts. At any time, you may see falcons or hawks flying among the rock formations. Seeing a **Peregrine Falcon** chasing some of the **Rock Doves** that also make a home in the rocks is a great thrill.

Clark's Nutcrackers can also sometimes be seen higher on the slopes, although often you'll only hear them. This is good swallow country, and the three common species—**Barn**, **Tree**, and **Violet-green swallows**—are found here. You'll probably also see **Common Ravens** flying near the rocks and **American Crows** working in the meadows below, where you should also find **Black-billed Magpies**. Check, too, for **Turkey Vultures** circling overhead.

One caveat about this trail before you begin. This area is known for sudden and serious summer thunderstorms that come over Lumpy Ridge with little warning. Keep an eye on the weather. There's not much cover. Either hit the trail early to avoid the storms or start after the afternoon thunderstorms have cleared the parking lot.

To begin this walk, take the lower trail from the information sign. It's the Black Canyon Trail, and you'll see a sign for it. A climber's trail also leaves from north of the information sign and can easily be mistaken for the main trail. For a mile or so, you'll be walking through a grassland interspersed with ponderosa pines and a few clumps of atypical

Northern Goshawk

aspens, twenty-foot trees with trunks big enough to support forty- and fifty-foot trees.

This grassland provides an excellent opportunity to see sparrows and wrens. **Vesper Sparrows** may be found, along with **Chipping Sparrows.** Watch, especially in spring, for both **Brewer's** and **Clay-colored sparrows.** In the thicker cover, particularly uphill toward the rocks, look for **Green-tailed Towhees. Mountain Bluebirds** may also be seen in the meadows.

You should find **House Wrens** without any trouble, and you may see the more uncommon **Rock Wren**, although it's typically only a migrant. From the look of the land, you'd have to believe **Canyon Wrens** would be here, but they're rare in RMNP. They're more common in the foothills and lower mountain canyons, but there are historical records from elevations as high as Trail Ridge Road. I've only seen one in the Park and it was at Lumpy Ridge. There are a few other reports of them from Lumpy Ridge and from the Gem Lake Trail.

If you're going to add a new bird to the Park checklist, it may be along Black Canyon Trail. If you've spent any time in the canyons of the southwest, you might be reminded of them along this trail. Wandering birds may be attracted to the area for the same reason. Since we've had both a **Black Phoebe** and a **Black-throated Sparrow** at Lake Estes, only a couple of miles from Lumpy Ridge, and an **Acorn Woodpecker** along McGraw Ranch Road, a few miles east, I think anything might turn up, especially in the spring and fall. **Townsend's Warblers** (in August and September) and **Lazuli Buntings** have been recorded along the Black Canyon Trail.

For the scenery here, you can be grateful to the Muriel MacGregor Trust and Rocky Mountain National Park. Without them, this would likely be another subdivision with mundane but expensive houses spread across the meadow below. Instead, the open grassland through which you walk, the hay meadows below, and the astounding rock formations above will take you back in time and make you realize why people were drawn to this mountain park in the first place. The grasslands in the Estes Valley are mostly gone now, given over to suburbia. Wetlands have vanished under reservoirs. Only the rocks seem unassailable … at least until you find some rock climbers on the sheer walls of Lumpy Ridge.

As you scan for birds, the climbers are difficult to miss as they hang from fingernail holds. It is only when you seen a tiny human suspended on the side of one of the rock formations, such as The Book or The Pear, that you can fully appreciate the immensity of the scene before you.

As you wander along the trail, watch for aspens with nest holes in them. They may be the homes of **Red-naped Sapsuckers**, **Northern Flickers**, and **Downy** and **Hairy woodpeckers**. A **Williamson's Sapsucker** may occasionally be seen. (A naturalist who leads bird trips here has seen one pursued by a **Peregrine Falcon**, a double delight for him, if not for the sapsucker.) Nest holes may also house **Northern Pygmy-Owls**, and the forest edge is good habitat for them, too. The trail wanders in and out of Park property, by the way, and you should respect the no-trespassing signs that MacGregor Ranch has put up to protect its land.

When the trail runs along the edge of the ponderosa pines, **Mountain Chickadees** and **Steller's Jays** are often seen, as are **Townsend's Solitaires**. **Pygmy Nuthatches**, as well as **White-breasted** and **Red-breasted nuthatches**, like this kind of open forest. The **Pygmy Nuthatches** may be easiest to find, due to their incessant chatting. When you find a flock, be sure to check for the other nuthatches and for **Brown Creepers**, since mixed flocks are very common, except during nesting season in June and July.

Add to this list **Mountain Bluebirds** and the very occasional **Western Bluebird**, **Pine Siskins**, **Cassin's Finches**, **House Finches**, **Red Cross-bills**, **Yellow-rumped Warblers**, **Cordilleran Flycatchers**, **Western Wood-Pewees**, and **Western Tanagers**, and you see that there is a good chance of seeing many birds along the way. Overall, the trail is not as birdy in total numbers of birds as some other locales, but the number of different species you may see should be typical of the other sites in this book. The raptors and the unusual scenery of the area make it a special place to watch birds in any case.

The trail traverses the grassy slope below Lumpy Ridge and meanders along the edge of the hay meadow. The meadow is an inviting area, but remember that MacGregor Ranch is a private trust. Anywhere in the West, it's not considered polite to walk through a rancher's hay field. In short, don't walk across the fields to access the riparian willows along Black Canyon Creek. Even from a distance, you'll hear **Red-winged**

Blackbirds, and you may hear or see **Common Snipe** if you're here in the evenings. The birds you'd find along the creek are more easily and more politely found other places.

As you walk along, you'll see a gate ahead on the trail as it crosses the top of the hay meadow. Watch for a wet draw coming down from a small aspen grove on the hill above, about 100 yards before the gate. The trail splits briefly at this point to avoid a particularly wet area. In July, August, and September, look for **Blue Grouse** here. Often you'll hear grouse before you see them, if you're paying attention. One day I stopped near this draw to scope a sparrow. As I was working on it, I thought I heard an owl giving a soft, repeated, low hoot up the hill. I took three steps toward the sound, and a young Blue Grouse exploded from beneath my feet. That was my owl. The owl-like mewing and various clucking noises of grouse with young can give away their location if you're listening for them.

At the gate at the end of the grassland section of the trail, you'll be a little over a mile from the trailhead. Go through the gate, being careful to close it behind you. Walk west to the dirt road you'll see. The meadows here are particularly good for sparrows, and you should find **Green-tailed Towhees** readily during the nesting season. Go left on the road toward an aspen grove where you may find **Northern Flickers** and the other woodpeckers mentioned above. The wet meadow near the aspen may also have **Blue Grouse**; it's perfect habitat for them.

After checking out the aspen and meadows, work your way back along the meadow edge in the vicinity of the road. Watch for accipiters, such as **Sharp-shinned Hawk**, seen here occasionally. **Dusky** and **Cordilleran flycatchers** may be found, along with an assortment of nuthatches, chickadees, and other birds. **Yellow-rumped Warblers** will be easier to find here than along the trail you've been on. This is one of the few places I've found a **Plumbeous Vireo** in the National Park, and you may hear and see **Mourning Doves**, an uncommon bird in the Park.

AFTER YOU'VE BIRDED the meadow and forest edges past the gate, you can hike to MacGregor Falls, continue on the Black Canyon Trail to its junction with the Cow Creek/Lawn Lake Trail, or return to your car.

If you or members of your party enjoy a destination for your hike, continue west on the dirt road. Follow it to a water treatment facility and find the marked trail to MacGregor Falls. The falls are about a mile-and-a-half from the gate, and you'll gain about 600 feet in elevation. The falls are small, but they're isolated and generally quiet unless a horseback group from one of the stables in town happens to be there. The walk is not particularly noteworthy for birds, but it will give you a breather from all the scenery.

You can also continue on the main trail from the gate, up and over the saddle to the trail that leads east to Cow Creek and west to Lawn Lake above Endovalley. The trail junction is about two miles up, and the hike is steep, climbing from 7,800 feet to 9,200 feet. I guess you can tell I wouldn't recommend it, but it may be worth your time to take the trail for a half-mile or so. It's one of the most reliable spots in the Park for **Western Tanagers.**

Both these extensions take you through forests where the bird life is fairly sparse and pretty predictable. If you're mainly interested in birds, I suggest you return to your car on the Black Canyon Trail. If you have extra time to spend in the area, you'll find the trail to Twin Owls on the east side of the parking area to be more interesting, both for birds and for scenery.

As you walk back to the parking area, it's almost as if you were on another trail. You'll find your attention is directed much more to the rock formations. You'll have a better view of The Book, that amazing, paginated piece of granite that climbers consider heaven, and you'll get a new perspective on the Estes Valley. Maybe you'll even find some new birds.

YOU SHOULDN'T MISS the chance to get up close and personal with the rocks and the birds of Lumpy Ridge. I think you'll find this one of your most memorable trips in the Park—both for the birds and for the scenery. And I hope you'll get to see the swifts and raptors for which this area is known.

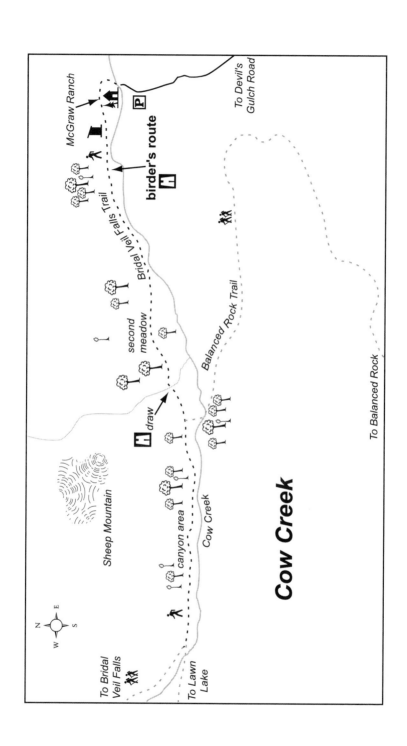

Cow Creek

N

To Bridal Veil Falls

To Lawn Lake

Sheep Mountain

canyon area

Cow Creek

draw

second meadow

Bridal Veil Falls Trail

Balanced Rock Trail

To Balanced Rock

McGraw Ranch

birder's route

P

To Devil's Gulch Road

7

Cow Creek

COW CREEK FLOWS THROUGH a little valley that is one my favorite places in Rocky Mountain National Park. Uncrowded and a bit out of the way, it's also a good place to find interesting birds. Most notably, the Cow Creek area has been one of the most reliable places in the Park to find **Northern Pygmy-Owl**, one of our specialties. The owls have nested here for many years. And **Blue Grouse**, another specialty, are fairly easy to find after mid-July, when family groups are on the move. Add to those great birds a mix of more common species and the chance for unusual ones, and you'll understand why I've included Cow Creek in this book.

The birding route I'll describe begins on the eastern boundary of Rocky Mountain National Park, a few miles northeast of Estes Park. You may hear the area referred to by the name of the popular hiking trail located there—Bridal Veil Falls—or by the name of the former dude ranch where the parking lot is located—McGraw Ranch. The ranch property now belongs to RMNP, and the buildings have been converted into a research and housing facility.

The trail follows a small mountain valley with a stream, beaver ponds, open grasslands, junipers, and aspen groves, all bordered by a mixed pine, spruce, and fir forest. Here, in one place, are nearly all the habitats of RMNP, except subalpine firs and alpine tundra.

Because Cow Creek is at relatively low elevation (7,800 feet), it might be a good starting place for your birding. It's good to take it easy the first day or two if you've come from a much lower elevation. This fairly level trail will help you get acclimated, especially because you'll hopefully be stopping a lot to look at birds.

Cow Creek is best from early June through early September, when the nesting birds are active. Earlier and later in the season can be chancy, and I have sometimes walked the trail without much bird company. Winter is the best time for **Northern Pygmy-Owls**, but this is still a good place to look for them in summer.

To Reach Cow Creek

At the intersection of Highways 34 and 36 in Estes Park, **reset your trip odometer to zero.** Take the Highway 34 Bypass north and west past The Stanley Hotel to the Devil's Gulch turn on MacGregor Avenue (0.4). Turn right (north) and drive to a dirt road on the left marked McGraw Ranch Road (3.9), where you'll turn.

Residents of this area were not thrilled, understandably, at the thought of increased traffic due to the purchase of the ranch by RMNP in 1988. They have tried to restrict access by, among other things, forcing the Park to limit parking. There is now a sign at the turn to indicate the status of the parking. Follow the dirt road over Lumpy Ridge and down to the old ranch, respecting private property by driving carefully and within the speed limit. There's a turnaround at the ranch and parking for sixteen cars alongside the road on the way back out. Bridal Veil Falls is a popular destination, and the parking lot usually fills early. Be there before 8 A.M. or come in late afternoon when the **Northern Pygmy-Owls** may be more active and the parking lot may be empty.

What You'll Find

The trail to Bridal Veil Falls is 3.2 miles long, but the best birding is from the trailhead to the Lawn Lake Trail cut-off, about two miles in. After you've parked, walk back to the turnaround where you should find a trail sign. The location of the trailhead may be changed due to the conversion of the ranch buildings, but it should be clearly marked. Begin by checking out the area around the buildings, including the man-made pond and beaver ponds west of the turnaround. **Mallards** usually nest on the pond, and you may also find **Spotted Sandpipers** near the beaver ponds. In the trees near the buildings, look for **Mountain Chickadees** and **Pygmy Nuthatches**. **Red-breasted** and **White-breasted nuthatches** are fairly common.

Most summers **Cordilleran Flycatchers** nest in the vicinity of the buildings, sometimes in surprising numbers. They seem to prefer close association with human habitation when available, and anywhere you find a cabin in the woods you should listen for the distinctive, rising "too-sweet" call of this "easy" *Empidonax*. Their nests are often placed under eaves or similar structural edifices. This is probably the best place in the Park to find one easily.

Follow the trail west, where you'll soon find a restroom. In the next half-mile, you'll be walking on an old roadbed through an open meadow with a few ponderosas, spruces, and aspens. This is not the birdiest part of the trail, but there are lots of possibilities. **House Wrens, Violet-green** and **Tree swallows**, and **Yellow-rumped Warblers** are common. Watch the willows near the stream for **Wilson's** and **MacGillivray's warblers** (early and late summer), **Song Sparrows**, and the occasional oddity, such as **Black-headed Grosbeaks. Black-billed Magpies** like the meadow but are not always present. You may get lucky and see a **Williamson's Sapsucker** in the mixed aspen and ponderosas north of the trail, too. They've nested here in recent years.

Northern Pygmy-Owls often nest in the general area you'll be walking through, sometimes in the aspen groves up the hill to the north and sometimes across the creek and up the hillside to the south. Although diurnal, they are most active in early morning and late afternoon. Overcast conditions can keep them active throughout the day. Once the female begins incubating, the birds are quiet. This makes them tough to find from mid-April through June. Once the juveniles are out, you may find them from their begging calls as the family feeds together. Other times of the year, listening for the owl's repeated, whistled call is the best way to locate one. Study your tapes, but remember that it's illegal to use them in the Park.

As you walk along the path, listen for **Townsend's Solitaires** calling from the tops of nearby evergreens. The recurring single note carries, so be prepared to walk farther than you think if you decide to pursue one.

Strangely, solitaires are less vocal in summer than they are at other seasons. Incidentally, the solitaire's call note can sometimes be mistaken for that of a **Northern Pygmy-Owl**, so you should listen to both on your tapes. Although similar in tone, the owl calls constantly, while the solitaire's single note is repeated at longer intervals.

Especially in the spring and early summer, this area can hold lots of sparrows. **White-crowned Sparrows** may be in the streamside willows, and the occasional **Brewer's Sparrow** or **Clay-colored Sparrow** can be found in the grasses. **Chipping Sparrows** are common residents all summer. In August, watch for migrating **Lark Sparrows**. Where trees stand in the meadow, watch and listen for flycatchers. Cow Creek is one of the best places to find **Olive-sided Flycatchers**. Look for them high in spruce and fir trees, especially on dead tops.

You'll soon come to a place where the stream runs right next to the trail. This is usually a birdy area, with mixed flocks in spring, as well as late summer and fall. They can keep you busy for an hour and give you ten to fifteen species, including the uncommon **Townsend's Warbler**, which migrates through in August and September. One late August day, my wife and I found a single flock with seventeen species, including five warblers (**Yellow-rumped**, **Wilson's**, **MacGillivray's**, **Virginia's**, and Townsend's), three species of nuthatches, three kinds of flycatchers, and a good assortment of other mountain birds. That may help explain why I consider this area to be so good!

After a half mile or so, the trail becomes a single track and climbs to a second meadow, this one with small aspens sprinkled throughout it. From this meadow to the Lawn Lake Trail cut-off, you'll find the most productive birding. The second meadow has been one of the best places in Rocky to find **Northern Pygmy-Owls**. On several occasions in summer I've seen them during the day in this section of the trail, but early mornings and late afternoons are better. This is the area we visit to add the species to our Christmas Bird Count.

One October, walking out at dusk, my wife and I heard at least two and perhaps as many as four **Northern Pygmy-Owls** in the last mile before reaching the trailhead, including one at the ranch buildings. We found the pygmy-owls again on the Christmas count in December, and

Northern Pygmy-Owl

they were there in February, too. They are year-round residents in this area. But remember that in summer they call infrequently and are more difficult to find.

We have also seen a **Great Horned Owl** hunting near the stream in this area, and **Long-eared** and **Flammulated owls** have been reported along the trail. Both are rare in the Park. The trail through the second meadow also produces **Blue Grouse** hens and chicks after midsummer, although it's not ideal habitat for them since it's fairly dry and open. But this *is* a great area for woodies. I've seen **Hairy Woodpeckers, Northern Flickers**, and **Red-naped Sapsuckers. Williamson's Sapsuckers** also nest here some years.

A **Three-toed Woodpecker** was reported along the trail one year, and the next year a pair nested near the stream in this area. I should warn you again that Three-toed Woodpeckers are not as regular or reliable as you may think, based on your experience with other woodies. They are notorious for setting up shop in a place for a year or two and then disappearing. Still, Cow Creek has been a good place to find Three-toed Woodpeckers, in this section of the trail and above the Lawn Lake cutoff, closer to the falls.

All the while you walk the trail, it's a good thing to pay attention to the sky overhead. Except in midsummer when they're generally at higher elevations, listen for the gravelly, jay-like calls of **Clark's Nutcrackers**. They can be seen flying from one margin to the other when they're present. Raptors nest on Lumpy Ridge to the south and Sheep Mountain, the prominent rock face to the north and west, and you may see **Red-tailed Hawks** and **Prairie Falcons**. **Peregrine Falcons** have nested on Sheep Mountain off and on for several years. **White-throated Swifts** also nest there, but they're seldom low enough to be identifiable without a scope.

In the forested parts of the trail, don't be surprised if you see an accipiter, either a **Sharp-shinned Hawk** or a **Cooper's Hawk**, especially in spring. The Park's first confirmed nesting for Sharp-shinned Hawks was reported in 1998 in the Cow Creek area. The forest right along the trail is probably not extensive enough to attract a **Northern Goshawk**, although one may fly from one side of the valley to the other, giving you a longer look than you're likely to get in the deep forest.

NEAR THE WEST END of the second meadow, before the trail enters the pines and firs, you'll cross a small gully. The trail dips into a streambed lined with alder and understory plants. This is an excellent area for birds and worthy of some time spent seeing what comes along. I've found **Ruby-crowned Kinglets**, **Western Tanagers**, *Empidonax* flycatchers, **Western Wood-Pewees**, **Red-naped Sapsuckers**, **Pygmy**, **White-breasted**, and **Red-breasted nuthatches**, and many other birds just by spending a little time here before continuing. An **Olive-sided Flycatcher** has been a regular for several years. Watch for one perched near the tops of the dead aspens north of the trail.

The aspens immediately after the gully are good hunting ground for woodpeckers and sapsuckers. Along with the more common species, watch especially for **Williamson's Sapsuckers**. A friend from Texas identified an **Acorn Woodpecker** along here one year, although it wasn't until the bird showed up the next day at a feeder at a home along the McGraw Ranch Road, causing great excitement for local birders, that she thought to tell us. After all, Acorn Woodpeckers are common birds in west Texas!

You'll soon come to the cut-off for the Balanced Rock Trail. **Three-toed Woodpeckers** have nested down this trail at the stream crossing, and you may want to take a quick side trip to check out the area. Drop down the trail to the bridge and continue to an open area on the right about fifty yards from the bridge. Watch for **Williamson's Sapsuckers** on the way down and back.

Return to the main trail, which soon enters the ponderosa pines again with more spruces and firs evident. Junipers add even more diversity to the tree life. It's a good area to get out your *Rocky Mountain Tree Finder*, a keyed guide, and start learning your trees. This is one of my favorite parts of the trail for birds. Keep an eye out for the flycatchers, including **Olive-sided** and **Dusky flycatchers**. **Hammond's Flycatcher** is also present farther along the trail in spruces and firs. This is another good place to find **Western Wood-Pewees**, too. While you're sniffing the trunks of the ponderosas to see if they're butterscotch, vanilla, strawberry, or the elusive chocolate variety, watch for **Brown Creepers**, an elusive variety of bird.

White-breasted and **Red-breasted nuthatches** and **Mountain Chickadees** should be in this area, and there's a better chance of seeing **Ruby-**

crowned **Kinglets** here than in other sections of the trail. They're easier to find in the spring and early summer when their songs resound through the woods. If a raven's voice was as loud in relation to its size, it would be a fog horn.

A little farther along the main trail, past the path to Rabbit Ears back-country camping site, there's a section of narrower, canyon-like country. I've seen **MacGillivray's Warblers, House Wrens, Green-tailed Towhees,** and several species of sparrows on the hillside above the trail. The wooded areas are also good for **Townsend's Solitaire, Western Tanager,** and **Red-naped Sapsuckers.**

The vegetation opens up again as you exit the small canyon, and soon you'll find a sign for the trail to Lawn Lake. If you kept your eyes closed, at least to birds, and walked the trail to this sign, it would take a little over an hour. But since you're birding, it probably will have taken two hours or more. The Lawn Lake Trail soon goes through a dense forest that is not particularly interesting in terms of birds, so you can return to the trailhead at this point or continue the hike to Bridal Veil Falls.

You may pick up some of the higher-elevation birds, such as **Hermit Thrush** or **Pine Grosbeak,** along the falls trail. Even better, **Three-toed Woodpeckers** have been reported regularly from the area where the trail enters the spruce/fir forest not far from the trail junction. In any case, the falls make a nice side trip. It's about a mile and another hour up from this point. The last section of the trail is steep and narrow, with a little rock scrambling required.

My wife and I have taken to hiking the Bridal Veil Falls Trail beginning in mid-afternoon. This takes us to the falls in late afternoon, after most of the people have come and gone. It also lets us walk out at dusk, increasing our chances for some owling.

Late afternoons are also a good time to find **Blue Grouse** along the trail. Once the chicks are ambulatory and the family groups are traipsing about, beginning in mid-July, you'll have a good opportunity to find them. We've seen as many as three families in one day.

One warm July evening, we heard birds calling in the second meadow on the way down. They were pretty far away, but I thought initially that they were **Northern Pygmy-Owls**, perhaps a family group. In tone, it was a pygmy-owl, but the call had an odd, two-note cadence. I imitated the call by whistling. Three or four minutes later, a bird swooped by us in the near dark and landed on the trail ten feet away. This was definitely not an owl on the ground—it was an even more unusual bird, new to our personal Rocky Mountain National Park bird list. We'd found a **Common Poorwill**, evidently escaping the foothills heat by taking a mini-vacation in the mountains. We found poorwills again the next year in July, closer to the ranch buildings.

Walking out late can bring many surprises, but be sure to leave yourself over two hours to walk out from the Lawn Lake Trail. Although the trail at the bottom end is easy enough to walk in the evening, this is bear and mountain lion country, too. We've seen bear sign, and we know of someone who hunts mountain lions successfully just a couple of miles outside the Park boundary near here. Those kind of surprises you don't need. Your chances of an encounter with either animal do increase as it gets dark. You should never travel alone or run on a trail in mountain lion country, particularly in the late afternoon or evening. You can read more about bears and lions in Chapter 11.

Besides, you want enough light on the way back to see the birds and to catch sight of the Rabbit Ears rock formation (and, we think, the whole bunny) on the south side of the trail, best seen on your way down.

I HOPE YOU FIND lots of birds at Cow Creek, and I hope it's a special place for you, too. You'll find more spectacular scenery in your other wanderings, but I doubt you'll find a more subtly beautiful area in which to enjoy birds. Mostly, I hope you're fortunate to find two birds that I would consider target birds for this area: **Northern Pygmy-Owl** and **Blue Grouse**. Even one of those two hard-to-find species would be great.

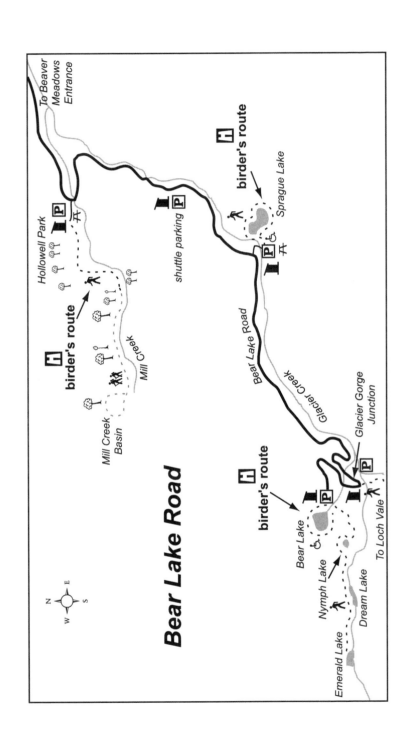

Bear Lake Road

To Beaver Meadows Entrance

Hollowell Park

birder's route

Mill Creek Basin

Mill Creek

shuttle parking

birder's route

Sprague Lake

Bear Lake Road

Glacier Creek

Glacier Gorge Junction

birder's route

Bear Lake

To Loch Vale

Nymph Lake

Dream Lake

Emerald Lake

N
W — E
S

8

Bear Lake Road

BEAR LAKE ROAD LEADS to some of the most heavily used areas in Rocky Mountain National Park—Sprague Lake, Glacier Gorge, and Bear Lake. The last two areas have trails that lead to some of the Park's most scenic and accessible lakes and waterfalls. Although birders will generally do better elsewhere in the Park, you'll likely spend some time in these areas. In fact, you probably cannot be said to have visited Rocky without going to Bear Lake, one of the Park's landmarks.

As long as you're there, you may as well bird, right? There are at least two good reasons to do so. Sprague Lake and other areas along the road provide another opportunity to see **Black Swifts**, and **Gray Jay**, a species that is sometimes difficult to find, is often sighted at Bear Lake and its associated trail system.

A word of warning. So crowded are the Bear Lake and Glacier Gorge parking areas that a free shuttle service runs most of the summer and into September. Attempts to find parking at either place after, say, 8 A.M. or 9 A.M. (and often much earlier at Glacier Gorge) will usually be fruitless from Memorial Day to Labor Day, so plan ahead. You may wish to take the shuttle from a lower parking area if you go later in the day. Signs just before the shuttle parking area indicate the status of the Bear Lake parking lot.

Because of these crowded conditions, I'll take you to Bear Lake first, marking the mileages of side trips on the way up. I'll start the mileage over at Bear Lake so you can make those stops on the way down, if you wish.

To Reach Bear Lake Road

Enter the Park at the Beaver Meadows Entrance. **Reset your trip odometer to zero here.** Take the first left for Bear Lake Road (0.2). Drive over the North Lateral Moraine and into Moraine Park, covered in Chapter 2. Continue across the eastern end of Moraine Park to the bridge over the Big Thompson River (2.2).

I'll mention the recommended birding stops for your return trip or a second trip some other day; these areas include Hollowell Park, Sprague Lake, and Glacier Gorge. *You should go directly to Bear Lake first to have the best opportunity to find some solitude, some birds, and a parking space.*

After you leave Moraine Park and travel around the South Lateral Moraine, the road briefly follows Glacier Creek. You'll join this picturesque mountain stream again in a few miles and follow it all the way to Glacier Gorge Junction. Note a paved road on the right to Hollowell Park (3.8), one of the return-trip birding areas.

Continue on Bear Lake Road to the shuttle parking area on the right (5.1); the entrance to Glacier Basin Campground is on the left at the same point. Although the shuttle parking area isn't a birding stop, you should note its location. Just before the turn into the parking area, a flip-up sign indicates if the parking lot at Bear Lake is full. If the sign is not up, you're good to go. If the sign is up, park here and ride the free shuttle to Bear Lake.

A short distance beyond the shuttle parking area, note the left turn to Sprague Lake (5.8), a side trip that should be saved for later. As you travel up the valley of Glacier Creek beyond Sprague Lake, you'll find several turnouts, many of which could be productive if you wish to stop and bird on the way back. Any time spent in this beautiful part of the Park is well spent.

The next mileage note is for Glacier Gorge Junction (8.7), a parking area in a switchback on the Bear Lake Road. The Glacier Gorge hike described later in this chapter should be done on a separate day. Past Glacier Gorge Junction is the end of the road, Bear Lake, at 9,475 feet (9.4).

What You'll Find—Bear Lake

At Bear Lake, you'll find an array of trails and a bewildering array of tourists of a most amazing variety. The habitat is just right—there are restrooms, a small book stand, and Park Service volunteers to answer questions. If we only had a field guide to tourists, we could tick off a bunch of species here!

If you need a **Gray Jay** for your list, Bear Lake could be the place. The jays are, of course, attracted by the people and the picnics. They can sometimes be found right at the trailhead. Other times you'll see them along the trails. They are more common early and late in the summer, but they can be found anytime. Recently enforced National Park rules against feeding animals have probably had some impact on the number of jays here. In comparison to the **Steller's Jays** and **Clark's Nutcrackers** that are often in the area, **Gray Jays** tend to be quiet and sedentary. Don't overlook them. Check the trees near places people congregate, such as picnic stops and overlooks.

Start your search by taking the Bear Lake Nature Trail, to the right at the trailhead. This handicapped-accessible loop trail follows the shore of the lake. Like the other trails and lakes in this area, it's not particularly birdy. The higher elevation limits species, and human disturbance plays a part. Still, you should see (or at least hear) **Ruby-crowned Kinglets** and **Hermit Thrushes**. The west side of the lake has a wet inlet area that can be good for **Lincoln's Sparrows. Warbling Vireos** and **Cordilleran Fly-catchers** may also be seen in this area. **Red Crossbills** sometimes fly over, and there's the chance for a **Pine Grosbeak.**

As you walk the nature trail, remember to look up. **Black Swifts** nest in the high country near here. You'll likely find **Violet-green Swallows** first, but the two species are sometimes seen together. And you won't be able to *not* look at the scenery. It's spectacular. The view of the northwest face of Longs Peak from Bear Lake is one of the grandest views of that great mountain anywhere in the Park.

If you're still looking for a **Gray Jay**, you may want to take the trail to Nymph, Dream, and Emerald lakes. Return to the trailhead after completing the Bear Lake Nature Trail and review the trail signs to these beautiful, high-country lakes. The trail is too crowded for my taste; it's even paved for quite a distance. Still, this is a very scenic area, and you will likely enjoy the relatively easy hike to Nymph Lake (.5), Dream Lake (1.1), and Emerald Lake (1.8).

Besides Camp Robbers, as **Gray Jays** are called in the Rockies, you should watch for other high-elevation birds of the subalpine forest. I've seen **Pine Grosbeaks** and **Red Crossbills** here. **Golden-crowned Kinglets** whisper from the spruces and firs, and **Hermit Thrushes** will likely be singing, although this is a tough place to pursue them. **Yellow-rumped Warblers** and **Mountain Chickadees** are fairly common along the trail.

If you've arrived a bit late and find lots of company, you might want to try to get away from the crowds by taking the Flattop Mountain Trail that leaves the Bear Lake Nature Trail on the north side of the lake or the Lake Haiyaha Trail that leaves the Emerald Lake Trail just below Dream Lake. Both trails provide opportunities for the birds mentioned above.

At the end of your Bear Lake birding adventure, you will probably have time to stop at some of the turnouts you've seen on the way up and at Sprague Lake and Hollowell Park for busier birding. **Reset your odometer to zero as you leave the Bear Lake parking area.**

What You'll Find—Glacier Gorge Junction

Shortly after you leave the Bear Lake parking lot, you'll come to the Glacier Gorge parking area (0.7). It's unlikely that you'll find a parking spot here or at the overflow parking (0.9) after about 7 A.M., and the hike I'll mention here really takes a whole day, in any case.

If you've read other birding guides that cover Rocky Mountain National Park, you'll probably recognize Loch Vale as a recommended hike for **Black Swifts**. The trail to Loch Vale and trails to several other destinations leave from the Glacier Gorge trailhead. Any of these trails can produce good high-elevation birding, but the hike to Loch Vale takes you to a known nesting area for Black Swifts. They nest on cliffs near or behind waterfalls at high elevations. Conventional birding wisdom suggests being at a known site early enough or late enough in the day to see the birds leave from or return to the nesting area. For many visiting birders, it's impractical to be at Loch Vale or any other Black Swift site in RMNP early or late enough in the day because it would require hiking in the dark.

One local birder who's been to Loch Vale more times than she can probably count has never seen a swift there. I've never seen one there, either. But neither of us have been there at dawn or nightfall. Another local birder, who went with a researcher to survey swifts as they return to their nests, saw one just at dark. Too dark for an identifying, life-bird look, he told me, and he also told me how fun the hike out in the dark was.

In short, I think a visiting birder interested mainly in **Black Swifts** should spend the day he or she would use to make the Loch Vale hike birding in Wild Basin (Chapter 3) instead, watching birds all day while having what is probably a better chance of seeing a Black Swift. The hike to Ouzel Falls, described in the Wild Basin chapter, presents an even better opportunity to see swifts, with excellent birding along the way. However, many people must have seen swifts at Loch Vale, and the scenery is magnificent.

Loch Vale is reached by a 2.7-mile trail with an elevation gain of about 940 feet. This doesn't sound like much, but the trail begins at an elevation of 9,240 feet and ends at 10,180 feet, so those not used to the altitude should take it easy and make a day of it. Take the trail to Alberta Falls and continue to the trail junction two miles in. Here one trail leads south to Mills Lake and Glacier Gorge. Take the other trail to Loch Vale. You'll reach a lake named The Loch in less than a mile. If you wish to continue to Glass Lake and Sky Pond, you'll find the trail becomes less maintained, and the hike turns into a rock scramble between the two higher lakes. **Black Swifts** reportedly nest at Timberline Falls between The Loch and Glass Lake.

On the way up, you should have seen many of the regular mountain birds, but you may be fortunate enough at these higher elevations to find **Red Crossbills** or **Pine Grosbeaks**. My life-bird **Golden-crowned Kinglet** came from the trail junction for Mills Lake and Loch Vale.

As you're hiking, you should keep a concentrated look out for the **Black Swifts**—it might shorten your hike. As I've mentioned, swifts range high in the sky and can easily be missed or, at a glance, mistaken for swallows. Stop often on the trail—you may be grateful for the break—and scan the sky. Be sure to check out any flocks of swallows, especially later in summer, for swifts.

Whether or not you find a swift, I hope you'll decide the hike was worth it. As I always tell visiting flyfishers, hike to a lake for the sake of the hike itself. If you catch some fish, that's just a bonus. Trout on the feed in high-country lakes, you see, can be as difficult to find as **Black Swifts**.

What You'll Find—Sprague Lake

Between Glacier Gorge and the next stop at Sprague Lake (3.5), you'll find several small turnouts that you may wish to explore. The birds will be typical of the subalpine forest, although riparian areas and aspen groves provide more diversity than Bear Lake offers. None of the areas will likely be particularly busy with birds, but you never know what you'll find. One lucky birder spotted a **Kentucky Warbler** in midsummer at one of these turnouts.

Take the right turn to Sprague Lake. The lake and nearby beaver ponds provide some waterfowl viewing and a chance for tourist-foraging birds, such as **American Crows**, **Gray Jays** (early and late in summer), **Steller's Jays**, and the occasional **Clark's Nutcracker**. Picnic areas, restrooms, and stables attract a crowd to the area anytime after 9 A.M., but if you get there early, you'll find a walk around the lake very pleasant. There are great views across the lake from the east side, so take your camera.

From the parking area, walk east to the handicapped-accessible trail that circles the lake. **Ruby-crowned Kinglets**, **Pine Siskins**, and **Mountain Chickadees** are common. You'll likely find resident **Mallards** and perhaps some other ducks here, including **Blue-winged**, **Green-winged**, and **Cinnamon teal**, the latter three mostly during migration. **Ring-necked Ducks** sometimes nest here, as do **Spotted Sandpipers**. **Violet-green Swallows** should be flying over the lake, and where the boardwalk crosses the wetland at the southwest corner, check the beaver ponds for **Lincoln's Sparrows** and **Wilson's Warblers**. **Red-winged Blackbirds** are common, and a **Common Grackle** may even make an appearance. Grackles are currently rare in the Park.

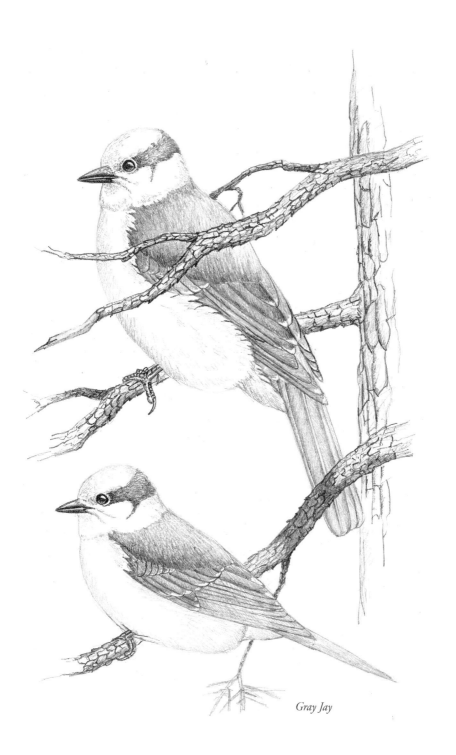

Gray Jay

At Sprague Lake, you should again check for **Black Swifts**. They range throughout the valley. Overcast conditions are particularly good times to look for them. As you walk the trail, you may see uncommon birds, such as **Western Tanagers**, in the spruce and fir forest surrounding the lake. **Hammond's Flycatchers** are sometimes seen on perches overlooking the lake, and you may see a **Belted Kingfisher** working the shallows or the beaver ponds near the lake. **Yellow-rumped Warblers** nest in the area. **Great Horned Owls** and **Northern Pygmy-Owls** have been seen regularly, too, so you might consider a late afternoon or early evening visit to the lake.

Don't forget to check the picnic area for the grubbers on your way out!

What You'll Find—Hollowell Park

After you've birded Sprague Lake, continue down Bear Lake Road to the left turn for Hollowell Park (6.3—or 5.5 if you skipped Sprague Lake) at a sharp turn in the road. Take the paved road to the parking area near the picnic tables and restroom. At 8,500 feet, you'll be 1,000 feet lower than you were at Bear Lake, and the difference in bird life will astound you. Mill Creek runs through this open grassland, creating a diverse riparian area that attracts sparrows and warblers. Lodgepole pine, Douglas fir, and spruce grow on the north-facing slopes, while the south-facing slopes host an open ponderosa pine forest. The trail through this area leads to Mill Creek Basin.

This is one of the better places in the Park to work on your high-country sparrows. The mixture of grasses and sage in close association with forest and riparian areas make this ideal habitat for many species, including **Vesper**, **Chipping**, and, rarely, **Brewer's sparrows**. **Green-tailed Towhees** and **Dark-eyed Juncos** are common summer residents, and **Lark Sparrows**, a common bird of the prairie, are sometimes found in August.

For sparrows, walk from the parking area west along the trail. The trail goes past a dead ponderosa about 100 yards from the parking lot, and that's where the good sparrow watching begins. Check the meadow north of the trail especially. I like to walk to the right of the trail, through the meadow about thirty yards from the trees. Sparrows often fly into bushes or nearby trees where they're easier to identify. A scope can be useful in this area.

In the grasslands, watch also for **Black-billed Magpies, Violet-green, Barn, Cliff,** and **Tree swallows, House Wrens,** and **Mountain Blue-birds. Broad-tailed Hummingbirds** can be found where wildflowers bloom. A **Golden Eagle** sometimes makes an appearance overhead.

While birding the meadow, you'll find a horse trail that cuts across it. Follow it back to the main trail and continue west. The trail will curve left, heading south toward the timber. This part of the trail can bring unexpected sightings. It's one of the few places where I find **Black-headed Grosbeaks** regularly. They fly back and forth from the willows to the scattered pines on the west slope. **Western Tanagers** do the same. Watch for **Green-tailed Towhees** in the low shrubs on the west slope as you near the trees. For the last few years, I've regularly seen a **Sharp-shinned Hawk** here, too, just inside the trees. A pair probably nests in the forest near the creek.

If you have time for a hike, continue on the trail to Mill Creek Basin, 1.7 miles from the trailhead. It winds along Mill Creek, climbing through mixed aspen and pine to a lovely meadow where you can take a short loop trail and return. Since there's no lake or waterfall along this trail, it's quieter than other trails along Bear Lake Road.

You're likely to find a good variety of mountain birds along the trail, including **Red-naped Sapsuckers, Dusky Flycatchers, Steller's Jays, Townsend's Solitaires, Mountain Chickadees, Ruby-crowned Kinglets, Pygmy, Red-breasted** and **White-breasted nuthatches, Yellow-rumped Warblers,** and **Dark-eyed Juncos,** but you'll also have the chance of seeing some of the more unusual birds—**Northern Goshawks, Brown Creepers, Red Crossbills,** and **Pine Grosbeaks.** Although those species aren't regular anywhere along the trail, the mix of aspen, ponderosa pines, and spruces makes this a place where you can hope for any, or all, of them. And although I've yet to find one, the aspen groves and meadows in Mill Creek Basin probably have **Blue Grouse,** so keep an eye out.

Bird the aspen and pine forest along the trail as far as you wish, then return to your car. On the way back, stick closer to the willows and beaver ponds south of the trail. I often see **Wilson's** and **MacGillivray's warblers** and **Song** and **Lincoln's sparrows** in this area. Check the riparian willows for **Willow Flycatchers**. **Yellow Warblers**, uncommon in the Park, may be seen in or near the tall spruces along the creek.

You may like this area well enough to plan a separate trip starting earlier in the day. In any case, after a morning with the crowds at Bear Lake and Sprague Lake, Hollowell Park is refreshing.

WHETHER YOU TAKE the long hike to Loch Vale or just the birding walks I've recommended, I hope you'll enjoy your time in one of the most scenic areas of the Park, the Bear Lake Road. And I certainly hope you will be lucky enough to spot a **Black Swift** and pick up that notorious, picnic-loving **Gray Jay** (a.k.a. Canada Jay, Whiskey Jack, Camp Robber).

PART THREE

Nearby
Birding Spots

9

The Estes Valley

THE MOUNTAIN PARK SURROUNDING the village of Estes Park is comprised of grasslands interspersed with ponderosa pines, Douglas firs, junipers, streamside willows, balsam poplar, and (mostly introduced) aspen. Lake Estes and Mary's Lake punctuate the relative dryness of the area.

The Estes Valley is different in habitat from most of Rocky Mountain National Park, and you'll find some interesting birding in the now-residential grasslands. The opportunity to bird this area is most important in winter when access to trails and roads in RMNP is limited, as is the Park's bird life. In summer, a tour of the residential areas can turn up some species you might have trouble finding in Rocky.

I call the auto tour I've put together for you the Bluebird Loop. That's not a great name for it in winter, but this chapter is written mainly for the summer birder. I don't usually recommend spending time in your car when you should be out walking or hiking for your birds, but you'll have the chance to pick up some species you might not see elsewhere, such as **Calliope Hummingbird**, **Band-tailed Pigeon**, and **Red Crossbill**. If nothing else, it's good to have something like this for a recuperation day or when the weather is not conducive to outdoor activities or when everyone else in your family wants to go shopping.

This chapter also includes information on birding the YMCA grounds, one of the best birding spots outside Rocky Mountain National Park. Whether or not you take the Bluebird Loop, you should visit the YMCA during your stay in the area.

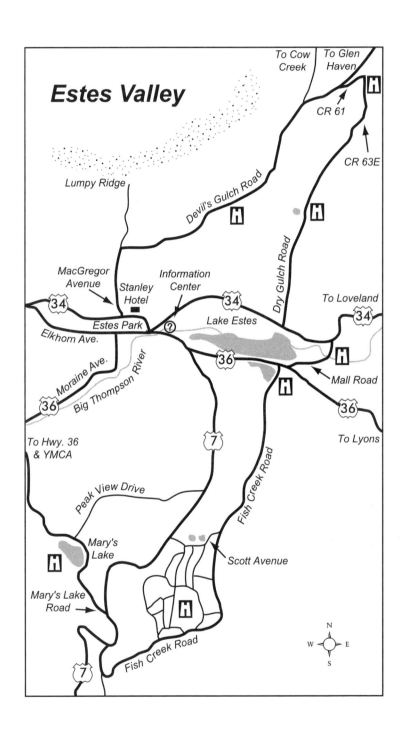

To Reach the Bluebird Loop

The loop begins at the intersection of Highways 34 and 36. **Reset your trip odometer to zero here.** Take the Highway 34 Bypass past the Stanley Hotel to begin the loop. Watch for the turn to Devil's Gulch on Mac-Gregor Avenue (0.4) and turn right (north). Continue to MacGregor Ranch Road (1.1) on the left.

What You'll Find—The Bluebird Loop

If you don't have the time to take the Lumpy Ridge walk (Chapter 6), you may wish to drive up the MacGregor Ranch Road to the RMNP parking area and try for **White-throated Swifts** and raptors from there. The Ranch has a museum, which you might especially enjoy if you're taking the loop drive on a cold, rainy day.

Continue on Devil's Gulch Road. On the right, the tall fence with the angled top that looks like it belongs at a prison once held the elk used to reintroduce a herd to the area. The success of that reintroduction is legendary. Turnouts along the next couple of miles provide the opportunity to see **Red-tailed Hawks** and **Prairie Falcons. Loggerhead Shrikes** can sometimes be spotted in summer and **Northern Shrikes** in winter. **Western Bluebirds** are occasionally seen on roadside fences.

Take the angled right turn onto County Road 61 (4.2). The dry grasslands on both sides of the road are good for **Mountain Bluebirds** in spring and summer and for migrating sparrows and other birds in spring. Check carefully in April and May for **American Pipits** and **Horned Larks**, resting and waiting for good weather before continuing on to the tundra for summer breeding. **Western Meadowlarks** will also sometimes be here in spring and have occasionally nested.

Turn right on County Road 63E (4.7), Dry Gulch Road, and pull immediately into the parking area on the left (east). This is a good place to watch for **Prairie Falcons**, especially in May and June when they're courting and setting up their breeding territory. For a number of years, a pair has nested in the vicinity, probably on Eagle Rock, which you'll see to the south on the east side of the road. **Northern Saw-whet,**

Northern Pygmy-, and **Flammulated owls** have all been reported from this vicinity, incidentally.

The habitat on both sides of the road here attracts sparrows, swallows, and bluebirds in summer, but it can be good at any time of year. **Black-billed Magpies** are often seen in the trees to the north. In summer there's usually water beside the parking area, flowing from a small dam on the other side of the dirt road. This source of water in an otherwise dry environment attracts birds from the grasslands and nearby forests. **Cliff** and **Barn swallows** are common, and you'll likely see **Vesper Sparrows**. Other sparrow species may be seen drinking and bathing in the water. Walk along the road on both sides and keep an eye on the water. There'll often be a surprise, such as **Red Crossbills**, if you spend some time here. Doing so will improve your chances of seeing the falcons, too.

From this parking area to the Highway 34 intersection ahead, you should find **Mountain Bluebirds**; look for them along the fence lines. Continue south on Dry Gulch Road and watch for willows and a pond at a turnout on the right (6.4). **Mountain Bluebirds, Black-billed Magpies, Song Sparrows, House Wrens, Red-winged Blackbirds**, and other birds are attracted to the pond, which is private.

Continue to Highway 34 (7.6). Turn left on the highway and then right on Mall Road (8.1). Just past the miniature golf course and over the bridge, pull off on the right and stop (8.3). Glass the man-enhanced wetlands and pond on the right. This is particularly productive during spring migration when a variety sandpipers, unusual waterfowl, and **White-faced Ibis** can be present. **Soras** have nested in the area under the willows on the south side of the pond for several years. **Tree Swallows** use nest boxes near the pond, and **Common Snipe** nest in the wetlands.

Continue to the intersection with Highway 36 (8.8) and turn right. Go a short distance and turn left on Fish Creek Road (8.9), before the highway crosses the lake. Pull into a turnout a little farther along the lake (9.0) and check for waterfowl. Scan the power poles along the causeway for **Prairie** and, rarely, **Peregrine falcons**. A pair of Prairie Falcons usually hunts from these perches throughout the summer, and this is the most reliable spot I know to find them. If you spot one, you may want to drive closer and then return to this turnout to continue to the loop.

Mountain Bluebird

Continue to a turnout near the Fish Creek inlet (9.2). **Spotted Sand-pipers** can often be seen along the shore throughout the summer. You should bird the willow area on foot, working your way south to the gauging station next to the stream. This is an excellent area in spring, when migrants are in, but it can produce good birding after mid-July when birds have dispersed in family groups. Look for **Song Sparrows, Black-capped** and **Mountain chickadees, Pine Siskins, Yellow** and **Yellow-rumped warblers, Black-headed Grosbeaks,** and **House Finches.**

Continue along Fish Creek Road, checking the willows along the stream for **Black-billed Magpies** and **Red-winged Blackbirds. Black-headed Grosbeaks** are fairly common some summers. At Scott Avenue (10.8), turn right and take the first left on Lakeshore Drive (10.9). During migration, the two ponds on your right attract waterfowl, particularly **Ring-necked Ducks,** and the willows below the lower pond can be busy with warblers. **Common Grackles** and **Red-winged Blackbirds** are here in summer.

We're now at a freelance part of the tour where you should check out residential feeders. Any road south of the ponds leads into Carriage Hills, a large subdivision with meadows and ponderosas. It's bounded by Fish Creek Road on the east and south and by Highway 7 on the west. You can't get very lost in it, although it may seem so at times. Other residential areas are nearby. Please respect private property by staying on roads.

Check out bird feeders in these areas. In winter, local birders visit the area to see **Brown-capped, Gray-crowned,** and **Black rosy finches.** You can't miss the flocks. There will sometimes be as many as 200 rosy finches feeding at one house. They cover the deck. They cover the roof. They fly off in a cloud. Winter feeders also attract **Cassin's Finches, Evening Grosbeaks,** and **Red Crossbills.**

Even in summer, **Brown-capped Rosy Finches** come down from the tundra to hit sunflower-seed feeders during bad weather. Remember that while it may only be cloudy and rainy in the Estes Valley, it can be snowing on Trail Ridge Road. Expect to find fewer rosy finches, perhaps only a handful. Since it's likely to be a bad-weather day if you take the Blue-bird Loop in summer, it's worth a try.

In summer, **Black-headed** and **Evening grosbeaks** also come to feeders. Starting in mid-July, **Red Crossbills** are sometimes seen at sunflower-seed feeders. **Cassin's Finches** may also be found. In the summer, **Band-tailed Pigeons** feed where corn or sunflower seeds are offered, and this may be your best chance to find one. Otherwise, you'll need a whole lot of luck, since there are no reliable places in RMNP to see them. There are no winter records for Band-tailed Pigeons.

Broad-tailed Hummingbirds are common at feeders, and you should watch for **Rufous Hummingbirds** beginning in mid-July. They are uncommon in the Park but common at feeders at this elevation. **Calliope Hummingbirds** are rare visitors in July and August also, but they are easier to find at the YMCA, described later in this chapter. Rarely a **Black-chinned Hummingbird** may also visit in late summer.

After you've covered residential areas to your satisfaction, find your way back to Fish Creek Road, turn right, and take it to Highway 7, where you should **reset your trip odometer to zero**. Turn right on Highway 7 and proceed to Mary's Lake Road (0.4). Turn left and go to Mary's Lake (0.8). Although it seldom attracts interesting birds in summer, Mary's Lake is worth a visit in other seasons when **Common Goldeneyes** and **Common Mergansers** are found, along with rarer visitors, such as **Barrow's Goldeneye** and **Trumpeter Swan**. The water stays open year-round, since it's piped underground from Grand Lake through a thirteen-mile tunnel. From here it drops through a tunnel to Lake Estes and becomes part of the Big Thompson Project irrigation system.

Just past the commercial campground at Mary's Lake, you can return to town or continue to the YMCA. To return to town, turn right on Peak View Drive (1.3) and continue back to Highway 7 (3.0), where you can turn left to return to Highway 36 (4.6) and your starting point. There are residential areas along the way that are worth checking for the feeder birds you may have missed.

What You'll Find—YMCA Grounds

To visit the YMCA grounds, one of the better birding areas outside Rocky Mountain National Park, continue on Mary's Lake Road to the

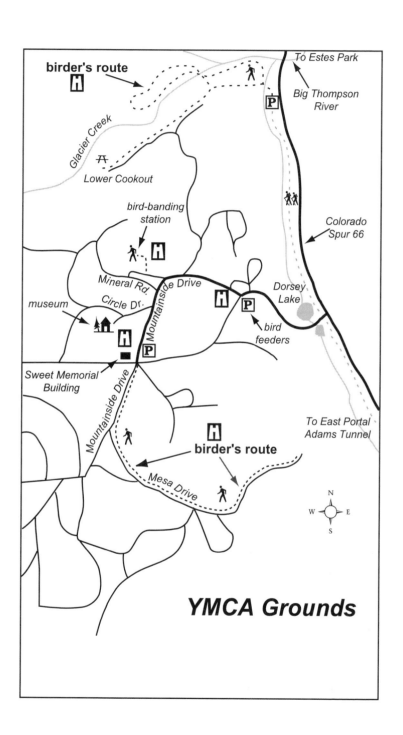

YMCA Grounds

stoplight at Highway 36 (3.0) where you'll turn left. You may also take Highway 36 (Moraine Avenue) from town, as if you were heading to the Beaver Meadows Entrance, to reach this intersection. At the stoplight, **reset your trip odometer to zero.** Travel west from the intersection, keeping in the left lane, and turn left on Colorado Spur 66 (0.2) where a sign indicates the turn to the YMCA.

Proceed to the bridge over the Big Thompson River (1.7) and park in the large turnout on the right just past the bridge (1.8). There's a horse trail through this parking area; don't park too near it or you'll have stirrup dings on your car. Begin your birding by following the horse trail back toward the bridge. Where it fords a small stream, follow the footpath closer to the road, which joins a utility road going west. You'll enter YMCA grounds at this point. Go around the gate, locked to prevent vehicular access, and continue a few yards to a trail intersection.

Take the trail to the right. It's a nature trail leading toward the river (and also a horse trail—be sure to yield to horse traffic by stepping off the trail). You should start picking up birds right away. **Ruby-crowned Kinglets, Mountain Chickadees, Western Wood-Pewees,** and **Yellow-rumped Warblers** can be found in the ponderosas. **Violet-green Swallows** will likely be overhead. Near the stream, watch for **Lincoln's Sparrows.** This is a reliable place to find an **American Dipper,** also. You'll have good, open views of the stream along the trail.

Continue on the trail as it follows the stream, keeping an eye and ear out for the occasional **Belted Kingfisher** and the common **Broad-tailed Hummingbird.** The trail meets the main trail from the YMCA grounds to Rocky Mountain National Park at a bridge over Glacier Creek. Cross the bridge and explore the excellent riparian area. If you haven't seen an **American Dipper,** walk downstream to the right and sit at the confluence of the Big Thompson River and Glacier Creek. You'll have great views of both rivers and should soon see one.

The better habitat is to the left. Follow the edge of the wet area as far as you wish, staying on the dry hillside to avoid tramping down the meadow grass. Watch for **Cordilleran Flycatchers, Pine Siskins, Lincoln's Sparrows,** and many other species as you work this area. You may be fortunate enough to see a **Cooper's Hawk** hunting in the forest openings on the other side of the creek. When you're ready to return to the bridge, climb the small hill on your right to the open ponderosa forest and walk back along the horse trail. **Brown Creepers** and **Pygmy Nuthatches** may be found here, and you should watch overhead. A **Prairie Falcon** can sometimes be seen in this area.

Cross the bridge again and stay on the main YMCA trail to a dirt road and go right. Work your way west along this road to the picnic area. Watch for **Northern Flickers, Townsend's Solitaires,** and the other species already mentioned. **Northern Pygmy-Owls** are occasionally seen in this area. You can continue on a trail along the stream for over a mile beyond the picnic area, if the birding's good. Otherwise, return on the dirt road to your car.

From where you're parked to the YMCA entrance is about a half mile. Depending on bird activity, you may wish to walk the horse trail in that direction, letting the birds determine how far you go. Then return to your car and drive to the entrance road, just beyond a pond on the right (2.3). Turn right to enter the YMCA grounds.

Just after the road levels out from the climb up the hill, turn in to a parking lot at the first buildings on the left. There are both seed and hummingbird feeders visible from your car on the east side of the buildings. Many species may be seen here. Watch for **House Finches, Pygmy Nuthatches, Pine Siskins,** and **Dark-eyed Juncos.** More unusual birds include **Black-headed** and **Evening grosbeaks, Cassin's Finches,** and **Red Crossbills.** In winter, active feeders on the YMCA grounds attract **Brown-capped, Gray-crowned,** and **Black rosy finches.**

At the hummingbird feeders, you should find **Broad-tailed Hummingbirds** all summer and **Rufous Hummingbirds** after the first week in July. **Calliope Hummingbirds** may be found from mid-July through August. There seems to be one or two here or at other feeders on the YMCA grounds every year. After you've viewed the feeders from your car, walk around the building to check the other feeders in the back.

After you've birded the feeders, scan the meadow across the road from the parking area for **Mountain Bluebirds.** A **Northern Goshawk** is a regular resident of the YMCA grounds each summer and may be seen hunting ground squirrels in open areas in early mornings, so watch for it here and in similar habitats.

Return to your car, exit from the lower end of the parking area, cross the entrance road, and proceed on Mountainside Drive ("Mt. Side" on the street sign). Fifty yards past the miniature golf course, stay straight on a dirt road where the paved road curves left. Turn right immediately onto a short cut-off road and park. Walk down the private drive straight ahead of where you've parked, just to the left of a small cabin. Follow an obvious trail to the left just before you reach the fence to benches you should see there, about twenty yards off the driveway. This is currently the bird-banding area, where seed and hummingbird feeders are established. Scott Rashid, the illustrator of this book, runs a banding program here that is open to the public. (Check at Sweet Memorial, mentioned later, for information on dates and times for the bird-banding demonstrations.)

The wet slough you can view from the benches is excellent for many species. The list of observed and banded species is a long one. Highlights include **Hammond's, Dusky, Cordilleran,** and **Least flycatchers, Black-headed Grosbeaks, Red Crossbills, Cassin's Finches, MacGillivray's, Virginia's, Yellow-rumped (Audubon's),** and **Townsend's warblers,** and **Rufous** and **Calliope hummingbirds**. Many of the usual mountain birds are also on the list. **Sharp-shinned** and **Cooper's hawks** have been seen, as well as the occasional **Northern Pygmy-Owl**. Once Scott even banded a **Blue Grouse** here!

Return to Mountainside Drive and turn right. Turn right on Circle Drive before you come to the first large building on the right. The Lula W. Dorsey Museum, an older building, is immediately behind it. Turn left on a dirt road into the museum parking area, where you'll find more feeders. **Calliope Hummingbirds,** in particular, may frequent one set of feeders and not the others, so check carefully for North America's smallest bird. **Cassin's Finches, Chipping Sparrows,** and **Dark-eyed Juncos,** among other seed-eaters, are found here.

Return to Mountainside Drive and turn right. The building on the corner is Sweet Memorial, where you'll also find feeders. Park in the lot on the left and check them out. You can get information on YMCA programs and activities, including the bird-banding program, in Sweet Memorial. Snacks, cold drinks, and restrooms are also available.

From this point on, you should bird on foot. Most of the rest of the YMCA is a residential area, and you should respect the comfort and privacy of the people who stay here by walking, not driving, through the grounds. It's a short walk over to the auditorium building, for instance, where **Cliff Swallows** nest. You can also explore the area south from the museum or up the hill from Sweet Memorial. A good way to explore the area in that direction is to walk up Mountainside Drive to Mesa Drive and continue on it to the left as far as you like.

The YMCA is a popular destination and an excellent lodging choice if you're visiting with a group that includes non-birders. Reservations usually need to be made far in advance, however. The YMCA rents cabins by the week and also has motel-style accommodations.

After birding the YMCA grounds, return to Spur 66 and turn right. Continue 1.4 miles to the end of the road and up a dirt road past the entrance to the Estes Park Campground. There you'll find a small reservoir. This is the East Portal, where water from Grand Lake comes out of the tunnel on its way to Mary's Lake and Lake Estes. On the way up, check for birds such as **Pine Grosbeaks** (regular in winter) and **Red Crossbills** in the spruces and firs. There is a trail along the right side of the road from the YMCA entrance to the reservoir. You can access this trail from turnouts along the way, providing you with good birding areas away from the road in several places.

ALTHOUGH I HOPE your visit does not include bad weather, the Bluebird Loop and a trip to the YMCA may save the day if it does rain (or snow!). And it's an opportunity to find some species, such as **Band-tailed Pigeons** and uncommon hummingbirds, that may elude you otherwise.

10

Lake Estes

LAKE ESTES IS A YEAR-ROUND PLEASURE for birders, but it's particularly exciting from September through May. The lake is at least partially open all year due to relatively warm water flowing through the tunnel from Mary's Lake. We've found **White-winged Scoters** in December and **Caspian Terns** in May. A **Long-tailed Duck (Oldsquaw)** appeared one November, and four **Sabine's Gulls** one September. Both **Tundra** and **Trumpeter swans** have shown up on winter days. **Barrow's Goldeneyes** are occasionally on the lake in fall and spring, and **Wood Ducks** and **Hooded Mergansers** sometimes spend the fall, winter, and spring on the lake in the company of the resident **Mallards**.

Not only does the lake itself offer good birding, but a small area of riparian willows at its northwest corner, situated between the lake and the Big Thompson River, is a great migrant trap, with spring sightings of eastern warblers uncommon to rare in Colorado, such as **Blackpoll**, and visitors from the west, such as **Sage Sparrow**. This area was designated a bird sanctuary in 1997 in recognition of its importance to migrating songbirds and waterfowl.

Any bird seems possible at the lake and the bird sanctuary, as you will see by looking at the checklist included as an appendix. Lake Estes and the Matthews-Reeser Bird Sanctuary, with a combined list of over 220 species observed, should definitely be on your itinerary if you're here in April or May, and it's worth checking at any time of the year.

It's difficult to understand how a mountain lake and surrounding habitats can attract so many species, many of them rare to Colorado.

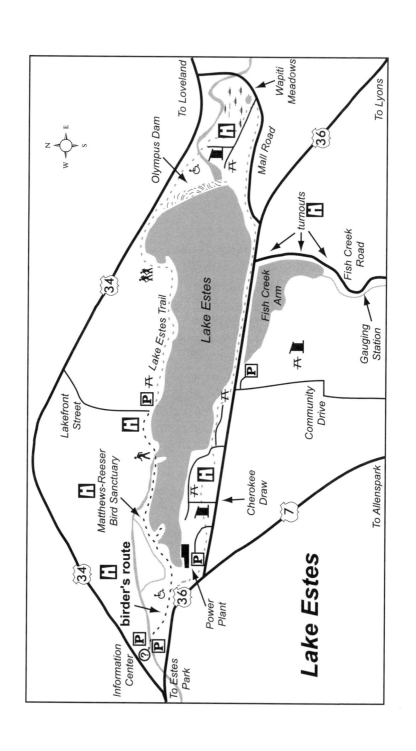

Lake Estes

Among those exotics are eastern warblers, such as **Ovenbird, Magnolia, Hooded, Blue-winged, Chestnut-sided**, and **Palm warblers**. They occur along the Front Range of Colorado in the spring, and there are hot spots in the state where these warblers congregate due to habitat and circumstance. An island of trees along Crow Creek in the Pawnee National Grassland is obviously going to attract warblers blown off course. But why does Lake Estes attract them, and how do they get here?

Then there are the species that occur more commonly farther west, such as **Black-throated Gray Warbler, Black Phoebe**, and **Golden-crowned Sparrow**. These species have to come over the Rockies to find Lake Estes. And, finally, there are the true exotics, the vagrants, such as **Sabine's Gulls** and **White-winged Scoters**. What are *they* doing up here at 7,800 feet in a small mountain park?

Whatever the cause, it's a bit of paradise for local birders in spring and a solace during the hard times of winter. Let's first take a look at Lake Estes and then a detailed, guided walk through the Matthews-Reeser Bird Sanctuary.

To Reach Lake Estes

Lake Estes is located directly east of downtown Estes Park. Highway 36 parallels its south shore, where there is an access road, and crosses over the Fish Creek Arm of the lake on a causeway. Highway 34 is just north of the lake, and side streets lead down to the lake's shore.

What You'll Find—Lake Estes

I'll let the checklist in the appendices give you the particulars on the birds you may find at the lake. Spring migration (March 1–June 1) is definitely the most interesting time, with migrating waterfowl and shorebirds present. Waterfowl highlights include **Common Loon, Eared, Horned, Clark's**, and **Western grebes, Canvasbacks, Green-winged, Blue-winged**, and **Cinnamon teal, Buffleheads, Ruddy Ducks**, and **Hooded Mergansers**. Herons, egrets, and other waterbirds can also be found, including **Double-crested Cormorants, Great Blue Herons, Snowy Egrets,**

Cattle Egrets, Black-crowned Night-Herons, and White-faced Ibis. Sandhill Cranes also make an occasional appearance.

An assortment of shorebirds passes through, including **Semipalmated Plovers, American Avocets, Willets, Greater** and **Lesser yellowlegs, Solitary Sandpipers, Long-billed Curlews, Marbled Godwits, Least Sandpipers, Long-billed Dowitchers,** and **Wilson's Phalaropes.** You can also find **Franklin's Gulls, Forster's Terns, Bald Eagles,** and **Ospreys** at this time of year.

In summer, the lake will often have only **Common Mergansers, Mallards,** and **Canada Geese.** Still, you may find **Spotted Sandpipers, Double-crested Cormorants, Ospreys,** and the odd **Caspian Tern. California Gulls** are fairly common but somewhat unpredictable. **Prairie Falcons** and, rarely, **Peregrine Falcons** hunt the area from perches on the power poles throughout the summer. If you don't make a special trip to the lake in summer, at least keep your eyes open as you drive by.

Fall migration (August 15–October 15) is not as exciting as spring migration, but many of the same species make a return appearance. We had a five-day visit by several **Sabine's Gulls** one September, and the lake's sole record for **Black-headed Gull,** a very good bird anywhere inland, came in October. **Townsend's Warblers** can be found in the trees along the lake and in the sanctuary. **Bald Eagles** often make an appearance in fall, too.

Winter has its highlights, also. Since the water's open, any misguided rarities seem to hit the lake, and they often stay for a period of time. There's nothing like finding a flock of **White-winged Scoters** on your way to the grocery store! **Trumpeter Swans** sometimes appear in November.

The area below the dam, Wapiti Meadows, provides great spring birding and is the summer home to **Soras, Common Snipe, Spotted Sandpipers,** and **American Dippers.**

LET'S TAKE A TOUR of the lake. Start by driving the dirt road marked "Cherokee Draw," off Highway 36 a short distance east of the power plant. Between Memorial Day and Labor Day, there's currently a day-use fee to enter by car here. (You can park in the power plant parking lot and walk the paved Lake Estes Trail to this area without cost in summer, if you like. You can also enjoy free access to the lake using Lakefront Street, described below, and other points.)

Drive east along the lake shore. Check the lake for waterfowl, gulls, and terns. In spring, the shoreline may have waders, such as **Solitary Sandpipers**, **White-faced Ibis**, and **American Avocets**, and the grassy areas can be loaded with migrants, such as **Savannah**, **Brewer's**, and **Clay-colored sparrows** and **Sage Thrashers**. **Bullock's Orioles** are sometimes seen in the trees along the shore in May. In summer, watch for **Spotted Sandpipers** and **California Gulls**. Near the end of the road, before it meets the highway again, take a short spur east to a picnic area that provides a good view of the lake's main body of water. Walk along the Lake Estes Trail east from here to scope out unusual birds. Be sure to check those power poles for **Prairie Falcons**, too.

Return to the highway and turn left. If you're here during spring migration, turn right on Community Drive just before the causeway and take an immediate left into a parking area. Drive or walk the dirt road along the lake to explore the west side of the Fish Creek Arm and the grassy areas up the hill toward the high school. Migrating sparrows like this area, and some years you'll find dozens of **Sage Thrashers** and sometimes **Sage Sparrows**.

Continue across the causeway and turn right on Fish Creek Road. Stop at any of the turnouts next to the lake to scope Fish Creek Arm and check the power poles for **Prairie Falcons**. You may also want to take a closer look at the Fish Creek inlet area ahead. A **Golden-crowned Sparrow** took local birders by surprise one day in May. **Blue-winged Warblers**, **Northern Waterthrushes**, and **Yellow-headed Blackbirds** have also been seen here. In summer, after young have fledged, you may find a variety of resident birds here.

Stop at a turnout near the inlet and walk south along the willows on the west side of the road. In the future, a trail and a bridge over Fish Creek is planned for the inlet area. For now, do not use the old wooden bridge to cross the stream. It's unsafe (as you'll observe). If you want to bird this area further, park at a turnout near the intersection of Fish Creek Road and Brodie Drive, just around the curve. Walk to Brodie

Prairie Falcon

and cross the stream using the road. Walk north along the west side of the stream to the inlet area.

AFTER YOU'VE BIRDED the inlet, return to Highway 36 and turn right. Take a left on Mall Road, less than a tenth of a mile. In about a half-mile, turn left on a dirt road toward Olympus Dam. (In summer there is a fee for using this area.) Stop long enough to check out the Wapiti Meadows wetland, a natural marsh enhanced by water released from the waste treatment plant. **Soras** often nest under the willows on the south side of the pond. **Tree, Barn,** and **Cliff swallows** are common, as are **Red-winged Blackbirds. Mallards** and **Canada Geese** use the pond for nesting and rearing young. In spring, migrating waterfowl and shorebirds are found here.

Continue toward the dam, taking the right fork to the river. In April and May, an amazing assortment of sparrows, pipits, and warblers can be found in these grasslands and the riparian area along the stream. **Eastern** and **Western kingbirds** are uncommon migrants, and **Mountain** and **Western bluebirds** are seen as they pass through. The Big Thompson River is a good place to stop and watch for **American Dippers**, which are here year-round. **Spotted Sandpipers** may be seen along the river, and **Yellow Warblers** nest in the riparian trees and shrubs.

Return to Mall Road and turn left to Highway 34 where you'll make another left. You'll pass the marina and travel along motel row to near the top of the hill where you'll make a left turn on Lakefront Street. This road leads to the lake near the Big Thompson River inlet and allows a good view of the larger body of the lake. You can walk the Lake Estes Trail east to check out birds on the lake or walk west to access the Matthews-Reeser Bird Sanctuary. The typical access to the sanctuary is from the west and is described below.

To Reach the Matthews-Reeser Bird Sanctuary

To bird the Lake Estes Trail and the Matthews-Reeser Bird Sanctuary, park at the Estes Park Information Center just east of the junction of

Highways 34 and 36. There are entrances to the Information Center from both highways. From the Highway 34 parking lot, find the signs for the Lake Estes Trail. Cross the footbridge over the Big Thompson River and continue walking east. From the Highway 36 parking lot, find the trail at the east end of the parking lot and walk east.

What You'll Find—Matthews-Reeser Bird Sanctuary

The Matthews-Reeser Bird Sanctuary at the northwest corner of the lake is the most popular local birding spot during spring migration. It's especially exciting during the warbler waves in May, with the third week in May usually the best birding. The sanctuary was named for two longtime birding couples from Estes Park—Ted and Lois Matthews and Warner and Ruth Reeser.

Ted Matthews lived in Estes Park most of his life. As a child, he attended the opening ceremony for Rocky Mountain National Park in 1915. Among many accomplishments, he and his wife published wildlife photographs, with credits including the *Peterson Guide to Western Bird Nests*. The bird sanctuary was created on March 11, 1997, and Ted and Lois were able to attend its opening later that spring. Both have since passed away.

Warner Reeser is well-known throughout Colorado for his leadership in birding activities. He and Ruth lived in Denver before retiring to Estes Park. They have been fixtures at the lake for many years, and I've relied on their records of sightings at the lake and within RMNP throughout this book.

Even though it's a small area, it's difficult to predict what you'll find in the Matthews-Reeser Bird Sanctuary in April and May and again in September and early October. In 1995, a **Black Phoebe** took up a ten-day residence. In 1996, a **Red-eyed Vireo** and an **Ovenbird** were among the highlights, along with a **Black-throated Sparrow**. In 1997, a **Sage Sparrow** and a **Palm Warbler** were exciting new finds. In 1998, a **LeConte's Sparrow** made the news and gave me my 600th ABA-area life bird. In 1999, a **Hooded Warbler** and a **Northern Parula** were birds of note. And in 2000, a **Prothonotary Warbler** was big news.

I must note, however, that in the summer months the sanctuary can be bereft of anything but **Yellow Warblers, American Robins, Common Grackles,** and **Violet-green** and **Cliff swallows.** I can't recommend you take time away from birding in Rocky Mountain National Park during June, July, and early August to visit it.

LET ME GIVE YOU the local's spring tour from the Information Center parking lot described above. The trail first runs alongside the golf course for about 100 yards. In spring, but especially in May, you should check out the open grasslands of the golf course, here and farther along the trail, for **Long-billed Curlews, Savannah Sparrows, Mountain Bluebirds,** and **Bobolinks.** When you reach a prominent cottonwood to the left of the trail, you've entered the best spring birding area in the Estes Valley.

That cottonwood is the Oriole Tree, a favorite hangout of **Bullock's Orioles** when they're visiting in May. It's also a good place to find **Yellow-rumped** and **Yellow warblers,** but the best warbler hunting is ahead. Just past the tree, check out the unvegetated area to the left where a sign warns you to stay off the golf course. Pay particular attention to the willow row that extends toward the golf course. When the sparrows are coming through, any species on the Lake Estes checklist is possible here. Sometimes it seems *any* sparrow might show up. Look for the regulars: **White-crowned, Lincoln's,** and **Song sparrows. Spotted** and **Green-tailed towhees** and the uncommon **Harris's Sparrow** may be found, and the willow area is a good **Brown Thrasher** site.

After you've checked the willows, turn your attention to the utility yard to the right of the trail. We call this the Sparrow Cage, because the fenced gravel yard and surrounding grassy areas are so attractive to the sparrows that migrate through. Keepers of the trail didn't find the utility yard attractive, however, and they put a privacy fence around it. Still, check out the fence, what you can see of the area inside, and the grassy areas on the east.

A **Black-throated Sparrow** was found here, sitting on top of the fence. More commonly, you'll see the first **Clay-colored** and **Brewer's sparrows** of the year here, on the fence or the ground nearby. The Clay-colored Sparrows arrive first, about the third week in April. The Brewer's are generally here by the end of the first week in May. Either bird can occur anytime in May. Be sure of your identification of these similar species.

On your left, you can follow an indistinct path along the east side of the willow row you birded for sparrows. Walk slowly as you drop down to the level of the stream. There are often good birds along the stream, and most springs it's unusual *not* to find **Common Snipe** here. To watch them rather than just spook them, go slowly and study the streamside closely. The **Green Heron** on the checklist came from this spot. Continue north far enough to check out the golf-course water hazard that birds tend to think of as a pond. For your own safety, it's not a good idea to enter the golf course proper, so return to the trail.

As you continue eastward, you'll find the willows on your left open up, providing a view of the small side stream. Watch for **Northern Waterthrush** in May and the more common warblers, including **Common Yellowthroat**. When we have **Yellow-breasted Chats**, they are most often seen along the stream here. This is also a good place to look for **Hermit** and **Swainson's thrushes** and the uncommon **Veery**. Throughout your walk, watch for accipiters; **Sharp-shinned** and **Cooper's hawks** and **Northern Goshawks** have been seen.

Continue on the trail, checking out both the willows on the left and the grassy area to the right. Before the trail was put in, **Killdeer** nested in the grassy area. They can still sometimes be seen migrating through, but the area is also attractive to more unusual migrants, such as **Rock Wrens**. **Mountain Bluebirds** sometimes use the birdhouse you'll see on the right. While you're birding here, you'll probably notice swallows flying overhead. **Barn**, **Violet-green**, and **Tree swallows** usually arrive by mid-April, with the **Cliff Swallows** coming in by the second week in May. **Barn** and **Cliff swallows** nest under the eaves of the power plant (along with **House Sparrows**). **Northern Rough-winged Swallows** and **Bank Swallows** make an occasional appearance during spring migration, also.

Willows attractive to warblers, vireos, and other birds grow along the left side of the trail as you enter the Matthews-Reeser Bird Sanctuary. You're now in the heart of things, in terms of spring migration. Notice that the sanctuary rules allow birding, walking, picnicking, fishing, and other quiet activities off the trail. It is okay to leave the paved trail, but please stick to established paths when you can. Some of those will have sticks and logs strewn across them to keep out bicyclists, but they are open to foot traffic.

As you pass the sanctuary sign, the trail curves northward. On your right is Night-Heron Pond, so called because **Black-crowned Night-Herons** used to roost here before the trail went in. When they're present, they are now more likely to be seen on Pine Point, a little farther ahead. Night-Heron Pond is excellent for migrants, especially unusual warblers. You should bird it thoroughly if you're here when the warblers are in town. **Blue-winged** and **Black-and-white warblers** and **Red-eyed Vireos** are exciting finds for local birders, but sometimes there's a bird good enough to warrant everyone's attention. A **Black Phoebe** took up residence at the pond for ten days one year, affording birders from around northern Colorado a good look.

The pond is also a reliable place for **Northern Waterthrush**. When there's one in town, it's likely to be here. Check the water's edge from the trail or by walking quietly down to the pond on the south side. You'll also likely find **Common Grackles** bathing and **Belted Kingfishers** fishing, as well as **Yellow-rumped** and **Yellow warblers** and **Common Yellow-throats**. **MacGillivray's Warblers** and **Gray Catbirds** are sometimes found in the shrubby trees between the pond and the main lake in May. Everybirdy likes the pond.

Return to the trail and continue past the pond. You'll soon see an informal path leading right to Pine Point. Another bird sanctuary sign is located here to remind people of the rules. Proceed downhill slowly. A very good birding area, The Swamp, is just a few yards off the paved trail on the left, but you may spook the birds if you're not careful. Many unusual warblers, such as **Ovenbird**, have been spotted here, and you may also find a **Sora**. Check for catbirds and chats, too. Because there is so much cover, this is a good place to sit down and wait for the birds to come to you.

Continue on the trail to Pine Point. This small peninsula of ponderosa pines can sometimes have a splendid assortment of birds, although it's just as often pretty empty. Watch for the thrushes here and check out the warblers. Most will be **Yellow-rumped**, but **Black-and-**

white, **Chestnut-sided**, and, rarely, **Magnolia warblers** have been seen on the Point. Check both sides of the peninsula for shorebirds and waterfowl in the shallow bays there. The east side provides another vantage point for The Swamp. One memorable spring day, Pine Point had **Indigo Buntings**, **Blue Grosbeaks**, and a **Blue-winged Warbler**. Birders were anything but blue that day!

Return to the trail and continue birding the willows on both sides as you walk east. This is Warbler Alley, and the birds can be thick, especially early on a May morning. Be prepared for anything! **Hooded Warbler** and **Northern Parula** have both been found here. The trail curves to the southeast at the end of this area, and on the left you'll find Catbird Corner. I've counted as many as forty **Gray Catbirds** in this small, shrubby meadow on a morning in May.

The trail affords views of the lake on the right and then enters The Narrows, where the river is close on the left and the lake on the right. You've left the boundaries of the bird sanctuary at this point. Surprisingly, some of our best birds have come from this unassuming part of the trail. **Marsh Wrens** are fairly common on both sides of the river in May. Before the trail was built, a pair nested here. **Common Yellowthroats** are, well, common on both the river side and the lake side. If you get lucky, you may find a rare warbler, such as the **Palm Warbler** seen here, in the willows and poplars. Watch also for **American Dippers** along the river and **Spotted Sandpipers** along the lake. The **LeConte's Sparrow** was first found in The Narrows.

Continuing on, the grassy areas before you reach the footbridge are good for migrating sparrows, and the finger of land extending into the lake on the right often has **Spotted Sandpipers** along its rocky shoreline. I've also seen **Cattle Egrets**, **Snowy Egrets**, and **White-faced Ibis** here, so I suppose any shorebird migrating through might be seen. On the river side of this peninsula, you may find mudflats with **Long-billed Dowitchers**, **American Avocets**, and **Western Sandpipers**, if the level of the lake is right.

The bridge marks the end of the best birding, although you can continue completely around the lake on the trail if you like. Unless, of course, it's May. Then you must, by local birder's law, return to your car through the area you've just birded. You're almost certain to find new birds on the way back.

ALTHOUGH MOST VISITORS will not be able to experience the excitement of birding Lake Estes and the Matthews-Reeser Bird Sanctuary in May when the warblers are in, any account of birding in Estes Park and RMNP would be incomplete without this chapter. After six months of winter weather and few birds, May in the sanctuary is just what we locals need to get our minds energized for summer birding.

PART FOUR

Trip Planning/ RMNP Birdfinding Guide

11

Planning Your Trip

ROCKY MOUNTAIN NATIONAL PARK, and Colorado in general, can surprise you in many ways. Good trip planning can take the hurt out of the unpleasant surprises and help you avoid some of the pitfalls any birding trip to an unfamiliar location can produce. In this chapter, I'll discuss when to come for the best birding, clothing you should bring, hazards you may face, and resources you can use.

When to Come

Spring: April 1–June 1

Spring is exciting to local birders, of course. Early in March the first **Mountain Bluebirds** arrive. Waterfowl and shorebirds start in March, too, but the highest numbers of them will come in April. In April and May, the summer birds are returning, and exciting migrants come to Lake Estes and RMNP.

May is the most likely month to produce rare vagrants at Lake Estes. The list of over 220 species for the lake and surrounding areas is amazing. To hit the peak of migration and enjoy reasonably good weather, be here for the last two weeks of May. Most of the mountain birds will be back, singing and establishing territories.

"Spring" months are chancy on weather. We don't have spring like most parts of the country do. March and April are our snowiest months, with occasional snowfalls of ten to twenty inches. High-elevation trails in Rocky will be snowy and may require snowshoes in April. The birding trails described in this book will be wet from snowmelt much of the

Estes Park Weather

	Jan.	Feb.	Mar.	Apr.	May	Jun.	Jul.	Aug.	Sep.	Oct.	Nov.	Dec.	Annual
Avg. high	37.9	40	44	52.9	61.8	72.2	78.5	76.7	70	60.1	46.6	40.1	56.8
Avg. low	15.4	16.7	20	26.6	34	40.8	46.1	44.7	37.6	30.1	22.6	18	29.4
Avg. temp.	26.7	28.4	32	39.8	47.9	56.5	62.3	60.7	53.8	45.1	34.6	29	43.1
Record high	61	65	68	77	83	92	93	96	89	85	75	66	
Record low	-38	-39	-26	-19	4	24	31	29	3	-9	-25	-30	
Monthy precip.	0.45	0.62	0.93	1.64	2.13	1.75	2.17	1.93	1.27	0.94	0.71	0.57	15.27
Record precip.	2.35	2.3	3.34	5.43	5.43	5.01	6.09	5.79	4.52	4.35	6.47	2.63	32.47
Avg. snowfall	6.7	10	12.5	11.2	2.4	0.2	0	0	0.6	2.7	6.8	8.2	83.7
Record daily snow	28	12	15	30	3	3	0	0	4	6	18	20	
Days over 90°	0	0	0	0	0	1	1	1	0	0	0	0	3
Days under 32°	7.8	5.6	4.1	0.9	0	0	0	0	0	0.4	2.9	6.9	28

Highest temperature: 96° on 8/2/47

Lowest temperature: -39° on 2/1/59

Most snowfall in a year: 148" in 1942

Most precip in one day: 3.59" on 8/1/76

Most snowfall in a month: 48" in Nov. 1946

Least snowfall in a year: 42" in 1931

Compiled by Colorado State University, Ft. Collins

time in spring, and Trail Ridge Road will not be open until late May. May is warmer but has frequent periods of cold, rainy weather. Lows are still in the 30s in May, and it can snow any day.

Summer: June 1–September 1

Most mountain folk live for the summer months. With average highs in the seventies and lows in the mid-forties to mid-fifties, it's perfect outdoors weather. For many people, summer is the only time they can visit the National Park, and it's also the best time to see the most birds.

Each of the three months is different in terms of birds. In early June, summer breeding birds, such as **Dusky Flycatchers**, are setting up territories. Males and females are busy building nests, so there are more birds out and about than there will be in a couple of weeks. Resident birds, such as **Pygmy Nuthatches**, are generally ahead of this schedule and may already be on nests.

By mid-June, almost all the species have established their territories. Nest building may be complete, but males still sing and defend territory. The birds are in their preferred habitat, making them easier to locate. For the next two to three weeks, there will be only half the birds available for viewing, since females, sometimes taking turns with males, are incubating.

By mid-July almost all the nesters are feeding young in the nest, and the rest have fledglings. This is a great time to be birding, because birds are still in their favored habitat, both males and females are making trips to the nest, and the young are vocal. Some species will already be feeding fledglings. **Blue Grouse** families, for instance, are ambulatory, and since the kids haven't learned to be quiet, it's a great time to find them.

By early August, almost all young will have fledged and will be at least partially self-sufficient. Family groups range farther and are less predictable in terms of location or habitat. Mixed groups begin to form for feeding efficiency and, perhaps, to prepare for migration. Until mid-August, when some birds begin to leave, this means the most number of birds are available for watchers. August is also a great time to see **Black Swifts**. They range farther from their nests, since the young are also flying by then. From mid-August on, birding becomes a feast-and-famine affair. You may walk a trail described in the book without finding many birds until a feeding flock of 100 birds of ten or more species crosses your path.

Summer weather is generally great with lots of sunshine, and a typical afternoon thunderstorm, just when you need a little cooling off. The storms usually dissipate in an hour or two, leaving clearing skies for the sunset. Early June can be chilly with winds and cold rain. And a cold front can bring snow on any day of the year, even the Fourth of July.

In August we have monsoons, stormy weather from the southwest. They usually last three or four days and bring atypical, overcast days with significant precipitation, sometimes throughout the day and night. They typically occur about the second week of August. I hope you miss them.

Fall: September 1–November 1

The summer-only birds are migrating by early September. Throughout the month, you can find those amazing mixed flocks. In Chapter 7, I describe one of those flocks, found in late August. There were seventeen species, including five different warblers, in the flock. Not all of the flocks are that spectacular, but any time you find birds in September, you'll likely find several species together.

There are fall migrants at Lake Estes, in more limited numbers than spring, and **Townsend's Warblers** are here for the only time during the year. By mid-September, a significant number of birds will be gone. By early October, almost all of the summer birds will have left.

September and October are gorgeous months. The days are crisp and clear with little precipitation. The fall colors are lovely in early October. Trout are feeding and elk are bugling. You won't find as many birds as the season progresses, but you won't soon forget a trip to Rocky Mountain National Park in the fall.

Winter: November 1–April 1

A trip to Rocky can be fun any time, but there are definitely better times for the birds. In winter, there simply won't be many birds. Along the

Front Range of Colorado at elevations of 7,800 feet and above, the environment is inhospitable. The weather is cold, and the wind blows. A lot. As I've mentioned, the Christmas Bird Count list is usually sparse, typically forty-five to fifty species.

So, winter is not a good time to come for the birds. If you find yourself here, there are a few benefits. One of those is the ease with which you may find **Brown-capped Rosy Finches** at feeders. Using Chapter 9 as your guide, visit residential areas in the Estes Valley and the YMCA. Throughout the winter season, but especially when the weather is bad, rosy finches by the hundreds can be seen at one feeding station.

Along with the **Brown-capped**, expect to find many **Gray-crowned Rosy Finches** and one or two **Black Rosy Finches**. The latter two species are only found here in winter. **Cassin's Finches, Red Crossbills,** and **Evening Grosbeaks** are all commonly found at feeders in the winter, too. Lake Estes and Mary's Lake are open all year. Unusual waterfowl can occasionally be present on either lake. **Tundra** and **Trumpeter swans** are rare visitors. **Barrow's Goldeneyes** and **Hooded Mergansers** are uncommon but regular.

You may find **Pine Grosbeaks** more easily when they're driven down by the weather. **Townsend's Solitaires** sing incessantly during winter, probably to defend feeding territories. And **Northern Pygmy-Owls** and **Boreal Owls** call more regularly. On the other hand, a walk through the woods can be very lonely. Lovely, but lonely. The company of **Mountain Chickadees** and **Dark-eyed Juncos** is all you can expect in many places.

Estes Park winter temperatures average only about ten degrees colder than Denver, but temperature alone does not determine comfort. With our low humidity, thirty-five degrees isn't bad if the wind's not blowing. But it almost always is, dropping wind-chill readings to uncomfortable levels. Peak gusts are often in the range of thirty miles per hour with a steady wind blowing day and night. In the last seven years, we've averaged about eighty-seven inches of snow with regular but infrequent storms of one to six inches of snow. Driving can be hazardous during and after storms, but generally the roads are clear, with patches of snow and ice.

Pygmy Nuthatch
Mountain Chickadee

Temperatures are lower, winds higher, and snowfall greater in the higher elevations of the National Park. If you enjoy snowshoeing or cross-country skiing, winter is a good time for solitude with the solitaires. Many areas of the Park are closed to vehicular traffic in winter. These include Trail Ridge Road, Old Fall River Road, and access roads to Endovalley Picnic Area, Fern Lake, Wild Basin trailhead, Upper Beaver Meadows, and others.

I HOPE THIS SEASONAL run-down will help you decide when to come or, if you don't have much say in it, what to expect when you get here. Any time you get to spend in Rocky Mountain National Park is good time. Being here when the birds are plentiful is even better.

What to Wear

It can snow in RMNP any day of the year! If you want to use every day of your vacation on something besides watching TV in your motel room, you'd better be ready for the weather.

There's one thing you can count on about mountain weather—it's variable. It can change dramatically in a few minutes. As we natives like to remark, if you don't like the weather, wait fifteen minutes. The need to accommodate rapid changes has led mountain people to use the layering method of dressing.

Start out an early June morning on Trail Ridge Road in your zip-off pants, sweater, coat, stocking cap, and gloves. By mid-morning, you still need the sweater. An hour later at a lower elevation, a long-sleeved shirt and a regular hat are sufficient. After lunch, the zip-off pants become shorts and your shirt sleeves are rolled up. Later, the shirt comes off and you're down to a T-shirt and shorts. As evening approaches, clothing is added back for warmth. A day pack carries any additional clothing, a raincoat, and maybe wind pants.

The first rule is, even in midsummer, don't come without clothing for cold weather. A sweater and a good jacket, preferably wind-proof, will suffice most of the time, but if you have room for gloves and a real coat, it may keep you out in the field on a cold day.

Second, bring rain gear. A hooded raincoat is vital, and rain pants are good, especially if you'll be hiking. You should expect an afternoon thunderstorm almost every day of the summer. It may not happen, but you should be prepared for one. How good your rain gear needs to be depends on how far you'll be from your car and how wet you're willing to get. Remember, too, that Colorado rain, especially mountain rain, is cold.

For almost all the birding trips in this book, tennis shoes or lightweight, low-cut hiking boots will be fine. I prefer boots since the soles are designed for safe footing on rocks. You may not get wet feet on any of the trips, unless you make a mistake, get caught in rain, or like to bird in the morning when the dew's still on the ground. (In other words, you should waterproof your boots!) One final word on footwear. Don't wear boots with aggressive soles on the tundra—you won't need the traction and they tear up the delicate vegetation.

Bring a wide-brimmed hat and wear sunglasses with ultraviolet protection. Our high-altitude sun is brutal on skin and eyes. If you burn easily, wear long-sleeved shirts and long pants all day or apply plenty of high-SPF sunscreen.

All that said, if you see me out birding in the summer, I'll be wearing shorts, a T-shirt with a long-sleeved shirt over it, low-cut, Gore-Tex® boots (I make mistakes while walking, especially in **Black Swift** country), and a wide-brimmed hat. I'll have a fanny pack big enough for a raincoat, some snacks, and my field guides, with two water bottles attached. In my car will be long pants, a hooded sweatshirt, a lightweight pair of gloves, and a jacket or coat.

Hazards

Although generally outside the realm of this book, I want to discuss briefly a few of the hazards you may face. You may come to Rocky Mountain National Park with concerns about bears and mountain lions and rattlesnakes. Lightning is a more likely threat, and you should be aware of health concerns like altitude sickness, sunburn, and hypothermia. (And, perhaps, what you'll do if you become lost following my directions …)

Weather

My number-one concern when I'm birding in the Park is lightning. I've read that the Front Range of Colorado has more lightning strikes than anywhere else in the country. Almost every summer storm is turbulent enough to create lightning. It can even strike during a snowstorm! It's the nature of storms in the Rockies to develop quickly and move fast. Some areas you'll be birding put you in terrain where it's difficult to see developing storms, most of which come from the west during summer. The first warning may be a lightning strike on the ridge above where you're walking.

So, watch the weather. Any build-up of cumulus clouds can signal a thunderstorm in the making. If you see lightning or hear thunder, you should start working your way back to your car, where you'll be best protected. If you're caught in a storm, stay in the timber as much as possible. Don't pick the tallest tree to stand under or trees separated from the main forest.

The worst place to face a severe thunderstorm is the tundra. It's only happened to me once, and I don't intend to let it happen again. Ever. It was terrifying. Visit the tundra in the morning when skies are clear and get off the mountain when you see storm clouds forming. Storms build even more quickly up top.

Also associated with storms is the possibility of becoming hypothermic, losing enough body heat to lower your internal temperature. It can happen at surprisingly mild temperatures if the wind is blowing or you're wet. The first indication of trouble is constant shivering. If you experience that, return to your car immediately and get warm. If you're a distance from your car, you may need help, because what follows shivering is disorientation and incoherence. Be sure to tell your birding partner or even a stranger on the trail what's happening and have them help you out. Ask for help before you don't know enough to do so.

Health

Altitude sickness is probably the most common health complaint of visitors. Like motion sickness, it doesn't affect everyone, but when it hits, it can be miserable. According to a pamphlet prepared by Timberline Medical in Estes Park, altitude sickness most commonly occurs over 6,000 feet. If you're driving to RMNP, you have time to acclimate, but if you're flying to Denver from sea level, you're more susceptible. The pamphlet recommends that you stay a day in Denver before driving to the mountains.

There is no way to determine who may suffer from this ailment, and your predisposition to it can change from year to year. Mild altitude sickness is not serious, but it's no fun. Symptoms usually occur eight to twenty-four hours after arrival. They include headache, flu-like symptoms, and difficulty sleeping. Moderate altitude sickness brings a more severe headache that does not respond to conventional remedies, breathlessness with exertion, and loss of coordination.

Acclimatization is crucial to avoiding altitude sickness. Your first few days at high elevation should not be strenuous. Drink plenty of liquids before and during exercise. Some people also benefit from a high-carbohydrate diet. Should you experience symptoms associated with altitude sickness, you should probably seek medical attention.

Incidentally, feeling a bit lazy, sleeping soundly (and sometimes too late in the morning for good birding), and having a hearty appetite are the most common "symptoms" of being at high elevation. Enjoy them.

Insects

We have mosquitos, and deer flies and horse flies are bothersome at times. Black flies are found in some wet areas, particularly along streams and ponds. All can be avoided by wearing appropriate clothing and using an insect repellent if necessary. The latter is seldom necessary.

Ticks are most active from mid-April through mid-June, and you can become infected with Colorado tick fever or Rocky Mountain spotted fever through tick bites. Both are serious diseases; neither is fatal if treated. Lyme disease is not a concern at this time. Only a small percentage of ticks carry any disease, so don't panic if you find one attached to you.

To prevent the tick from becoming attached, wear light-colored clothing, especially when hiking in brushy areas—it makes checking for ticks easier. Our ticks are big enough to see, about the size of a match head. Team up with your partner to check areas you can't see. After a day in the field, do a strip search. Attached ticks should be removed carefully and slowly, so that all body parts come out. Use tweezers and pull the head very gently. Do not squeeze the body. Never attempt any other way of removing one. Take your time. Let the tick become tired of holding on. Treat the area with antibiotics, and you should be okay. If you do have flu-like symptoms, which may not show up until after your trip, seek medical help.

Snakes

This is a short section. There are no poisonous snakes in the Estes Valley or Rocky Mountain National Park to my knowledge. The cut-off for rattlesnakes is about 7,500 feet in elevation at this latitude, so it's possible a rattler might be at the very lowest elevations in the area. I've never seen one.

Falls

The steep Rocky Mountains provide many opportunities for injuries from falls. Beware of steep drop-offs along trails and be sure to stay back from the edges of precipitous snow fields. Birders are notorious for watching the trees and skies instead of their feet. This is not a good place to make that mistake.

Drowning

A number of people have drowned in recent years, several of them children. The pretty mountain stream where you're watching for dippers can be deadly, especially early in summer when run-off makes currents dangerous. Footing is slippery and rock stability is uncertain next to rivers. Currents are swift, and underwater rocks can render you unconscious.

Animals

Bears, mountain lions, elk, and moose can present hazards to you, but none are a real threat to your safety unless you're uninformed or very, very unlucky.

RMNP has a healthy population of black bears, as does the Estes Valley, but you'll have to be lucky to see one. (There are no known grizzly bears in Colorado.) They're cautious and smart enough to avoid people, at least in the Park. Residential areas and campgrounds may have bears that are habituated to people, and they present more of a danger. A bear-related fatality occurred in 1977 at a campground adjacent to RMNP.

Bears will leave you alone if you don't pose a threat. You can pose a threat by surprising them or happening on a sow and cubs. That's the luck part of the deal. Should you see a bear, leave the area. Stay calm—never run from a predator. Stop and back away. Talk aloud to let the bear know you're there. In close contact, talk softly and calmly as you back away. Be sure to keep children close to you or within sight in campgrounds and anywhere in the Park.

The Colorado Division of Wildlife has a pamphlet entitled "Living with Wildlife in Bear Country," which you might like to request. Contact information is given at the end of this chapter. Bears go about their business unless threatened or surprised, but birders have one disadvantage—they generally walk along very quietly. In dense shrubbery, you should make noise. Talk aloud to let wildlife know you're around.

I've only seen one bear in RMNP, sometime in the 1970s. It was eating a cookie offered by the driver of a car at Farview Curve on Trail Ridge Road. More recently a tourist told me he'd seen a bear run up a nearby hillside just before I arrived to bird in Hollowell Park. That's it for bears.

You're not likely to see a mountain lion in the Park, either, let alone encounter one along a trail. They are secretive, cautious animals. Bears, in comparison, just gallumph along. Mountain lions, however, have been known to prey on humans. A young boy was killed by a mountain lion on the west side of RMNP when he strayed from his family on a hike. Another Colorado fatality involved a high school student who was jogging alone on a trail near his school.

I've only seen three mountain lions in Colorado in my life, all along roads at lower elevations. Still, I think the number of encounters between lions and humans will increase. It's inevitable. Most of the advice given for bears applies to encounters with lions. Stay calm. Talk calmly but firmly. Back away if you can. Do not run. Face the lion and stand tall. Make yourself appear bigger if you feel threatened—raise your arms or open your jacket and spread it above your head. The greatest threat is to children. Don't allow them to wander away on the trail or to play alone or in small groups unsupervised, especially in the early morning and at dusk. If you encounter a lion on the trail, gather your children next to you or pick them up. They must not run away.

The biggest liability you'd face as a birder would be in going alone very early or late in the day. Your biggest asset is your alertness. If you can see a lion early, you can avoid a confrontation. The Colorado Division of Wildlife also has a pamphlet entitled "Living with Wildlife in Lion Country," which you may also wish to request.

Even elk can pose a hazard. Bull elk during the fall rut are formidable animals. Do not approach them. A cow elk in June can be just as much a threat. Cows hide their calves nearby while they graze. If you walk too near an unseen calf, a cow elk will likely charge you. They can do real damage by rearing and using their hooves. I was nearly driven into Lake Estes by a cow elk one spring before I learned this lesson. You may also encounter moose on the west side of RMNP. They're just generally cantankerous if approached too closely or surprised. They will charge, and they mean business when they do.

Having said all that, if you're lucky enough to see a bear or mountain lion, it will probably be a highlight of your trip, not a life-threatening encounter. Be aware of the presence of all these animals. Be cautious around them. Respect them. And enjoy the experience.

Crime

Estes Park is a very safe community. Serious crime is rare, but the summer season always shows an increase in criminal activity. All national parks have some crime, usually breaking into cars. Follow any recommendations given in Rocky Mountain National Park's newspaper-style handout you'll receive when you enter the Park. At the present time, I'd advise you not to worry beyond their recommended measures.

Where to Stay

There are, of course, a multitude of motels, bed-and-breakfasts, and other lodgings in and near Estes Park. I suggest you contact the Estes Park Chamber Resort Association to find an appropriate one. Their phone number is listed below. You might also visit web pages found by searching the internet. For birders, a good lodging choice would be the YMCA. They rent cabins, usually by the week, and rooms, and the grounds offer excellent birding. There are lots of activities for non-birding family members. Be forewarned that summer reservations at the YMCA need to be made well in advance.

If you're camping, you'll also have good birding "at home." In general, you should make reservations if you intend to camp in the National Park. If you don't have reservations, you should try to be at the campgrounds between 10 A.M. and noon, when campers are checking out. For the best birding, I'd choose Moraine Park Campground in Rocky (reservations accepted). There's good birding in the campground, and you can walk to the Cub Lake Trail. My second choice would be Aspenglen, a smaller campground located near the Fall River Entrance (no reservations). If you can't get a site in the Park, try Olive Ridge Campground, a Forest Service site south of Estes Park on Highway 7. Many of the closer commercial campgrounds are fine for RVs, and some are comfortable enough for tenting. The Chamber Resort Association can help.

I HOPE THIS RUN-DOWN of trip-planning basics will help you, especially if you're traveling to Rocky Mountain National Park for the first time. Locals are friendly and full of advice on where to eat, what to do, or where to get help. Don't be afraid to ask, if you can find one of us among all the tourists. The Chamber Resort Association Information Center at the junction of Highways 34 and 36 just east of town is a great place to stop for any kind of help, advice, or information.

Directory

General Resources and Lodging

Estes Park Chamber Resort Association: 800-443-7837 or
970-586-4431
Information Center: intersection of Highways 34 and 36
www.estesparkresort.com

YMCA of the Rockies: 970-586-3341

Estes Park Police Department: 970-586-4600; emergencies: 911

Rocky Mountain National Park: 970-586-1206 (information);
emergencies: 970-586-1399 (or 911 after hours)
www.nps.gov

Colorado Division of Wildlife, Northeast Regional Office:
970-484-2836

Campgrounds

Rocky Mountain National Park Campground Reservations:
800-365-2267
http://reservations.nps.gov

Olive Ridge Campground, Forest Service information: 970-586-3440

Commercial campgrounds: Contact the Chamber Resort Association
at the number above

Medical Care

Estes Park Medical Center (hospital): 970-586-2317
555 Prospect Ave.

Timberline Medical Urgent Care: 970-586-2343
131 Stanley Ave.

12

Where to Find Birds in Rocky: A Species-by-Species List

MY SELECTION OF BIRDS for a Rocky Mountain National Park birdfinding guide may puzzle you. I've included many more birds than an experienced RMNP birder knows to expect. You can thank my wife for this. When we get ready for a birding trip to unfamiliar territory, she likes to get out the bird books, look at the maps, and make a list of the species we may see that are not common at home, particularly the ones that would be lifers. She's suggested that I write this section for a person such as herself, and I think it's a good idea.

The birds included here are those that have a range that includes the Rockies, plus the vagrants seen at Lake Estes and other areas. To the best of my knowledge, if you don't see it listed, it hasn't been found in the area. Not yet, anyway.

Although I've listed many birds not associated with the Rockies, they're generally treated briefly. Those of more interest to visiting birders are described in greater detail with the best, most reliable spots I know to see them. I've made references to specific chapters when it's important to read more detailed information on the birds and where to find them. References to Collister and Kleinschnitz are from annotated RMNP checklists published in 1970 and 1947 respectively.

Mountain specialties and other high-interest birds are shown in boldface to help you sort through the list.

Keys: 1 = common   sp = spring (April 1–June 1)
       2 = fairly common   sr = summer resident/visitor (June 1–Sept. 1)
       3 = uncommon   f = fall (Sept. 1–Nov. 1)
       4 = rare   wv = winter visitor (Nov. 1–April 1)
       5 = accidental   yr = year around

Loons, Grebes

Common Loon, 3, sp/f: Uncommon migrant at Lake Estes.

Pacific Loon, 5: One recent November record at Lake Estes.

Horned and Eared Grebes, 4, sp/f: Rare migrants at Lake Estes.

Pied-billed Grebe, 4, wv/sp: Seen occasionally at Lake Estes in spring migration. Found on two recent Christmas Bird Counts, with one bird staying most of one winter.

Clark's and Western Grebes, 4, sp: Both recorded at Lake Estes and Mary's Lake over the years in migration. Occasionally seen in summer. Common in summer on plains reservoirs.

Pelicans, Herons, Allies

American White Pelican, 4, sp/f: Fall wanderers as early as August. Spring birds reported on Trail Ridge Road, riding thermals over the mountains.

Double-crested Cormorant, 2, sp/sr/f: Regular visitors, especially during spring and early summer. Young birds show up in summer and stay until fall migration. Check Fish Creek Arm of Lake Estes.

American Bittern, 4, sp: Historical records for RMNP from Moraine Park and the Colorado River valley. (I saw one near my house one spring, sitting among the rabbit brush.)

Great Blue Heron, 2, sp/f; 3, sr: Fairly common in spring at Lake Estes, especially on Fish Creek Arm. One or two are around nearly every summer. Also found in the Kawuneeche Valley.

Snowy Egret, 4, sp: Rare migrant at Lake Estes, late April or early May.

Cattle Egret, 4, sp: Rare migrant at Lake Estes.

Green Heron, 5: Two spring records, both along the side stream in the bird sanctuary at Lake Estes.

Black-crowned Night-Heron, 3, sp: Seen nearly every April and May in the bird sanctuary at Lake Estes. Spring reports from Endovalley in RMNP.

White-faced Ibis, 3, sp: Uncommon but regular migrant at Lake Estes mid-April through May. Also found in Endovalley, in wet meadows near Fall River and Fan Lake. One found dead at Lily Lake. Usually seen in flocks of ten to thirty, often during or after a spring storm.

Swans, Geese, Ducks

Tundra and Trumpeter Swans, 5: The occasional Tundra Swan has probably always been possible at Lake Estes, especially in fall. In 1996 and 1997, Trumpeters also migrated through in the late fall, one at Mary's Lake and two at Lake Estes. In 1999, a Trumpeter spent ten days in early February at Lake Estes.

Snow Goose, 4, sp: Rare at Lake Estes in early spring.

Canada Goose, 1, sp/sr/f; 3, wv: On the increase here, as they are along the Front Range of Colorado. In the past few years, status changed from uncommon migrants to nesters at Lake Estes, wintering over some years. Like elk, now are regular nuisances on the golf course next to the lake. Recently seen regularly on Fan Lake in Endovalley.

Wood Duck, 3, sp; 4, wv: Uncommon in Colorado, with a few breeding populations. Sometimes appears in spring at Lake Estes. One occasionally spends the winter.

Mallard, 1, yr: Most common duck at Lake Estes and in RMNP.

Gadwall, 2, sp/f: Fairly common in spring and fall at Lake Estes.

Northern Pintail, 3, sp: A few show up irregularly at Lake Estes beginning in February.

American Wigeon, 2, sp/f: Fairly common during both migrations at Lake Estes.

Northern Shoveler, 2, sp: Fairly common but sporadic migrant at Lake Estes.

Cinnamon Teal, 3, sp/f: Seen occasionally at Lake Estes in mid-April. Also found in the wetlands below the Lake Estes dam. Very occasionally, Cinnamon Teal will be seen on Fan Lake and on beaver ponds in Moraine Park.

Blue-winged Teal, 2, sp; 3, f: Regular spring migrant and uncommon fall migrant at Lake Estes, other area lakes, and the wetlands below the Lake Estes dam.

Green-winged Teal, 2, sp; 3, f: Regular spring migrant and uncommon fall migrant at Lake Estes. Also found in smaller ponds, lakes, and in the wetlands below the Lake Estes dam.

Canvasback, 3, sp/f: Always a treat. Occasionally found with Redheads at Lake Estes.

Redhead, 1, sp/f: Common during both migrations at Lake Estes.

Ring-necked Duck, 1, sp/f; 2, sr; 3, wv: Common in migration and possible in winter at area lakes. Apparently nests at Lily Lake, Sprague Lake, and other lakes.

Lesser Scaup, 1, sp/f: Common migrant beginning in March at area lakes.

Long-tailed Duck (Oldsquaw), 5: Rare visitor anywhere in Colorado. Records from mid-November through February at Lake Estes.

White-winged Scoter, 5: I've seen a raft of these rare stragglers at Lake Estes in December. One fall record from 1937 for Grand Lake.

Surf Scoter, 5: One recent winter record at Lake Estes.

Common Goldeneye, 1, wv/sp/f: One of the most common ducks at Lake Estes during winter.

Barrow's Goldeneye, 4, wv/sp/f: A mountain-lake bird that sometimes makes a winter stopover at Lake Estes or Mary's Lake. Also on the west side of RMNP in migration on Shadow Mountain Reservoir.

Bufflehead, 3, wv: Occasionally found at Lake Estes or Mary's Lake in late winter and early spring.

Hooded Merganser, 4, sp/f/wv: Rare migrant, found in spring and fall at Lake Estes. One spent most of the winter recently.

Common Merganser, 1, sp/f/wv; 2, sr: Usually found at Lake Estes and Mary's Lake from November through April. Fairly common in summer with a recent breeding record for Lake Estes.

Red-breasted Merganser, 5: On the RMNP checklist based on historical sightings from the 1950s. One recent sighting at Lake Estes.

Ruddy Duck, 3, sp/f: Uncommon at Lake Estes. Most sightings in spring. Not found every year.

Raptors

Turkey Vulture, 1, sr: Arrives for the summer in mid-April. Found throughout the Estes Valley and lower elevations of RMNP. Occasionally seen on the tundra.

Northern Harrier, 4, f: Occasionally seen in the open meadows of Horseshoe Park and Moraine Park in RMNP and wandering above timberline.

Cooper's Hawk, 3, sr: More common than Sharp-shinned but still not a bird to count on. Wanders from its usual timbered habitat to above timberline late in summer. Vantage points in Moraine Park and similar habitats give you the best chance to see one. Also hunts near bird feeders in residential areas and at the YMCA.

Sharp-shinned Hawk, 3, sr: A definite breeding record established in 1998, but probably a regular nester in the forests of RMNP and surrounding areas. Seen in Hollowell Park and the Cow Creek drainage, as well as Cub Lake Trail, Lumpy Ridge, and Moraine Park. Occasionally seen above timberline.

Northern Goshawk, 3, yr: Our mountain accipiter, always a thrill to see. More common than observations might indicate. Tends to stay in heavily wooded areas with small to medium-sized openings. The most common sighting is of a bird flying very fast through the forest, so know the field marks. Heavy-bodied and typically very dark gray in appearance. Experienced observers have little difficulty separating this species from the "daintier" accipiters. Little Horseshoe Park (Chapter 1), Lumpy Ridge, and Moraine Park have fairly regular sightings. The YMCA almost always has one, typically seen early summer mornings hunting ground squirrels.

Broad-winged Hawk, 5: Two records from Lake Estes in May.

Swainson's Hawk, 4, sp/f: A common hawk of the prairie in summer, but rare at this elevation. Check hawks flying over the Estes Valley in May. A recent sighting in May over Lumpy Ridge near Twin Owls. Historical sightings include late summer flights of several Swainson's Hawks above timberline.

Red-tailed Hawk, 1, yr: Common resident that helps control the Wyoming ground squirrel population.

Ferruginous Hawk, 3, f: Late summer visitor to the tundra. One seen recently in the Estes Valley. A summer breeder on the Pawnee National Grasslands.

Rough-legged Hawk, 4, f/wv: Late summer observations from the 1960s over the tundra. Historical sightings during winter. One recent Christmas Bird Count record.

Bald Eagle, 3, wv/sp/f; 2, sr: Typically seen two or three times a year near Lake Estes, staying for a week or more at a time. Summer resident at Shadow Mountain Reservoir on the west side of RMNP.

Golden Eagle, 3, yr: Uncommon resident. Altitudinal migration makes them less common in winter. Seen along Dry Gulch Road, at Lumpy Ridge, and above open meadows in RMNP, including Horseshoe Park, Moraine Park, and Hollowell Park. Occasionally seen over the tundra.

Osprey, 2, sp/f: Fairly common in spring and early summer. If suitable nesting sites were available, Ospreys might nest here. Only one or two birds are usually found, with most sightings at Lake Estes. Common summer resident at Shadow Mountain Reservoir on the west side of RMNP.

Merlin, 4, sp/f/sr: I've only seen one Merlin here, a single bird at Lily Lake in July. A few other recent reports. A couple of accepted breeding records, plus one unconfirmed, from RMNP. More common at lower elevations.

American Kestrel, 3, sr: Common on the plains, but only a few summer birds at this elevation. One seen on the 2001 and 2002 Christmas Bird Counts. Listed as a common resident by Kleinschnitz in 1947.

Prairie Falcon, 2, sr; 4, yr: Several nesting pairs reported every year. Dry Gulch Road in the area near Eagle Rock is a regular site. A pair usually hunts around Lake Estes every year and may be seen on the utility towers there (Chapter 10). Also found at Lumpy Ridge, Cow Creek, and the YMCA. The most common raptor of the alpine tundra.

Peregrine Falcon, 4, sr: For several years, a pair nested on the south face of Mount Olympus. In 1998, a pair nested on Sheep Mountain in the Cow Creek area. Scattered reports each year of summer birds in other areas of the Estes Valley where remote rock walls provide nesting sites.

Gamebirds, Grouse

Northern Bobwhite, 5: Introduced in the 1910s and not seen since, as far as I can tell. Still on the RMNP checklist.

Chukar, 5: I hesitate to include this, but I'd hate to have you record one of the mystery sightings of this species and not find note of it here. Reported from Lake Estes and from Pole Hill Road east of the Estes Valley off Hwy. 36. No known breeding populations of this bird anywhere near RMNP, but numerous sightings of birds escaped from game-bird farms on the plains. Historical Park records for this species from the 1940s.

Ring-necked Pheasant, 5: Once common enough in the foothills to make it into RMNP boundaries. The last record, until I saw one in 1983, was from the Beaver Point area (Mary's Lake Road and Hwy. 36) in 1961. My sighting was of a cock bird running across Mary's Lake Road, just south of Hwy. 36! I'd just moved up to the mountains and thought I'd lost my mind. If you see one, don't report it. People will only wonder about you. I know. (Then again, a local birder reported one in 2001.)

Blue Grouse, 2, yr: A true nemesis bird for many birders who'll never believe they're fairly common. Camouflaged and quiet, Blue Grouse are prone to freeze as you approach. Get yourself in grouse country and let these friendly and curious birds pay you a visit. Easiest to find in July and August when young birds are ambulatory but haven't learned to lie low. Try along the road between the Cub Lake trailhead and the Fern Lake trailhead at first light (Chapter 2). Sometimes seen in the Fern Lake trailhead parking lot! If you don't find them on the drive in, walk back along the road. I found three families in one day in July in the Cow Creek area. Also seen at Rainbow Curve on Trail Ridge Road, at Lumpy Ridge, and in Wild Basin. In short, they're everywhere … unless you need one for your life list.

White-tailed Ptarmigan, 3, yr: Another nemesis bird. Residents on the tundra. A few winter reports at lower elevations. Medicine Bow Overlook on Trail Ridge Road is a reliable spot. See Chapter 4 for other specific locations and tips on finding them. You'll need time, sharp eyes, and some luck, but with determination, you should find ptarmigan in RMNP.

Greater Sage-Grouse, 5: On the RMNP list from before the construction of Shadow Mountain Reservoir. Some populations may remain in the Willow Creek area adjacent to the west boundary of the Park, but your best bet for sage-grouse is Arapaho National Wildlife Refuge near Walden. If you're on a Colorado tour, you should also try to find a Gunnison Sage-Grouse. (See *A Birder's Guide to Colorado* for details.)

Wild Turkey, 4, yr: More common at lower elevations of the foothills. Turkeys have been seen on several recent Christmas Bird Counts near Glen Haven and the YMCA. No place in the area can you *expect* to find one.

Coots, Rails

Common Moorhen, 5: One record from August 1939 for Lily Lake.

American Coot, 3, sp; 4, sr/wv: Uncommon migrant and rare visitor at Lake Estes. A few historical breeding records from Lake Estes, beaver ponds in the Colorado River Valley, and Shadow Mountain Reservoir.

Virginia Rail, 4, sr: A rare breeder. Historical records from Lily Lake, Hidden Valley, Mill Creek, Endovalley, and Sheep Lakes. Now seen regularly only at the beaver ponds on the Cub Lake Trail with an occasional sighting at Lily Lake.

Sora, 2, sr: Fairly common summer nester. Sometimes seen in spring migration at the bird sanctuary at Lake Estes. A pair has nested at the Wapiti Meadows Wetlands below the dam for several years. Also found nesting nearly every year in the wetlands south of Lily Lake and at the beaver ponds along the Cub Lake Trail. Possible in Hollowell Park, Endovalley, and Moraine Park in riparian wetlands. Also reported from Shadow Mountain Reservoir and riparian wetlands along the Colorado River.

Cranes, Shorebirds

Sandhill Crane, 4, sp/f: Typically seen in the vicinity of Lake Estes, often along the shore or on the nearby golf course.

Semipalmated Plover, 4, sp: One or two show up at Lake Estes irregularly, usually in early May after a storm.

Killdeer, 1, sp; 3, sr: Arrive in March and common all spring. The shores of Lake Estes can sometimes be alive with them during unsettled spring weather. Far less common in the fall. Formerly nested in grassy areas near Lake Estes and still may nest in the meadows west of Fish Creek Arm. Found at ponds and lakes in the Estes Valley and on both sides of RMNP.

American Avocet, 3, sp: Uncommon to fairly common at Lake Estes in April and May, sometimes in flocks of thirty or more.

Greater Yellowlegs, 3, sp: Uncommon but regular migrant at Lake Estes in early April. Also seen at Sheep Lakes in RMNP.

Lesser Yellowlegs, 3, sp/f: Uncommon but regular migrant at Lake Estes in mid-April. Also seen at Sheep Lakes in RMNP. A few fall records.

Solitary Sandpiper, 3, sp: Uncommon but regular spring migrant at Lily Lake and in the Wapiti Meadows Wetlands below Lake Estes during May. A few Park records from Sheep Lakes, beaver ponds in Moraine Park, and Grand Lake.

Willet, 3, sp: Uncommon but regular spring migrant at Lake Estes.

Spotted Sandpiper, 1, sr: Our most common wader. Hundreds can be seen along the shores of area lakes in May as some migrate through and others begin to set up breeding territories. Found in summer along the shores of RMNP lakes such as Lily Lake and Fan Lake, near the Fish Creek inlet of Lake Estes, and along the banks of larger streams, such as the Big Thompson and Colorado rivers.

Long-billed Curlew, 3, sp: A surprise find in May when storms bring a few to the golf course north of Lake Estes. An historical sighting along Trail Ridge Road in the summer.

Marbled Godwit, 4, sp: Rare migrant at Lake Estes. Historical record of a flock of fifty from Sheep Lakes in May 1946.

Baird's Sandpiper, 4, sp: A rare find at Lake Estes in early April. Historical sightings on the alpine tundra at elevations of 12,000–13,000 feet in summer.

Western Sandpiper, 3, sp: An unusual find at Lake Estes after April storms. Park records from Sheep Lakes.

Semipalmated Sandpiper, 3, sp: Found occasionally at Lake Estes in early May.

Least Sandpiper, 3, sp: Late April sightings from Lake Estes.

Long-billed Dowitcher, 3, sp: Sometimes appears for a day or two at Lake Estes after early May storms.

Short-billed Dowitcher, 4, sp: One or two records at Lake Estes in early May.

Common Snipe, 1, sp/sr: Nests in wet meadows and riparian areas of the Estes Valley and RMNP. Arrives as early as the third week in March. Relatively easy to find (if you call walking in wet meadows easy) in Endovalley, around Lily Lake, in Moraine Park, and in Hollowell Park. The winnowing sounds of the spring nuptial flights provide evening serenades through June.

Wilson's Phalarope, 3, sp: Uncommon April/May migrant at Lake Estes and Fan Lake in Endovalley.

Red-necked Phalarope, 4, sp/f: One or two records in mid-May at Lake Estes. Park sightings include an August report from The Loch (about 10,000 feet!) and a September report from Bear Lake, both from the 1950s.

Gulls, Terns

Pomarine Jaeger, 5: Historical record from Lake Estes in November 1957.

Bonaparte's Gull, 4, sp: Seen only a few times in late April at Lake Estes.

Black-headed Gull, 5: Warner Reeser found one in October near Lake Estes.

Franklin's Gull, 3, sp/f: Large flocks sometimes seen at Lake Estes, particularly in April and May. Seldom remain for more than a day. Fall accounts of Franklin's migrating at high elevation, including over Trail Ridge, are numerous, and a flock of 500–1,000 was reported in October 1960 at Lake Estes.

Ring-billed Gull, 3, sp: Seen occasionally at Lake Estes in April and May. Common on the eastern plains.

California Gull, 2, sp/sr: Common at Shadow Mountain Reservoir and Lake Granby just outside the Park's western boundary, where they may nest. East-side sightings are less common, but there are fairly regular spring sightings beginning in March at Lake Estes and regular summer sightings of one to six birds on area lakes, including Lake Estes and Fan Lake in RMNP. No known nesting records on the east side.

Herring Gull, 3, wv: Common on the plains, but irregular winter records here, all from Lake Estes.

Thayer's Gull, 5: One made a stop in January 1999 at Lake Estes; another was reported in September 1999.

Sabine's Gull, 5: One found dead on the road near Beaver Meadows Entrance in 1990. No other records until September 2000, when four turned up at Lake Estes during a snowstorm.

Black-legged Kittiwake, 5: One sighting from Lake Estes in spring.

Caspian Tern, 5: I found six at Lake Estes one day in May.

Common Tern, 5: No records until September 2000, when one turned up with the Sabine's Gulls noted above.

Forster's Tern, 4, sp/f: Fairly common on the eastern plains, but makes only rare appearances at this elevation, usually at Lake Estes.

Black Tern, 4, sp: Rare at Lake Estes in mid-May. A straggler from the plains, where it is fairly common but local. Seen historically at Sheep Lakes, Mary's Lake, and on the west side at Grand Lake and Shadow Mountain Reservoir.

Doves, Pigeons, Cuckoos

Mourning Dove, 2, sr: Found in meadow areas and broken woods around the Estes Valley and, less commonly, at the lower-elevation areas of the Park. Try Beaver Meadows if you want one for your Park list.

Rock Dove, 1, yr: Not included in Allegra Collister's 1970 edition of *Birds of Rocky Mountain National Park*, but common today in many parts of the Estes Valley. Within Park boundaries, occurs much less frequently; regular only at Twin Owls on Lumpy Ridge.

Band-tailed Pigeon, 3, sr: Another nemesis bird. Fairly common, but finding one—or telling birders where to find one—is another matter. Locals who feed corn or sunflower seeds may have them all summer, so birding residential areas within the ponderosa pines is worth a try (Chapter 9). You may find a family flock of a dozen or so birds flying in Moraine Park or along Park trails. Overlooks on Trail Ridge Road at elevations up to 11,000 feet may also be productive. Band-taileds are distinctive, with their great banded tails and noisy wing beats at take-off. Their uniform color and more direct flight helps separate them from Rock Doves, which have variegated plumage, whitish underwings, and the habit of soaring with wings held in a V-shape. No self-respecting Band-tailed would do that! Any pigeon you see in the Park, except along Lumpy Ridge, is likely to be this species. Band-tailed Pigeons arrive in late April and leave in mid-September. No winter records.

Yellow-billed Cuckoo, 5: Two records from July, one near Twin Sisters and one in Endovalley.

Owls

Long-eared Owl, 4, sr: Very few records, although they apparently have nested in the Park. Historical sightings come from Wild Basin and Moraine Park. Recent accounts from Cow Creek and Endovalley. More common at lower elevations; winters on the plains.

Great Horned Owl, 2, yr: Can be heard in many areas of the Estes Valley and RMNP up to 9,000 feet. Sighted in Cow Creek, Moraine Park, Upper Aspenglen, residential areas of Estes Park, near Mary's Lake, and many other areas.

Boreal Owl, 4, yr: Even more difficult to find than Northern Pygmy-Owls without hearing them. Complicating this is the Boreal's scarcity, their silence except during winter and early spring, and their habitat requirements, the tall spruce/fir forests of the high country where access is difficult in winter. Most people seeking this bird travel to Cameron Pass, between Ft. Collins and Walden, where a paved road offers miles of roadside access to the proper habitat. Even so, many birders return having heard the owl but not having seen it. To try for a Boreal, walk in its habitat along Trail Ridge Road (Chapter 4), particularly at Hidden Valley (9,200 feet) and Many Parks Curve (9,600 feet). Boreals are almost strictly nocturnal and do little, if any, calling in summer.

Northern Saw-whet Owl, 3, yr: Uncommon on both sides of RMNP to 10,000 feet. Reports of this owl come from Upper Beaver Meadows, Moraine Park, Hidden Valley beaver ponds, and Endovalley. They prefer damp, riparian areas with dense spruce and fir trees. Known nests have been in cavities in aspen. Heard calling near homes in the Estes Valley each spring as they move up to their nesting territory.

Flammulated Owl, 4, sr: Rare in terms of sightings but "uncommon and difficult-to-locate" is probably more accurate. Heard in the ponderosas, but the soft calls do not carry well. Collister listed them as "formerly a rare summer resident." She lists records only from 1890 and 1903, but one was heard in the Lily Lake area recently (at 4:00 A.M.). Injured birds have been found on Dry Gulch Road and at Park Headquarters, so they *are* here. This bird is strictly nocturnal and so quiet and secretive that it's simply not found. Prefers mature ponderosa forests but can occur in mature aspen. More common in southern and western Colorado.

Eastern Screech-Owl, 4, yr: Very few records of this little owl. Reports of its call from Moraine Park, Hollowell Park, and the Colorado River Valley are given by Collister. Generally found at the lower elevations of the plains and foothills.

Northern Pygmy-Owl, 3, yr: One of our most sought-after species, but difficult to find in summer. Quiet during nesting and feeding (May through August), making them tough to locate. Winter birds tend to talk more, and finding one in December or January is easier. Most reliable location is Cow Creek, where a pair has nested for several years (Chapter 7). They have also been regulars over the years at Endovalley and Little Horseshoe Park. The Black Canyon Trail is a good possibility, as is Cub Lake Trail. Seen in the burn on the Ouzel Falls Trail and along the birding trail in Wild Basin, and also at the YMCA. Your best bet is to be out early in the morning or late in the afternoon when the birds are more likely to be feeding and/or calling. Overcast days prolong their activity. Without hearing them, you'll have to get lucky, even in the right habitat.

Nighthawks, Swifts

Common Poorwill, 4, sr: Rare summer visitor in the lowest elevations of RMNP. More common in the lower foothills. Recent sightings from Bridal Veil Falls Trail along Cow Creek (Chapter 7). Seen in the second meadow and near the ranch buildings early evenings in July and August. Very few other records.

Common Nighthawk, 3, sr: Usually found each summer in lower elevation mountain parks, such as Moraine Park, and in the Estes Valley, but also seen in Wild Basin and many other RMNP sites. Irregular in occurrence. Best located by their calls in early evening.

Chimney Swift, 4, sp/sr: One visited the area of the bird sanctuary at Lake Estes in late May. At least one Park record in July over Trail Ridge.

Black Swift, 3, sr: Arrives in late May and stays through mid-September. Nests at high-elevation sites, often behind or near waterfalls, but seen flying throughout nesting-site drainages. Reliable nesting populations in these drainages: North St. Vrain (Ouzel Falls above Wild Basin), Glacier Creek (Timberline Falls in Loch Vale), and Big Thompson (waterfalls above Odessa Lake). May be away from nests for most of the day. Common wisdom is to find a nesting area and be there at daybreak or nightfall to see the birds leaving or returning, but this is difficult in Rocky for most people, since you have to hike in or out in the dark. Some trips to Ouzel Falls, the most accessible site, starting in predawn light have been successful, especially on overcast days. Try to find the birds feeding lower in the drainages. In July and August, sightings at lower elevations increase as birds range farther from their nests. Overcast days drive the birds down. Best places to try, in order of reliability: 1. Wild Basin along the basin birding trail and the Ouzel Falls Trail (Chapter 3); 2. Moraine Park, along the Cub Lake Trail; 3. Any stop along the Bear Lake Road, Sprague Lake and higher. Also the Loch Vale Trail. Here's my formula for finding Black Swifts. When you're in those drainages, *keep looking up.* Swifts feed at higher altitudes than swallows, and you just won't see them unless you make yourself look for them and maybe even scan for them with binocs. If you see a group of swallows, be particularly watchful, since swifts are often found with swallows but flying higher. Cloudy days are ideal, since it's easier to spot swifts against the light background. A low ceiling is even better, and there are reports of swifts at tree level when that occurs. Prolonged, stormy weather can drive swifts down in elevation all the way to the plains.

White-throated Swift, 2, sr: Common at one place in the area, Lumpy Ridge. Can be seen almost any summer day above the Twin Owls formation. Use your binocs to scan the sky above the rocks; unless there's very cool or stormy weather, this should be an easy find. May nest on Sheep Mountain in Cow Creek and are also found occasionally in Wild Basin, where they could be mistaken for Black Swifts. Found infrequently in Endovalley.

Hummingbirds, Kingfishers

Blue-throated Hummingbird, 5: Accidental in fall at hummingbird feeders.

Magnificent Hummingbird, 5: Accidental in fall at hummingbird feeders.

Black-chinned Hummingbird, 4, f: More common in western Colorado, but occasionally shows up in the Estes Valley as a late August or early September visitor.

Calliope Hummingbird, 3, sr: Arrives in the Estes Valley in July after nesting elsewhere. Many years there are few reports, making them more rare than uncommon. Check out the feeders at the YMCA and at residences in the Estes Valley.

Broad-tailed Hummingbird, 1, sr: If you miss this one, you're not paying attention. Buzzing trill of the male's wings is a trademark. Found throughout RMNP and at every hummingbird feeder at the YMCA and local residences.

Rufous Hummingbird, 2, sr/f: Presumptive hummers that arrive in July as visitors with the sole intent of taking over every hummingbird feeder. The bright orange of the male is distinctive, as is the attitude. Check the YMCA's feeders beginning in July (Chapter 9).

Belted Kingfisher, 2, sp/sr; 4, f/wv: Fairly common in spring and summer on many streams and lakes on both sides of RMNP and in the Estes Valley. Try the Big Thompson River near the YMCA, the willow carr at Wild Basin, and Sprague Lake. Occasionally overwinters along the Big Thompson River below Lake Estes.

Woodpeckers

Acorn Woodpecker, 5: Established at a few locations in southwestern Colorado. A pair recently bred in the foothills near Loveland. The arrival of one at a home in Estes Park the next summer still has to be considered accidental. A nearby sighting at Cow Creek was likely the same bird.

Red-headed Woodpecker, 4, sp/f: Evidently more common in years past, since there are a number of historical RMNP sightings. Seen recently at Lake Estes in May, in Upper Beaver Meadows in June, and in Horseshoe Park.

Lewis's Woodpecker, 4, sr/f: Records for July through September from various locations in the Estes Valley and the Park, but most are from the 1940s, '50s, and '60s. Only two recent reports from residential areas for this species, which is more common in the foothills.

Williamson's Sapsucker, 3, sr: Another favorite target bird for visitors. Found in aspen groves intermixed with pines and spruces. The determined birder should be able to locate one in Upper Beaver Meadows (Chapter 5), the most reliable spot. Also try Endovalley, Wild Basin, Cow Creek, and the Cub Lake Trail. Females are very different from males in appearance and may be mistaken for a juvenile Northern Flicker at first glance.

Red-naped Sapsucker, 2, sr: Difficult to miss in proper habitat at many of the birding spots in this book, particularly Endovalley. Nests in or around aspen groves in mixed forests, especially near riparian willows where it may surprise you to find them foraging on the thin willow branches. Arrives in April and leaves by October.

Downy Woodpecker, 3, yr: More abundant in the foothills and plains, but found throughout RMNP, usually at lower elevations but seen all the way to timberline. Try Endovalley and Cub Lake Trail.

Hairy Woodpecker, 2, yr: More common than the Downy in RMNP and the Estes Valley. Possible at many of the sites in the book, including Endovalley and Upper Beaver Meadows.

Three-toed Woodpecker, 4, yr: One of the best finds, but unpredictable, both in numbers and in year-to-year location. Most recent sightings from Endovalley, Upper Beaver Meadows, and Cow Creek (Chapters 1, 5, 7). One to three pairs have nested in Endovalley the last few years, east and west of the alluvial fan on both sides of the road and on the trail to the bog pond at the picnic area. Upper Beaver Meadows birds found near burn areas. Cow Creek birds seen in the vicinity of the Balanced Rock Trail cutoff as it nears the stream and nearer Bridal Veil Falls. Also found in Wild Basin, near Copeland Lake and farther west near the roadside ponds (Chapter 3). Nests in aspen near pines or spruces. Look for active nest holes. The white of the bark will be worn away where the tail rests below the entrance hole. Very quiet, both in call notes and pecking sounds. Strips bark during feeding rather than drilling holes, so look for trees with peeled bark.

Northern Flicker (red-shafted race), 1, sr; 3, yr: Occurs throughout RMNP and the Estes Valley in summer. Migrates altitudinally, making it uncommon in winter. Found at Endovalley and many other sites. Park records of yellow-shafted race from the 1960s.

Flycatchers

Olive-sided Flycatcher, 3, sr: Fairly common in the right habitat, but not here in great numbers. Look for it at the top of dead trees or on a high, dead limb. Call is distinctive. Distributed throughout the Park. Cow Creek is usually a reliable place to find one. Cub Lake Trail and Wild Basin also regularly have them. Sometimes seen near the Endovalley Picnic Area and along the Flattop Mountain Trail above Bear Lake. Nests to timberline.

Western Wood-Pewee, 1, sr: Common in ponderosa/aspen forests at most sites in the book. Know the call, and you'll find the bird.

Cordilleran Flycatcher, 2, sr: The whistled call of this *Empidonax* in June and July may first attract your attention. Its overall yellow to yellow-green coloration and teardrop-shaped eye ring should help sew up the identification, separating it from Dusky and Hammond's.

Often nests under eaves of buildings or other manmade structures, but also found in remote areas. For several years, one or two pairs have nested at the McGraw Ranch buildings at Cow Creek. Almost all sites in this book can have them.

Willow Flycatcher, 3, sr: Found in riparian willow areas along streams and beaver ponds. Look for it along the Cub Lake Trail after it turns west and in the willows in Hollowell Park and Wild Basin.

Least Flycatcher, 4, sr: A few historical records for this species. One recently banded at the YMCA in spring. Hammond's has a similar call, so beware of identification by sound alone. Least's call is constantly repeated, Hammond's is not.

Hammond's Flycatcher, 2, sr: A fairly common *Empidonax* but difficult to separate from Dusky, with which it often occurs in areas such as the Cub Lake Trail. Habitat differences are often cited in field guides, but many sites in this book are in an overlap zone. Hammond's song, given on breeding territory in June, its feeding height, and physical characteristics help distinguish the two. Bring Kenn Kaufman's *Advanced Birding* for help. Cub Lake Trail, Endovalley, and Wild Basin are good places to see one.

Dusky Flycatcher, 2, sr: Usually found lower in elevation and lower in the tree than the Hammond's, but difficult to distinguish without close study and supporting evidence. Neither predominates at lower elevations of RMNP, although Hammond's is more common in higher elevation spruce/fir forests. Cub Lake Trail, Wild Basin, Cow Creek, and Endovalley are all good places for those who like to be frustrated by these two look-alikes.

Black Phoebe, 5: One spring record from the bird sanctuary at Lake Estes.

Say's Phoebe, 4, sp: One or two are seen at the bird sanctuary at Lake Estes nearly every spring.

Ash-throated Flycatcher, 5: One record from McGraw Ranch at Cow Creek and a recent June sighting at the alluvial fan in Endovalley.

Eastern Kingbird, 3, sp/f: Regular spring visitor to Lake Estes and lower-elevation meadows in RMNP. There are historical breeding records from 1911. In the past, recorded as a late summer and fall visitor.

Western Kingbird, 3, sp/f: Regular spring visitor to Lake Estes and lower-elevation meadows in RMNP, such as Moraine Park. Seen also along Dry Gulch Road. Rarely a late summer and fall visitor.

Shrikes, Vireos

Northern Shrike, 3, wv: Consistently found in winter in open areas around Lake Estes, along Dry Gulch Road, and in areas such as Moraine Park.

Loggerhead Shrike, 3, sp: Regular spring migrant at Lake Estes and along Dry Gulch Road.

Red-eyed Vireo, 4, sp/f: Makes an occasional appearance in May at Lake Estes. A few Park records, including one in September.

Warbling Vireo, 1, sr: Often heard before it's seen. Drab and often maddeningly difficult to spot high in the aspen trees it prefers. Sometimes sings from the nest, making it even more frustrating. Knowledgeable visiting birders have insisted on seeing this bird, although it's common in the East, because they believe it might be split to a separate species, so I've highlighted it in this list. The song of the western subspecies is quite different. Found throughout RMNP, usually in taller aspens. Watch and listen for them in Upper Beaver Meadows, Cow Creek, Endovalley, Wild Basin, and other sites.

White-eyed Vireo, 5: One banded in Moraine Park in summer.

Plumbeous Vireo, 3, sr/f: Very infrequent visitor to the area. Most records come from fall migration. More common in the foothills. A few historical reports of immatures and adults in RMNP in the summer months, and a recent sighting of an adult at Lumpy Ridge in July. Reports of several in Allenspark suggest that Wild Basin may also be a place to see one.

Jays, Magpies, Crows

Steller's Jay, 1, yr: Our common "blue jay." Found in all wooded areas of the Park. The white "eyebrow" distinguishes this race from those found in the Pacific Northwest.

Blue Jay, 4, sp: Rare visitor reported in RMNP as far back as 1932. Most recent sightings have been at Lake Estes and at residences in the Estes Valley in May, with some sightings as late as July.

Western Scrub-Jay, 4, sp/f: Collister lists a few fall records for this bird, but this species is better looked for in the foothills near Lyons and Loveland. Occasionally seen at residential feeders in spring.

Gray Jay, 2, yr: Camp Robber, Whiskey Jack, Canada Jay ... few birds have been known by as many names. Before the Park clamped down on hand-feeding at turnouts on Trail Ridge Road, this bird was easy to see, but now it sometimes takes work to find this high-elevation species. Try the Lake Irene Picnic Area on the west side of Trail Ridge Road. Also fairly common along the trail around Bear Lake and the trail up to Emerald Lake. Quiet and inconspicuous compared to other picnic grubbers.

Pinyon Jay, 4, sp/f/wv: Not common anywhere near RMNP, so it's always a surprise to find one. Seen once on the Christmas Bird Count. Other sightings are mostly from fall with a few spring sightings. Occasionally seen at residential feeders. Regularly seen in foothills above Lyons.

Clark's Nutcracker, 2, yr: Often seen at turnouts along Trail Ridge Road, especially Rainbow Curve. As hand-feeding is further restricted, you may find it a little difficult to locate one. They are widespread in the area, however, and if you're up on your calls, the Clark's will be easier to find. Noisy alone or in groups and usually heard before they're seen. Found at all of the areas described in this book at one time or the other. Likes to hang out near the picnic tables just west of the alluvial fan in Endovalley. Wild Basin, Little Horseshoe Park, and Moraine Park are also good areas. Found in Estes Valley residential areas when pine cones are plentiful. Abundance in any area depends on good cone production.

Black-billed Magpie, 1, yr: Easily found in many places in RMNP and the Estes Valley. Endovalley (Chapter 1) and Moraine Park have good populations. Dry Gulch Road and Fish Creek Road are also reliable places.

Common Raven, 2, yr: Not numerous, but widespread and should be found at many locales. Usually seen alone or in a small family group. A pair nested for several years in the spruce trees on the south side of

Clark's Nutcracker

the power plant at Lake Estes. Seen regularly at Lumpy Ridge and along Trail Ridge Road. Large size, huge beak, V-shaped tail in flight, and hoarser call help differentiate ravens from crows.

American Crow, 1, yr: Common at all seasons near Lake Estes. Usually seen in larger groups, seldom alone. Seen less commonly in the open areas of RMNP, including Moraine Park, Endovalley, and Trail Ridge Road.

Larks, Swallows

Horned Lark, 1, sr: This amazing species, thought of as a prairie nester, also nests on the alpine tundra. Passes through the Estes Valley in April on the way up. Along with American Pipits, the most common birds of the tundra in summer.

Purple Martin, 5: One record from Estes Park in 1939.

Northern Rough-winged Swallow, 4, sp: Infrequent migrant to Lake Estes. Usually seen in late April. Not seen every year. A few Park records, all from spring.

Bank Swallow, 4, sp: A few records from Lake Estes in late April.

Violet-green Swallow, 1, sr: A common breeder that often nests near dwellings, sometimes taking over bluebird boxes. Also nests in natural cavities and woodpecker holes, particularly in aspen. Look for them in the "Aspen Apartments" at Endovalley.

Tree Swallow, 1, sr: Common throughout the Estes Valley and RMNP in summer. Nests in cavities, particularly in aspen groves. Occasionally found above timberline.

Cliff Swallow, 1, sr: Common near buildings where colonies nest under eaves. The Lake Estes power plant and the auditorium on the YMCA grounds are good places to find them. Also look for them in the mountain parks, such as Hollowell Park, and restroom buildings at picnic areas.

Barn Swallow, 2, sr: Often found in conjunction with buildings and other manmade structures. Found more commonly in the Estes Valley, but check open areas of RMNP, such as Hollowell Park, Upper Aspenglen, and Moraine Park.

Violet-green Swallow

Chickadees, Nuthatches

Black-capped Chickadee, 3, yr: Sometimes difficult to find. Not as numerous as Mountain Chickadees. Can be seen at any of the locations featured in this book. They migrate altitudinally and are less common in winter.

Mountain Chickadee, 1, yr: Common nester in ponderosa and spruce/fir forests. You should have little trouble locating these delightfully scruffy chickadees at most of the sites in this book.

Red-breasted Nuthatch, 2, yr: Their "toot-toot" calls will help you locate one. Found in pine, spruce, and fir trees throughout RMNP. Try Cub Lake Trail, Cow Creek, and Wild Basin.

White-breasted Nuthatch, 1, yr: More raucous than the Red-breasted's, the call carries well and will help you locate the bird in pine, spruce, and fir trees throughout the Park. Try Endovalley, Upper Beaver Meadows, and Cow Creek. Populations in this area do not give the "yank-yank" call of eastern birds. Listen, instead, for a rapid "eh-eh-eh-eh-eh." Subtle differences in plumage are illustrated in *The Sibley Guide to Birds*. Some birders think the eastern and western races will be split into separate species, so I've highlighted it here.

Pygmy Nuthatch, 1, yr: I see Pygmy Nuthatches almost every day I'm out, but they seem to disappear when someone wants one for a life list. I'm tempted to call them fairly common, just so those birders who have a difficult time finding them won't feel bad. Most often seen in ponderosa pines, they should be easy to find in Wild Basin, Cow Creek, and at the picnic areas in Endovalley. Really they're everywhere in RMNP where ponderosas predominate, and they range into the spruce/fir forests as well. You'll often hear them twittering about before you see them, and they're almost always in feeding flocks of many individuals, except during nesting season when they can truly be difficult to find. Also check residential feeders in the Estes Valley and at the YMCA.

Brown Creeper, 3, yr: Always a treat. Designated uncommon, mostly because they're difficult to find unless you hear their high-pitched call. Well camouflaged. Investigate any bird flying from the top of a tree to the base of a nearby trunk. Found in ponderosa and spruce/fir forests. Watch for them in Cow Creek and Wild Basin.

Wrens

Bewick's Wren, 5: Seen a few times at Lake Estes during spring migration. There is one Park record for May.

House Wren, 1, sr: You're not looking very hard if you miss this bird, whose buzzings and trillings and scoldings will accompany you on many of the birding trips in this book in summer.

Winter Wren, 5: One September record from the Park and recent reports during the summer from Old Fall River Road and Calypso Cascades on the Ouzel Falls Trail in Wild Basin.

Marsh Wren, 3, sp: Uncommon but regular along the Lake Estes Trail in late April and early May.

Rock Wren, 2, sr: Making a comeback in RMNP. There are now a couple of sites where you have a good chance of finding one. Try the rocky areas of the alluvial fan in Endovalley (Chapter 1), especially the west side, or the base of Lumpy Ridge rock formations. Seen occasionally on the tundra. Each spring, the bird sanctuary at Lake Estes is inundated with migrating Rock Wrens.

Canyon Wren, 4, sr: Fairly common species of nearby foothills canyons. There ought to be more in RMNP than there are. May be at the limit of its altitudinal range. Best chance is at Lumpy Ridge, along the Black Canyon Trail in the vicinity of Twin Owls and west. One report from the Gem Lake Trail. A few scattered reports come from other areas, including one on Trail Ridge Road.

American Dipper, 2, yr: Another target bird, and a sometimes frustrating one for birders new to the area, probably because habitat requirements are difficult to understand. Found in streams of fifteen feet or wider, with white water, pools, and riffles. Nesting sites adjacent to the water include crevices in rocks, ledges in rocky overhangs, and structure under bridges. They establish breeding and feeding territories, just like any species, but territories are long and narrow, following streams. The problem for people trying to find this bird is generally one of time. Since there will be, at most, two birds (until young fledge) occupying any section of stream in summer, you'll often have to wait or walk the stream to find one. I suggest a lunch break next to a stream, giving you time for the bird to appear on its feeding forays. Try Roaring River in Endovalley where the stream comes down through the alluvial fan. Other good areas in RMNP: the confluence of the Big Thompson River and Glacier Creek near the YMCA, the Big Thompson River along the Fern Lake Trail, the North St. Vrain Creek near the Wild Basin trailhead, and Fall River in the Endovalley Picnic Area. A car trip down the Big Thompson Canyon on Hwy. 34, with frequent stops, is almost a sure bet. In winter, dippers are concentrated in the river below Olympus Dam at Lake Estes, the only open stream in the area, where you may also find them in summer.

Kinglets, Gnatcatchers

Golden-crowned Kinglet, 3, yr: Tough to find unless it's singing on territory in spring and early summer. A higher-elevation species, preferring dense spruce/fir forests. The most reliable place to find it recently has been the Endovalley Picnic Area, where it nests in the spruces and firs in the middle of the loop road. The birds disperse in July. Also try Old Fall River Road, the Bear Lake Nature Trail, and trails in Wild Basin.

Ruby-crowned Kinglet, 1, sr: Widespread in the Park. Fairly easy to find in spring and summer if you know its song. Because the bird is so small and tends to like dense spruce and firs, it's hard to pick out. Try the Cow Creek area, Cub Lake Trail, Endovalley Picnic Area, and Wild Basin. Know the song and you'll find the bird.

Blue-gray Gnatcatcher, 4, sp: One or two make an appearance at Lake Estes every spring. A few spring records for RMNP.

Solitaires, Bluebirds

Townsend's Solitaire, 2, yr: Fairly common throughout the Estes Valley and RMNP. Often heard before it's seen. The repeated single note, which might be confused with a Northern Pygmy-Owl call, carries well, so be prepared for a walk if you hear one calling up the side of a hill. Much more vocal in winter. Tends to perch at the top of trees when calling.

Mountain Bluebird, 1, sr: One of our jewels. Should be fairly easy to find, especially once the young are out in early July. Nests in aspen near open meadows, in areas such as Moraine Park and Endovalley. Can usually be found in nest boxes along Dry Gulch Road and Devil's Gulch Road and on the YMCA grounds. One found on the 2002 Christmas Bird Count.

Western Bluebird, 3, sr: Always a pleasant find; at the eastern boundary of its range. A few nesting pairs in Rocky and the Estes Valley every summer, but they are uncommon. Most sightings are in Moraine Park, Lumpy Ridge, Beaver Meadows, and Cow Creek. May be in nest boxes in residential areas. Try the nest boxes along Devil's Gulch Road and Dry Gulch Road.

Eastern Bluebird, 4, sp/sr: Infrequent visitor to RMNP and the Estes Valley in spring. A breeding pair raised a family at a residence in the area recently, and another pair, probably nesting, spent the summer near the Cub Lake trailhead.

Thrushes, Thrashers

American Robin, 1, sr; 3, wv: Almost as common in the forests of RMNP as they are in city parks across the country. Even seen regularly on the tundra in summer. Regularly seen in winter in the Estes Valley where juniper berries are available.

Veery, 4, sp: Rare spring migrant at Lake Estes. A few Park records, all from spring. Bird book maps suggest this species nests here, but I haven't found any in RMNP during breeding season. Still, you should check out any thrushes carefully.

Swainson's Thrush, 3, sr: Usually heard before it's seen. Although they breed at varying elevations and can be found in ponderosas, look for them in spruce/fir forests, usually in proximity to water. Endovalley and the trails in Wild Basin are good places to search. Drive the Old Fall

River Road early in the morning, stopping frequently to listen. Occasionally heard along Trail Ridge Road at higher-elevation turnouts.

Hermit Thrush, 2, sr: Like the Swainson's, the beautiful song usually tips you off to its presence. Secretive and shy, both thrushes usually take some work getting to and stalking for a look. Listen for them in higher spruce/fir forests, typically along streams. They can sometimes be heard singing near timberline as you walk the tundra. Readily found at Calypso Cascades along the Ouzel Falls Trail in July feeding young.

Gray Catbird, 2, sp; 3, f: At Lake Estes in mid-May, there's no missing them for about a week. Because of their numbers, it would seem possible that some may stay in RMNP to breed, but Park records for the bird are inconclusive. Makes an occasional appearance in September at Lake Estes.

Northern Mockingbird, 3, sp: Another regular visitor to Lake Estes in May with one or two sightings a year, usually for extended periods. Few Park records. More common on the eastern plains.

Brown Thrasher, 3, sp: Common on the plains, but mainly here as migrants at Lake Estes in May. A few records for RMNP, most from Moraine Park. A few years ago, one overwintered at a residence in Estes Park.

Sage Thrasher, 2, sp: Regular spring migrant, sometimes in numbers but typically one or two birds at a time. Found in grassy areas near the Fish Creek Arm of Lake Estes. A common breeder in the sagebrush country of North Park, especially in Arapaho National Wildlife Refuge, so its absence as a breeder in similar areas within RMNP seems unusual.

Starlings, Pipits, Waxwings

European Starling, 1, yr: Common in the Estes Valley and at a few lower-elevation sites in RMNP, using nesting holes in aspen. Less common in winter, especially in the Park. Collister lists the first Estes Valley record as 1946.

Sprague's Pipit, 5: One spring record from Wapiti Meadows below Lake Estes. This is a species thought to be more common in migration than sightings indicate, so it may be overlooked or in groups of American Pipits, with which a straggler might associate.

American Pipit, 1, sr: Migrates through the Estes Valley in spring, some as early as March but most in April and early May. Typically seen along lake shores. Common nesters on the tundra and should be easy to find on your ptarmigan walks. Sometimes blown back down by spring blizzards; they return in migration in September.

Bohemian Waxwing, 3, wv: Infrequent visitor during the depths of winter. Flocks of several hundred are seen in neighborhoods around the Estes Valley, usually in association with junipers.

Cedar Waxwing, 2, sp/f; 3, sr: Fairly common as a spring migrant at Lake Estes and less frequently seen through the summer. No nesting records for the Park. Find them in proximity to streams and rivers, where they're often seen fussing in streamside vegetation or flycatching over the stream. We who flyfish follow them when they're working a stream, for it surely means a hatch of mayflies is on. Watch along the Big Thompson River in Moraine Park, along Cow Creek, or in the Estes Valley along streams.

Warblers

Northern Parula, 5: One found at Lake Estes in May recently. At least one Park record from the Cub Lake Trail.

Orange-crowned Warbler, 2, sp/f; 4, sr: Regular in late April and early May at Lake Estes. One of the few spring migrants that also shows up in fall migration in September. Uncommon as a nester in RMNP in willow thickets along streams. I know of no regular place to find one.

Tennessee Warbler, 4, sp/f: A few records in May and September from Lake Estes.

Blue-winged Warbler, 4, sp: A rare find anywhere in Colorado. Found in the bird sanctuary at Lake Estes and in the willows at the Fish Creek inlet to Lake Estes in May.

Virginia's Warbler, 3, sr: Nests in Wild Basin and Moraine Park. The most reliable area is the north slope of Wild Basin above the picnic area at Copeland Lake (Chapter 3). The Cub Lake Trail often has one or more breeding pairs, and there are recent records from the Fern Lake Trail. Most easily found during the breeding season when males are singing. They favor substantial areas of dense shrubbery, six to twelve feet tall, usually on a hillside, and can be difficult to see even when they're singing. Found also during spring migration at Lake Estes.

Nashville Warbler, 4, f: Only records are from September, in the bird sanctuary at Lake Estes.

Yellow Warbler, 1, sp; 2, sr: Very common in spring migration, particularly at Lake Estes. A few nest in the bird sanctuary and below the dam. Also found in lower-elevation deciduous trees in RMNP, but considered uncommon. Try the balsam poplar grove in Moraine Park and streamside spruces in Hollowell Park.

Chestnut-sided Warbler, 4, sp/f: Only a few records over the years at Lake Estes, usually from the third week in May. One record from September of a first-fall bird at Lake Estes. One recent Park record in summer.

Magnolia Warbler, 4, sp: A record or two from Lake Estes, again usually in the third week in May. At least one historical Park record.

Black-throated Blue Warbler, 5: One record from the Cub Lake Trail during the summer my wife and I were in Michigan looking unsuccessfully for one for her life list.

Yellow-rumped Warbler (Audubon's), 1, sr: Common breeder throughout RMNP, present from mid-April to late September. Nests to timberline. Abundant migrant at Lake Estes in the spring.

Yellow-rumped Warbler (Myrtle), 2, sp: Fairly common for a couple of weeks in April/May at Lake Estes and in RMNP at Endovalley and Upper Beaver Meadows.

Black-throated Gray Warbler, 4, sp/f: A few records of this western species at Lake Estes in the spring and in the Park in August. One seen in September at Lake Estes.

Townsend's Warbler, 3, f: Found from late August through October at various locations in RMNP and at Lake Estes. Watch for them in mixed flocks of chickadees, nuthatches, and warblers. Wild Basin and Cow Creek are two areas with regular sightings of this species. Also check the bird sanctuary at Lake Estes in September.

Black-throated Green Warbler, 5: One record from Lake Estes in the spring and one in the fall from Moraine Park.

Grace's Warbler, 5: Only a couple of records in RMNP of this south-western warbler. Southwest Colorado is the closest reliable area for this species.

Palm Warbler, 4, sp/f: Two or three records during spring migration at Lake Estes in the second week of May and one fall record from the Estes Valley.

Bay-breasted Warbler, 5: One historical record from Cub Lake Trail in August. Since the species migrates occasionally along the foothills in spring, it's likely to be recorded at Lake Estes sooner or later.

Blackpoll Warbler, 5: One or two records from recent years at Lake Estes in the first week of May.

Prothonotary Warbler, 5: One spring record from the bird sanctuary at Lake Estes.

Black-and-white Warbler, 3, sp/f: Regular spring migrant at Lake Estes with one or two seen most years in mid-May. Stormy weather in fall can bring one in. I found a singing male on the Cub Lake Trail in late June.

American Redstart, 3, sp/f: Another regular spring migrant at Lake Estes. At least one fall record from the Park. Redstarts tend to stay around for a week or two when they come through. Typically found near Night-Heron Pond in the bird sanctuary at Lake Estes.

Ovenbird, 4, sp: Two Park records, one from the west end of Moraine Park in 1954 and a recent record from the bog pond at Endovalley Picnic Area, both in May. Two spring records from the bird sanctuary at Lake Estes.

Northern Waterthrush, 2, sp/f: Regular visitor to the bird sanctuary at Lake Estes in May. Found along the small creek on the north side of the Lake Estes Trail and in the Swamp along the trail to Pine Point. Other records come from Grand Lake and Onahu Creek on the west side of Rocky. When the birds come through in the second week of May, they could potentially be found along the banks of any of the area's small creeks.

Kentucky Warbler, 5: One summer report from Bear Lake Road.

MacGillivray's Warbler, 3, sr: Fairly common but difficult to locate. Stays close to the ground in brushy habitat. Can be found to timberline, but more common at lower elevations. Try to find it singing from the tops of streamside willows in June and early July—that's the easiest way to locate one. Found regularly along the Cub Lake Trail, both in the lower section and along the willows after the trail turns west, and along the lower part of the Fern Lake Trail. Recently nested in the willows south and north of the east alluvial fan trail in Endovalley. Seen regularly in the willow carr at Wild Basin. Also try Hollowell Park and its significant willow habitat. Occasionally found along Cow Creek Trail, especially where the trail goes along the stream beyond the Balanced Rock Trail junction. Easily found in May at Lake Estes.

Common Yellowthroat, 1, sp; 3, f: Difficult to miss in the bird sanctuary at Lake Estes from mid-April through May, but just passing through. Check out Night-Heron Pond and Warbler Alley. A rare migrant in RMNP.

Wilson's Warbler, 2, sr: Abundant during migration and fairly common to common nesters in the riparian areas of RMNP. Look for them along the river east of the stock ramp parking area in Endovalley and along the road close to the Endovalley Picnic Area. Willow Park on the Old Fall River Road usually has several nesting pairs. The open area overlooking the willows along the birding trail in Wild Basin is a reliable site. The marsh at Lily Lake often has nesting pairs. Look for them in Hollowell Park, also.

Hooded Warbler, 4, sp: At least one Park record from the Endovalley Picnic Area in May and one record of a female at Lake Estes in spring.

Yellow-breasted Chat, 3, sp: Irregular spring migrant at Lake Estes and in lower-elevation riparian areas within the Park. Not seen every year.

Tanagers, Grosbeaks, Buntings

Hepatic Tanager, 5: An historical record from the Longs Peak Trail.

Western Tanager, 3, sr: Uncommon throughout the Park and often frustrating to find. Easiest to find where the mixed ponderosa/spruce forests afford more open views. Often seen in or near burns. Watch for them on the Black Canyon Trail at Lumpy Ridge. Also found along the Cub Lake Trail, in Upper Beaver Meadows (particularly in the burn), in Beaver Meadows, in Endovalley and nearby Upper Aspenglen, in Hollowell Park just before the trail goes into the forest, and in Wild Basin. In short, they're just about everywhere in RMNP. Simply not abundant in numbers and therefore can be chancy.

Scarlet Tanager, 5: An historical record from Moraine Park.

Black-headed Grosbeak, 3, sr: Populations are erratic in this area. Sometimes fairly common, but may be declining locally. I've seen them several times at Hollowell Park just before the trail goes into the forest. Cow Creek is another possibility, but generally you'll need to get lucky to find this species. Watch for them in aspen/pine habitat and along streams at lower elevations. Occasionally seen in the bird sanctuary at Lake Estes and on the Estes Valley tour along Fish Creek, at residential bird feeders, and at the YMCA.

Rose-breasted Grosbeak, 4, sp: Rare spring visitor to the Estes Valley and RMNP.

Blue Grosbeak, 4, sp: Irregular visitor to Lake Estes in the spring. I found a female in Moraine Park near the balsam poplar grove in July.

Lazuli Bunting, 3, sp/f: Regular but uncommon visitor to Lake Estes and lower-elevation parts of RMNP in spring, less often in fall. Fairly common breeder in the foothills.

Indigo Bunting, 4, sp: Another pleasant surprise for spring birders at Lake Estes and other sites in the Estes Valley.

Sparrows

Spotted Towhee, 3, sp: Fairly common nester of nearby foothills. One or two make an appearance during spring migration almost every year. There are a few Park records, including an apparent nesting record from 1910.

Green-tailed Towhee, 2, sr: Found regularly as a nester in low shrubs and grassland edges in places such as Hollowell Park, Upper Beaver Meadows, Upper Aspenglen, along the Cub Lake and Cow Creek trails, and in the Lumpy Ridge area. Migrants arrive at Lake Estes in late April. More difficult to find after they quit singing in July.

Sage Sparrow, 4, sp: Another wanderer from the West with May records from the bird sanctuary at Lake Estes and the west side of the Fish Creek Arm.

Black-throated Sparrow, 5: One May record from the bird sanctuary at Lake Estes.

American Tree Sparrow, 3, wv: Small numbers present nearly every winter. Found on about two-thirds of the Christmas Bird Counts.

Brewer's Sparrow, 2, sp; 3, sr: Fairly common in grassy areas around Lake Estes in early May. Breeding records from Moraine Park and Beaver Meadows in RMNP. See Chapter 2 for directions on where to find breeding birds east of Cub Lake Trail. Also try Hollowell Park, Lumpy Ridge, and along the Cow Creek Trail.

Clay-colored Sparrow, 3, sp/f: Found every spring in limited numbers in the grassy areas around Lake Estes. Arrives in late April, shortly before the similar Brewer's Sparrow arrives. A few Park records as high in elevation as the tundra in fall.

Chipping Sparrow, 1, sr: Common to abundant, especially at lower elevations. You should find this bird fairly easily in Moraine Park, along the Cow Creek trail, in Hollowell Park, at Lumpy Ridge, and many other areas.

Baird's Sparrow, 5: One spring record from Lake Estes.

LeConte's Sparrow, 5: One record from Lake Estes in April, an individual that stayed almost a week.

Savannah Sparrow, 2, sp/f/sr: A fairly common spring and fall migrant at Lake Estes. Also nests in grassy meadows in the Park. Uncommon nesters in Moraine Park and Hollowell Park, but common in the Kawuneeche Valley on the west side of RMNP.

Vesper Sparrow, 1, sp/f; 2, sr: Vespers arrive in late April in numbers at Lake Estes. Favors open grasslands with low shrubs for breeding. Look in Hollowell Park and at Lumpy Ridge. Also found in residential areas with open grasslands and along Dry Gulch Road.

Lark Bunting, 3, sp: Colorado's state bird makes regular appearances in the grassy areas around Lake Estes in May. Several Park records, including some on the west side and some above timberline.

Lark Sparrow, 3, sp/f: Regular spring and fall visitor at Lake Estes. A few breeding records from RMNP.

Harris's Sparrow, 4, wv: Rare visitor to the Estes Valley in winter, with some individuals or small groups making extended stays at bird feeders. Seen on about ten percent of the Christmas Bird Counts.

Golden-crowned Sparrow, 5: One spring record from the Fish Creek inlet of Lake Estes.

White-throated Sparrow, 5: One September record from Lake Estes.

White-crowned Sparrow, 1, sr: A high-elevation breeder. Can be found in brush and willows, usually near water, in places such as Willow Park on Old Fall River Road, and in the krummholz along Trail Ridge Road, especially at Poudre Lake. Look for it on your ptarmigan walks. Seen at lower elevations in migration.

Fox Sparrow, 4, sp/sr: A rare breeder in RMNP. The only reliable spot to find one has been at the entrance to Endovalley Picnic Area (Chapter 1). Be careful not to disturb this very accessible pair. Stay on the road! If the bird's there, you'll hear the male singing and eventually see it. This is another species that seems ripe for splitting, so try to identify it by subspecies also. Occasional reports from the Estes Valley in spring, including one recently at the Wapiti Meadows Wetlands below Lake Estes.

Song Sparrow, 2, sr: Found along streams, beaver ponds, and wet areas, sometimes at high elevations. Fairly common along the lower Cow Creek Trail, in Endovalley, at Lily Lake, and in Wild Basin. Common in the bird sanctuary at Lake Estes.

Lincoln's Sparrow, 1, sr: A skulker that is common throughout the Park in low shrubs and willows near water but sometimes difficult to find. Look for this bird in suitable habitat in Endovalley, Wild Basin, Cow Creek, and Upper Beaver Meadows.

Dark-eyed Junco, Gray-headed, 1, sr; 2, yr: Common breeder throughout the Estes Valley and RMNP, nesting to timberline. Found on over sixty percent of Christmas Bird Counts.

Dark-eyed Junco, Oregon, 2, wv: Slightly more common than the Gray-headed in winter with greater numbers seen. Found on nearly eighty percent of Christmas Bird Counts.

Dark-eyed Junco, Slate-colored, 2, wv: Fewer numbers than the Oregon, but seen on over eighty percent of Christmas Bird Counts.

Dark-eyed Junco, White-winged, 3, wv: Seen on nearly fifty percent of the Christmas Bird Counts but in very limited numbers.

Smith's Longspur, 5: Seen once at Lake Estes. Many of the longspurs might be anticipated here based on field guide maps, but they are regularly seen only on the eastern plains.

Snow Bunting, 4, wv: A few sightings spread over several years. Seen at Lake Estes, in the grasslands along Dry Gulch Road, and in residential areas. A real find.

Meadowlarks, Blackbirds, Orioles

Western Meadowlark, 3, sp: Erratic wanderer from the plains, usually following spring storms. Found in the grassy areas around Lake Estes and rarely in meadow areas of RMNP, such as Moraine Park. Recently several birds spent the summer along Dry Gulch Road.

Bobolink, 3, sp: Groups appear at Lake Estes nearly every spring, with individuals seen occasionally in Moraine Park. Nesting colonies near Boulder and west of RMNP in the hay meadows of the Colorado River valley.

Brown-headed Cowbird, 2, sr: Now a fairly common breeder in the Estes Valley. Seen less commonly within RMNP in summer, but evidently increasing.

Yellow-headed Blackbird, 4, sp: Rare spring visitor at Lake Estes and Fish Creek Arm. Also reported from Moraine Park.

Red-winged Blackbird, 1, sr; 4, wv: Common in summer in suitable riparian habitat at lower elevations in RMNP. There are nearly always Red-wingeds in Wild Basin, in Moraine Park, and in Endovalley. Recorded on four Christmas Bird Counts.

Brewer's Blackbird, 2, sr; 4, wv: Fairly common nester in the Estes Valley and lower elevations of RMNP. Try Lily Lake. Less common at higher elevations, but some alpine sightings. Seen on two Christmas Bird Counts.

Common Grackle, 1, sp/sr; 4, wv: Abundant spring migrant at Lake Estes. Some stay to nest in the bird sanctuary. Uncommon in RMNP.

One recent record from Sprague Lake. Noted by Collister as "regrettably" extending its range into the mountains. Seen on two Christmas Bird Counts.

Bullock's Oriole, 3, sp: Seen occasionally at Lake Estes in the spring. A few Park records, some from the summer and at least one from the west side.

Baltimore Oriole, 5: One sighting at Lake Estes in May. Considered rare in Colorado except in the extreme eastern portion of the state.

Grosbeaks

Evening Grosbeak, 2, wv; 3, sr: Another unpredictable species, especially in summer when they are more common at lower elevations. Reported on over eighty percent of the Christmas Bird Counts. A fairly common but irregular visitor to feeders in the Estes Valley and the YMCA in winter, less so in summer. Few breeding records from RMNP.

Pine Grosbeak, 3, yr: In summer, found at higher elevations of RMNP. Winter brings them down to lower elevations and more accessible locations. Seen individually or in small family groups. Try the trails around Bear Lake, such as the Bierstadt Lake Trail or the Lake Haiyaha Trail. From Glacier Gorge, try Mills Lake or Loch Vale. In Wild Basin, watch for them along the Ouzel Falls Trail. Old Fall River Road gives access to correct habitat, the tall spruce/fir forests of the high country—stop at any of the turnouts and watch for them. Also seen occasionally in or near the Endovalley Picnic Area. Along Trail Ridge Road, stop at turnouts as you climb above Hidden Valley.

Finches, Crossbills

Gray-crowned Rosy Finch, 3, wv: Appears at feeders in the Estes Valley and the YMCA in winter, usually in the company of Brown-capped Rosy Finches. Found on over half of the Christmas Bird Counts. Early dates are from September in the alpine areas of the Park. Generally gone by April, although there is a late Park record in May.

Although the occurrence of this species must be considered uncommon, when you find them, they are likely to be in flocks of hundreds.

Brown-capped Rosy-Finch, 3, yr: The only rosy finch known to breed in RMNP. Difficult to locate on the tundra during nesting season, but found occasionally at Lava Cliffs and along the edges of snowfields beside Trail Ridge Road where they find insects easy to pick out against the white of the snow (Chapter 4). May be easier to find in early summer (road opening in May through early June) before they are on nests and in late summer (late July until road closure in September or October) when they are out and about as family groups. Check out accessible rocky cliffs along Trail Ridge Road, such as Lava Cliffs and areas near the Alpine Visitor Center. Glass the edges of snowfields along the road. All rosy finches need open ground on which to feed. Snowstorms can drive them down to residential feeders anytime during the spring and summer. Also found at feeders in the Estes Valley and the YMCA during winter storms, although they are less common and less numerous than Gray-crowned in that season. Seen on about a third of the Christmas Bird Counts.

Black Rosy Finch, 4, wv: Rare and seldom seen in numbers. Most observations are of a few individuals mixed with other rosy finches at feeders in residential areas and at the YMCA.

Cassin's Finch, 2, yr: A bird of the open ponderosa forests, ranging in summer to the krummholz near timberline. Cassin's Finches are distinguished from House Finches by a beefier appearance, the lack of breast streaking, the rosy red coloring (instead of true red), and the heavily marked facial patterns of both sexes. Look for them at Endovalley (especially Upper Aspenglen, Chapter 1), Wild Basin, Moraine Park, Upper Beaver Meadows, Beaver Meadows, and Little Horseshoe Park. Also check feeders in the Estes Valley and at the YMCA at any time of year. Not numerous, but you have a chance of finding them in proper habitat. Found on over eighty percent of the Christmas Bird Counts.

House Finch, 2, yr: Now common at feeders in the Estes Valley year-round. Seen on every Christmas Bird Count since 1981. In 1970, Collister described them as uncommon summer residents, so this expanding species seems to have found a home in the mountains.

Red Crossbill, 2, yr: Unpredictable, as the birds follow high pine-cone production. Some years difficult to find, other years abundant. Most years, somewhere in between. They range widely, both in habitat and elevation, but almost always associated with cone-bearing conifers (or sunflower-seed feeders). Typically heard in gregarious flocks in the highest reaches of trees. Often seen flying overhead in a noisy group. Familiarizing yourself with their calls makes it easier to find them. A tame species with little fear of man, they can usually be approached fairly closely. I've found them regularly in Wild Basin, Beaver Meadows, and Endovalley, but they are widespread in RMNP and the Estes Valley. A fairly common feeder bird throughout the year, so check residential areas and the YMCA.

White-winged Crossbill, 4, wv: A few records from RMNP, most of them in December and January. No recent records.

Common Redpoll, 4, wv: Driven south by winter storms, they make the rare bird alert in Colorado whenever they show up. Most reports are from the plains, but they also visit the Estes Valley, usually in late winter. Three Christmas Bird Count records since 1981, including one bird in 2002.

Siskins, Goldfinches

Pine Siskin, 2, yr: Fairly common at all elevations except tundra in summer. Abundant during spring migration at Lake Estes. Altitudinal migration brings them down to feeders in the Estes Valley in winter, but they can be seen in residential areas any time of the year. Recorded on nearly every Christmas Bird Count. Found throughout RMNP.

Lesser Goldfinch, 4, sp: Fairly common bird of the foothills and plains. Makes an occasional appearance at Lake Estes and residential feeders in the spring. Few Park records.

American Goldfinch, 2, sp/f; 4, wv: Sometimes abundant at Lake Estes in the spring. Common nester in the foothills, but no breeding records in this area, although there are now scattered summer reports of the species. Has appeared on about a third of the Christmas Bird Counts, including a high count of 132 birds in 1997.

House Sparrow, 2, yr: First reported in 1910. Now fairly common around buildings and houses throughout the Estes Valley and in the lower elevations of RMNP. Found on all Christmas Bird Counts since 1982.

Checklist of the Birds of Rocky Mountain National Park

This list includes 280 species that have been reported for this region, including Rocky Mountain National Park, Arapaho National Recreation Area, Estes Park, and Granby. It is arranged according to the A.O.U. Checklist. The park's interpretation office would appreciate receiving details of any unusual observations.

(Note: This list has been adapted from the official Rocky Mountain National Park checklist, which includes nearby areas as noted above. The abundance and occurrence status codes have been changed to conform more closely to the birdfinding guide included earlier in this book in order to avoid confusion. Copies of the checklist are available at RMNP headquarters.)

Key

Abundance

(Note: Multiple symbols reflect notable population changes from year to year.)

1 = common
2 = fairly common
3 = uncommon
4 = rare
5 = accidental

Season

(Note: Multiple listings reflect descending order of abundance.)

yr = year around
sr = summer resident or visitor
wv = winter visitor
m = migrant, late summer visitor
ir = irregular visitor

Preferred Habitat

A—Aspen

B—Wetlands

D—Douglas fir

F—In flight

G—Grassland, meadows

H—Hillsides, rocky sites

K—Krummholz

M—Dry brushland, sage

P—Pine

R—Wooded riparian

S—Spruce/fir

T—Alpine tundra

W—Aquatic (ponds, lakes, streams)

Loons, Grebes

___Pacific Loon: 5, m, W

___Common Loon: 3, m, W

___Pied-billed Grebe: 3, m/wv, W

___Horned Grebe: 4, m/wv, W

___Red-necked Grebe: 5, m, W

___Eared Grebe: 3, m, W

___Western Grebe: 2, m/sr, W

Pelicans, Herons, Allies

___American White Pelican: 4, m, W

___Double-crested Cormorant: 4, wv/m, W

___American Bittern: 4, m, WB

___Least Bittern: 4, m, WB

___Great Blue Heron: 3, m/sr, WB

___Snowy Egret: 4, m, WB

___Cattle Egret: 5, m, WB

___Green Heron: 5, m, WB

___Black-crowned Night-Heron: 4, m, WB

___White-faced Ibis: 4, m, WB

Swans, Geese, Ducks

___Tundra Swan: 4, m, W

___Greater White-fronted Goose: 5, wv, W

___Snow Goose: 4, wv/m, W

___Canada Goose: 3, m/sr, W

___Wood Duck: 4, sr/wv, W

___Green-winged Teal: 2, m/sr/wv, W

___Mallard: 1, sr/wv/m, W

___Northern Pintail: 3, m/wv, W

___Blue-winged Teal: 2, m/sr, W

___Cinnamon Teal: 3, m/sr, W

___Northern Shoveler: 3, m/sr, W

___Gadwall: 3, m/sr/wv, W

___American Wigeon: 3, m/wv, W

___Canvasback: 4, m, W

___Redhead: 3, m/wv, W

___Ring-necked Duck: 2, sr/m, W

___Lesser Scaup: 2, m/wv, W

___Long-tailed Duck: 4, wv, W

___Surf Scoter: 5, m, W

___White-winged Scoter: 5, m, W

___Common Goldeneye: 2, wv/m, W

___Barrow's Goldeneye: 3, m/wv, W

___Bufflehead: 3, m/wv, W

___Hooded Merganser: 4, wv/m, W

___Common Merganser: 2, wv/m/sr, W

___Red-breasted Merganser: 4, m, W

___Ruddy Duck: 3, m/wv, W

Vultures, Hawks, Eagles

___Turkey Vulture: 3, m/sr, FGH

___Osprey: 3, m/sr, W

___Bald Eagle: 3, wv, FW

___Northern Harrier: 3, m/yr, FGT

___Sharp-shinned Hawk: 3, m/yr, FPDS

___Cooper's Hawk: 3, m/yr, FPDS

___Northern Goshawk: 2, yr, FPDS

___Swainson's Hawk: 3, m/sr, FGT

___Red-tailed Hawk: 1, yr, FPG

___Ferruginous Hawk: 4, m, FGT

___Rough-legged Hawk: 3, wv/m, FGT

___Golden Eagle: 2, yr, FHTG

___American Kestrel: 2, sr/yr, FGAP

___Merlin: 4, m/sr, FG

___Peregrine Falcon: 4, m/sr, FGTH

___Prairie Falcon: 3, m/sr/yr, FTGH

Grouse, Ptarmigan

Need ___Chukar: 5, ir, HM *(rare)*

___Ring-necked Pheasant: 4, yr, G

___Blue Grouse: 2, yr, ADPS

Need ___White-tailed Ptarmigan: 2, yr, KT *fairly Common*

Need ___Greater Sage-Grouse: 4, yr, M *rare*

___Wild Turkey: 4, yr, RMP

___Northern Bobwhite: 5, yr, MGR

Rails, Coots, Cranes

___Virginia Rail: 3, sr, WB

___Sora: 3, sr, WB

___Common Moorhen: 4, m, WB

___American Coot: 3, m/sr/wv, WB

___Sandhill Crane: 4, m, FGW

Shorebirds

___Semipalmated Plover: 4, m, W

___Killdeer: 2, sr/m, WGB

___American Avocet: 4, m, W

___Greater Yellowlegs: 4, m, W

___Lesser Yellowlegs: 3, m, W

___Solitary Sandpiper: 4, m, W

___Willet: 4, m, W

___Spotted Sandpiper: 2, m/sr, W

___Long-billed Curlew: 4, m, WGT

___Marbled Godwit: 4, m, W

___Western Sandpiper: 4, m, W

___Least Sandpiper: 4, m, W

___Baird's Sandpiper: 4, m, WT

___~~Common~~ *Wilsons* Snipe: 2, sr/m, WB

___Wilson's Phalarope: 3, m, W

___Red-necked Phalarope: 4, m, W

___Pomarine Jaeger: 5, m, WF

___Franklin's Gull: 2, m, WFG

___Bonaparte's Gull, 4, m, WF

___Ring-billed Gull: 3, sr/m/wv, WF

___California Gull: 3, m/sr, WF

___Herring Gull: 4, wv/m, WF

___Sabine's Gull: 5, m, WF

___Caspian Tern: 5, m, WF

___Forster's Tern: 4, wv, WF

___Black Tern: 4, m, WF

Doves, Pigeons, Cuckoos

___Rock Dove: 3, yr, HF

___Band-tailed Pigeon: 3, sr/yr, PHF

___Mourning Dove: 3, sr/yr, GPMF

___Yellow-billed Cuckoo: 5, sr/m, R

Owls

Need ___Flammulated Owl: 4, sr, PD

___Eastern Screech-Owl: 3, yr

___Great Horned Owl: 2, yr, PRF

Need ___Northern Pygmy-Owl: 3, yr, APDSR *(uncommon)*

___Long-eared Owl: 4, ir, DPAR

Need ___Boreal Owl: 4, yr, SP *(rare)(spruce/Pine)*

Need ___Northern Saw-whet Owl: 3, yr, PD

Nighthawks, Swifts
___Common Nighthawk: 2, sr, FGPH
___Common Poorwill: 4, sr, FGPH
___Black Swift: 4, sr, FH
___Chimney Swift: 4, sr, FH
___White-throated Swift: 3, sr, FH

Hummingbirds, Kingfishers
___Magnificent Hummingbird: 5, m/sr, FAPR
___Black-chinned Hummingbird: 4, sr, FAPR
___Calliope Hummingbird: 4, m/sr, FAPR
___Broad-tailed Hummingbird: 1, sr, FAPDR
___Rufous Hummingbird: 2, m, FAPR
___Belted Kingfisher: 2, sr/yr, FW

Woodpeckers
___Lewis's Woodpecker: 4, m/sr, PAR
___Red-headed Woodpecker: 4, sr, PAR
___Red-naped Sapsucker: 2, sr, APRS
___Williamson's Sapsucker: 3, sr, PA
___Downy Woodpecker: 3, yr, RAPD
___Hairy Woodpecker: 3, yr, RAPD
___Three-toed Woodpecker: 4, yr/ir, PSDA
___Northern Flicker: 1, sr/yr, PDAR

Flycatchers
___Olive-sided Flycatcher: 3, sr, SDP
___Western Wood-Pewee: 2, sr, AP
___Willow Flycatcher: 3, sr, BR
___Least Flycatcher: 4, m, RA
___Hammond's Flycatcher: 2, sr, SD
Need ___Dusky Flycatcher: 3, sr, ARP *(uncommon)*
Need ___Cordilleran Flycatcher: 2, sr, PAR
          (fairly common)

___Black Phoebe: 5, m, RG
___Say's Phoebe: 3, m, GT
___Ash-throated Flycatcher: 5, m/sr, RP
___Cassin's Kingbird: 5, m, GR
___Western Kingbird: 3, m, GRT
___Eastern Kingbird: 4, m, GR

Larks, Swallows
___Horned Lark: 1, sr/yr, TG
___Purple Martin: 5, m, FAPD
___Tree Swallow: 1, sr/m, FAPG
___Violet-green Swallow: 1, sr/m, FAPG
___Northern Rough-winged Swallow: 4, sr, FGR
___Cliff Swallow: 2, sr/m, FGHR
___Barn Swallow: 1, sr/m, FGHR

Jays, Crows, Magpies
___Gray Jay: 2, yr, SDP
___Steller's Jay: 1, yr, PADS
___Blue Jay: 4, yr/ir, RPA
___Western Scrub-Jay: 4, ir, MR
___Pinyon Jay: 4, ir, MR
___Clark's Nutcracker: 1, yr, KSP
___Black-billed Magpie: 1, yr, GAPR
___American Crow: 2, yr, FGP
___Common Raven: 2, yr, FGPTHR

Chickadees, Nuthatches, Creepers
___Black-capped Chickadee: 2, yr, RAP
___Mountain Chickadee: 1, yr, PDSAR
___Plain Titmouse: 5, sr, RP
___Red-breasted Nuthatch: 2, yr, SPD
___White-breasted Nuthatch: 2, yr, PAR
___Pygmy Nuthatch: 1, yr, PD
___Brown Creeper: 2, yr, SDPR

Wrens, Dippers

___Rock Wren: 3, sr, H

___Canyon Wren: 3, sr/yr, H

___Bewick's Wren: 5, m, M

___House Wren: 1, sr/m, APDRH

___Winter Wren: 5, m, R

___Marsh Wren: 5, m, BW

___American Dipper: 2, yr, W

Kinglets, Gnatcatchers

___Golden-crowned Kinglet: 2, yr, SDP

___Ruby-crowned Kinglet: 1, sr/m, SDPA

___Blue-gray Gnatcatcher: 4, m/sr, RM

Bluebirds, Thrushes, Thrashers

___Eastern Bluebird: 4, m, PAG

___Western Bluebird: 3, m/sr, PAG

___Mountain Bluebird: 1, sr/m, APGT

___Townsend's Solitaire: 2, yr, PH

___Veery: 4, sr/m, RAH

___Swainson's Thrush: 3, sr, DSR

___Hermit Thrush: 2, sr, SD

___Wood Thrush: 5, m, R

___American Robin: 1, sr/m/yr, PGDR

___Varied Thrush: 5, m, R

___Gray Catbird: 4, sr, RM

___Northern Mockingbird: 4, m, RM

___Sage Thrasher: 3, m/sr/mG

___Brown Thrasher: 4, sr, RM

Pipits, Waxwings, Shrikes

___American Pipit: 1, sr/m, TG

?
.___Sprague's Pipit: 5, m, G

?
.___Bohemian Waxwing: 1, 4, ir, FPRM

___Cedar Waxwing: 1, 4, ir, PRM

___Northern Shrike: 3, wv, GMR

___Loggerhead Shrike: 4, m, GMR

Starlings, Vireos

___European Starling: 2, yr, GRPA

___Plumbeous Vireo: 3, sr, PA

___Warbling Vireo: 1, sr, ARB

___Red-eyed Vireo: 5, m/sr, RA

Wood Warblers

___Blue-winged Warbler: 5, m, BR

___Golden-winged Warbler: 5, sr, R

___Tennessee Warbler: 5, sr, RBAP

___Orange-crowned Warbler: 4, m/sr, RBAP

___Nashville Warbler: 5, m, RPA

___Virginia's Warbler: 3, sr/mRPA

___Northern Parula: 5, sr, R

___Yellow Warbler: 3, m/sr, RB

___Chestnut-sided Warbler: 5, sr/m, RM

___Magnolia Warbler: 5, m/sr, RPS

___Cape May Warbler: 5, m/sr, RS

___Black-throated Blue Warbler: 5, m/sr, RS

___Yellow-rumped Warbler: 1, sr/m/wv, SDPRA

___Black-throated Gray Warbler: 5, m, RMP

___Townsend's Warbler: 3, m/sr, DSPRA

___Black-throated Green Warbler: 5, m, RP

___Blackburnian Warbler: 5, sr, RP

___Grace's Warbler: 5, m, PR

___Palm Warbler: 5, m, R

___Bay-breasted Warbler: 5, m/sr, RS

___Black-and-white Warbler: 5, m, R

___American Redstart: 5, sr/m, R

___Worm-eating Warbler: 5, m, R

___Ovenbird: 5, m, RAP

___Northern Waterthrush: 5, m, WBR

___Connecticut Warbler: 5, m, R

___MacGillivray's Warbler: 3, sr, RB
___Common Yellowthroat: 4, m, BR
___Hooded Warbler: 5, m/sr, R
___Wilson's Warbler: 1, sr/m, BR
___Yellow-breasted Chat: 5, m, RM

Tanagers
___Hepatic Tanager: 5, sr, PR
___Scarlet Tanager: 5, sr, RP
___Western Tanager: 3, sr, PD

Grosbeaks, Buntings, Sparrows
___Rose-breasted Grosbeak: 4, m/sr, R
___Black-headed Grosbeak: 3, sr, RPA
___Blue Grosbeak: 5, m, R
___Lazuli Bunting: 4, sr, RM
___Indigo Bunting: 5, m, R
___Green-tailed Towhee: 1, sr/m, HPMR   *Need*
___Spotted Towhee: 4, m/sr/wv, HMR
___Brown Towhee: 5, sr, HMP   *need*
___American Tree Sparrow: 3, wv, GR
___Chipping Sparrow: 1, m/sr, PG   *Need*
___Clay-colored Sparrow: 5, m, GRM
___Brewer's Sparrow: 3, sr/m, MG   *Need*
___Vesper Sparrow: 2, m/sr, GT
___Lark Sparrow: 4, sr/m, G
___Black-throated Sparrow: 5, m, R
Need ___Sage Sparrow: 5, m, MG *(accidental)*
___Lark Bunting: 4, m, GTM
___Savannah Sparrow: 2, sr/m, GBT
___Fox Sparrow: 4, sr/m, RBH
___Song Sparrow: 2, m/sr, BR
___Lincoln's Sparrow: 1, sr, BR
___White-throated Sparrow: 5, m/wv, RM
___Golden-crowned Sparrow: 5, m, RB

___White-crowned Sparrow: 1, sr/m, KBR
___Harris's Sparrow: 4, m, RG
___Dark-eyed Junco: 1, yr, PDSRAH

Blackbirds, Meadowlark, Oriole
___Bobolink: 5, m/sr, G
___Red-winged Blackbird: 2, sr/m, BGR
___Western Meadowlark: 3, sr, G
___Yellow-headed Blackbird: 4, m, BR
___Rusty Blackbird: 5, m, BR
___Brewer's Blackbird: 2, m/sr, GRBW
___Common Grackle: 3, m/sr, RG
___Brown-headed Cowbird: 2, sr/m, GPRBA
___Bullock's Oriole: 3, sr/m, R

Finches
Need ___Brown-capped Rosy Finch: 2, sr/wv, TG   *fairly common*
___Gray-crowned Rosy Finch: 3, ir/wv, TG   *(uncommon)*
Need ___Black Rosy Finch: 4, ir/wv, TG *(rare)*
___Pine Grosbeak: 2, yr, SP
___Cassin's Finch: 2, yr, SP *(fairly common)*
___House Finch: 1, yr, PAMR
___Red Crossbill: 2, yr/ir, FSPDR
___White-winged Crossbill: 4, ir, SPR
___Common Redpoll: 4, ir/wv, G
___Pine Siskin: 1, yr, FSPD
___Lesser Goldfinch: 4, sr, RMPG
___American Goldfinch: 3, m/sr/wv, RG
___Evening Grosbeak: 3, yr/ir, PDS

Weaver Finch
___House Sparrow: 2, yr, G

Checklist of the Birds of Lake Estes

The following birds have been seen at Lake Estes and the Matthews-Reeser Bird Sanctuary. Sightings from adjacent areas—Wapiti Meadows below Olympus Dam, Fish Creek Arm and inlet, and the Lake Estes Trail—are included. An early arrival date for each species is given, if known.

The list covers 230 species, plus four subspecies. Many of the species are uncommon in the mountains; some are rare to Colorado. The abundance and season codes are based on their occurrence in this area.

Abundance codes:

1 = common, to be expected in proper habitat

2 = fairly common, not always seen

3 = uncommon, seldom seen but not a surprise

4 = rare, extremely unusual, often out of normal range

5 = accidental, far out of normal range.

Season codes:

yr = year-around resident

sp = spring migrant (April 1–June 1)

sr = summer resident or visitor (June 1–Sept. 1)

f = fall migrant (Sept. 1–Nov. 1)

wv = winter visitor (Nov. 1–April 1)

Loons, Grebes

___Common Loon: 3, sp/f, 4/15

___Pacific Loon: 5, wv, 11/1

___Horned Grebe: 4, sp, 4/12

___Eared Grebe: 4, sp/f, 4/8

___Pied-billed Grebe: 3, wv, 1/1

___Western Grebe: 4, sp, 4/8

*Need*___Clark's Grebe: 4, sp/sr *rare*

___American White Pelican: 4, sp/f, 4/24

___Double-crested Cormorant: 3, sp/f, 4/3

Egrets, Herons

___Great Blue Heron: 2, sp; 3, sr, 3/17

___Snowy Egret: 4, sp, 4/28

___Cattle Egret: 4, sp, 4/28

___Green Heron: 5, sp, 5/4

___Black-crowned Night-Heron: 4, sp, 4/13

___White-faced Ibis: 3, sp, 4/11

Swans, Geese, Ducks

___Trumpeter Swan: 5, wv, 2/6

___Tundra Swan: 5, wv, 3/15

___Canada Goose: 1, yr

___Snow Goose: 4, wv, 2/27

___Wood Duck: 3, sp, 4/6

___Mallard: 1, yr

___Gadwall: 2, sp/f, 3/14

___Northern Pintail: 3, sp, 2/17

___American Wigeon: 1, sp/f; 3, wv, 1/3

___Northern Shoveler: 2, sp, 3/10

___Cinnamon Teal: 3, sp/f, 3/29

___Blue-winged Teal: 2, sp/f, 4/17

___Green-winged Teal: 2, sp/f; 4, wv, 1/1

___Canvasback: 3, sp/f, 4/22

___Redhead: 1, sp; 3, wv, 1/1

___Ring-necked Duck: 1, sp/f/wv, 1/1

___Lesser Scaup: 1, sp/f, 2/26

___Long-tailed Duck: 5, wv, 11/18

___White-winged Scoter: 5, wv, 12/12

___Surf Scoter: 5, wv, 11/1

___Common Goldeneye: 1, sp/f/wv, 1/1

___Barrow's Goldeneye: 4, wv, 2/2

___Bufflehead: 3, wv, 3/5

___Hooded Merganser: 4, wv, 3/3

___Common Merganser: 2, yr

___Ruddy Duck: 3, sp/f, 4/11

Raptors

___Turkey Vulture: 1, sr, 4/6

___Northern Harrier: 4, sp/f

___Cooper's Hawk: 3, sr, 4/20

___Sharp-shinned Hawk: 3, sr, 4/20

___Northern Goshawk: 3, sr, 4/27

___Broad-winged Hawk: 5, sp, 5/19

___Swainson's Hawk: 4, sp/f

___Red-tailed Hawk: 1, yr

___Rough-legged Hawk: 4, wv, 12/16

___Bald Eagle: 3, sp/f/wv, 1/1

___Golden Eagle: 3, yr

___Osprey: 2, sp/f, 4/11

___Merlin: 4, sp/f

___American Kestrel: 3, sr, 4/19

___Prairie Falcon: 2, yr

___Peregrine Falcon: 4, sr, 5/3

Coots, Rails, Cranes

___American Coot: 3, sr, 4/11

___Sora: 4, sp; 3, sr, 5/11

___Sandhill Crane: 4, sp/f

Shorebirds

___Semipalmated Plover: 4, sp, 5/2

___Killdeer: 1, sp; 3, sr, 3/16

___American Avocet: 2, sp, 4/11

___Greater Yellowlegs: 4, sp, 3/29

___Lesser Yellowlegs: 3, sp, 4/10

___Solitary Sandpiper: 4, sp, 4/28

___Willet: 2, sp, 4/25

___Spotted Sandpiper: 1, sp; 2, sr, 4/15

___Long-billed Curlew: 3, sp, 5/8

___Marbled Godwit: 4, sp, 4/18

___Baird's Sandpiper: 4, sp, 4/8

___Western Sandpiper: 3, sp, 4/30

___Semipalmated Sandpiper: 3, sp, 5/1

___Least Sandpiper: 3, sp, 4/28

___Long-billed Dowitcher: 3, sp, 5/1

___Short-billed Dowitcher: 4, sp, 5/2

___Common Snipe: 1, sp; 2, sr, 3/23 *[Wilson's]*

___Wilson's Phalarope: 3, sp, 5/2

___Red-necked Phalarope: 5, sp, 5/15

Gulls, Terns

___Bonaparte's Gull: 4, sp, 4/11

___Black-headed Gull: 5, f, 10/24

___Franklin's Gull: 3, sp, 4/8

___Ring-billed Gull: 3, sp, 4/25

___California Gull: 2, sr, 3/17

___Herring Gull: 3, wv, 1/2

___Thayer's Gull: 5, wv, 1/10

___Sabine's Gull: 5, f, 9/23

___Black-legged Kittiwake: 5, sp

___Caspian Tern: 5, sp, 5/7

___Common Tern: 5, f, 9/23

___Forster's Tern: 4, sp/f, 4/28

___Black Tern: 4, sp, 5/15

Doves, Pigeons

___Mourning Dove: 2, sr, 4/27

___Rock Dove: 2, yr

___Band-tailed Pigeon: 4, sr, 4/28

Owls, Nighthawks

___Great Horned Owl: 3, yr

___Common Nighthawk: 3, sr, 6/30

Swifts, Hummingbirds, Kingfishers

___Chimney Swift: 4, sp, 5/22

___Broad-tailed Hummingbird: 1, sr, 5/2

___Rufous Hummingbird: 3, f, 8/15

___Belted Kingfisher: 1, sr; 3, wv, 1/2

Woodpeckers

___Red-headed Woodpecker: 4, sp, 5/28

___Red-naped Sapsucker: 3, sp/f

___Downy Woodpecker: 3, sr, 5/5

___Hairy Woodpecker: 3, sr, 5/1

___Northern Flicker: 1, sr, 3/22

Flycatchers

___Olive-sided Flycatcher: 3, sp/f

___Western Wood-Pewee: 3, sp/f

Need ___Cordilleran Flycatcher: 3, sp/f, 5/16

___Hammond's Flycatcher: 3, sp/f

Need ___Dusky Flycatcher: 3, sp/f, 5/13 *(uncommon)*

___Black Phoebe: 5, sp, 5/11

___Say's Phoebe: 4, sp, 4/8

___Eastern Kingbird: 3, sp, 5/8

___Western Kingbird: 3, sp, 5/29

Shrikes

___Northern Shrike: 3, wv, 2/10

___Loggerhead Shrike: 2, sp, 4/23

Vireos

___Red-eyed Vireo: 5, sp, 5/23

___Warbling Vireo: 3, sp/f, 5/31

Jays, Magpies, Crows
___Steller's Jay: 1, yr
___Blue Jay: 4, sr/wv, 5/13
___Western Scrub-Jay: 4, wv, 2/28
___Clark's Nutcracker: 3, yr
___Black-billed Magpie: 1, yr
___Common Raven: 2, yr
___American Crow: 1, yr

Larks, Swallows
___Horned Lark: 2, sp/f; 4, wv, 1/2
___N. Rough-winged Swallow: 3, sp, 4/22
___Bank Swallow: 3, sp, 4/19
___Violet-green Swallow: 1, sr, 4/3
___Tree Swallow: 1, sr, 4/8
___Cliff Swallow: 2, sr, 5/8
___Barn Swallow: 1, sr, 4/16

Chickadees, Nuthatches, Wrens
___Black-capped Chickadee: 3, sr, 4/8
___Mountain Chickadee: 2, yr
___Red-breasted Nuthatch: 3, yr
___White-breasted Nuthatch: 3, yr
___Pygmy Nuthatch: 1, yr
___Brown Creeper: 3, yr
___Bewick's Wren: 4, sp, 5/7
___House Wren: 1, sr, 4/19
___Marsh Wren: 3, sp, 4/13
___Rock Wren: 3, sp, 5/2
___American Dipper: 1, yr

Kinglets, Gnatcatchers, Solitaires
___Golden-crowned Kinglet: 3, sp, 4/14
___Ruby-crowned Kinglet: 1, sp, 4/3
___Blue-gray Gnatcatcher: 4, sp, 4/22
___Townsend's Solitaire: 2, yr

Bluebirds, Thrushes, Thrashers
___Mountain Bluebird: 2, sr, 3/6
___Western Bluebird: 3, sr, 4/18
___American Robin: 1, sr, 3/16
___Veery: 4, sp, 5/21
___Swainson's Thrush: 3, sp, 4/30
___Hermit Thrush: 3, sp, 4/20
___Gray Catbird: 1, sp, 5/9
___Northern Mockingbird: 3, sp, 5/5
___Brown Thrasher: 2, sp, 5/10
___Sage Thrasher: 3, sp, 4/13

Starlings, Pipits, Waxwings
___European Starling: 2, yr
___Sprague's Pipit: 5, sp, 4/28
___American Pipit: 3, sp, 4/22
___Cedar Waxwing: 2, sr, 5/7

Warblers
___Northern Parula: 5, sp, 5/16
___Orange-crowned Warbler: 3, sp/f, 4/27
___Tennessee Warbler: 4, sp, 5/23
___Blue-winged Warbler: 5, sp, 5/19
___Virginia's Warbler: 3, sp/f, 5/7
___Nashville Warbler: 4, f, 8/27
___Yellow Warbler: 1, sr, 5/5
___Chestnut-sided Warbler: 4, sp, 5/20
___Magnolia Warbler: 4, sp, 5/21
___Yellow-rumped Warbler (M): 2, sp, 4/13
___Yellow-rumped Warbler (A): 1, sr, 4/16
___Black-throated Gray Warbler: 4, sp
___Palm Warbler: 4, sp, 5/10
___Blackpoll Warbler: 4, sp, 5/3
___Prothonotary Warbler: 5, sp, 5/13
___Black-and-white Warbler: 3, sp, 5/15
___American Redstart: 3, sp, 5/11
___Ovenbird: 4, sp, 5/12

___Northern Waterthrush: 3, sp, 5/9

___MacGillivray's Warbler: 3, sp/f, 5/15

___Common Yellowthroat: 1, sp, 4/15

___Wilson's Warbler: 2, sp/f, 5/2

___Yellow-breasted Chat: 4, sp, 5/19

Tanagers, Grosbeaks, Buntings

___Western Tanager: 3, sp/f, 5/17

___Black-headed Grosbeak: 4, sr, 5/16

___Rose-breasted Grosbeak: 4, sp, 5/15

___Blue Grosbeak: 4, sp, 5/19

___Lazuli Bunting: 3, sp/f, 5/22

___Indigo Bunting: 4, sp, 5/19

Sparrows

___Spotted Towhee: 3, sp, 5/3

___Green-tailed Towhee: 2, sr, 4/25

Need ___Sage Sparrow: 5, sp, 5/5   *Accid -*

___Black-throated Sparrow: 5, sp, 5/20

___American Tree Sparrow: 3, wv, 11/1

___Brewer's Sparrow: 2, sp/f, 4/28 *fairly common*

___Clay-colored Sparrow: 2, sp/f, 4/22

___Chipping Sparrow: 2, sp/f, 5/2

Need ___Baird's Sparrow: 5, sp, 5/29 *Accid*

___LeConte's Sparrow: 5, sp, 4/25

___Savannah Sparrow: 1, sp, 4/8

___Vesper Sparrow: 1, sp/f, 4/15

___Lark Bunting: 4, sp/f, 5/15

___Lark Sparrow: 3, sp/f, 5/9

___Harris's Sparrow: 4, sp, 5/23

___Golden-crowned Sparrow: 5, sp, 5/5

___White-throated Sparrow: 4, f, 9/27

___White-crowned Sparrow: 1, sp/f, 4/26

___Song Sparrow: 1, sr, 3/12

___Lincoln's Sparrow: 1, sr, 4/18

___Dark-eyed Junco (Oregon): 2, wv

___Dark-eyed Junco (Pink-sided): 2, wv

___Dark-eyed Junco (White-winged): 3, wv

___Dark-eyed Junco (Gray-headed): 2, yr

Need ___Smith's Longspur: 5, sp *(accidental)*

___Snow Bunting: 5, wv, 1/3

Meadowlarks, Blackbirds, Orioles

___Western Meadowlark: 3, sp, 4/5

___Bobolink: 3, sp, 5/6

___Brown-headed Cowbird: 2, sr, 4/28

___Yellow-headed Blackbird: 3, sp, 5/19

___Red-winged Blackbird: 1, sr, 2/28

___Brewer's Blackbird: 1, sr, 3/22

___Common Grackle: 1, sr, 3/30

___Bullock's Oriole: 4, sp, 5/18

___Baltimore Oriole: 5, sp, 5/24

___Evening Grosbeak: 3, sr, 4/13

Finches, Crossbills, Siskins

___Gray-crowned Rosy Finch: 4, wv, 11/10

Need ___Cassin's Finch: 3, sp/f/wv, 3/22 *(uncommon)*

___House Finch: 1, yr

___Red Crossbill: 3, wv, 10/19

___Common Redpoll: 5, wv, 3/16

___Pine Siskin: 1, yr

___Lesser Goldfinch: 4, sp/f, 5/14

___American Goldfinch: 3, sp/f, 4/22

___House Sparrow: 1, yr

Annotated Bibliography of Useful Books

Bird Field Guides

Birds of North America, by Kenn Kaufman, Houghton Mifflin. Unlike the other guides listed here, this book uses photographs. Unlike other guides that use photographs, this one works well, due to the computer enhancements that produce photos that are typical of the species. The commentary is brief but very good, especially for the beginning birders for whom it was written. Recommended as a first guide.

A Field Guide to Western Birds, by Roger Tory Peterson, Houghton Mifflin. One in the series of bird guides that started it all. Peterson's illustrations are still the best, but the guide has two disadvantages. The maps are separated from the entries and only western birds are included.

Field Guide to the Birds of North America, Third Edition, National Geographic. National G, as birders call this guide, includes all North American birds in one book small enough to carry in the field. Maps are on the same page as entries. Text is detailed and covers subspecies and plumage differences. Illustrations were done by a number of people, so consistency and quality vary. Still, this is the book most experienced birders carry in the field.

The Sibley Guide to Birds, by David Sibley, National Audubon Society. The publication of this book marked another milestone in field guides, if you consider a book this large something you'd carry on your birding walks. More detailed, with many plumages and subspecies illustrated. Flight patterns and other identification keys are also detailed. Skimpy on text, but a book many experienced birders use for difficult identifications. We carry one in the car (and sometimes in our packs).

Advanced Birding, by Kenn Kaufman, Houghton Mifflin. This book will take you to the next level of identification skills. Don't let the title intimidate you. A beginner trying to identify a Dusky Flycatcher in RMNP can use this book and will learn from it. Covers many other troublesome species.

Books on Birding in Colorado

A Birder's Guide to Colorado, by Harold Holt, American Birding Association. The classic guide to Colorado birding, updated in 1997. Covers the entire state, concentrating on popular sites such as RMNP and Pawnee National Grass-lands. A great companion to this guide, if you're traveling elsewhere in the state.

Colorado Breeding Bird Atlas, edited by Hugh Kingery, Colorado Bird Partner-ship. A detailed guide to all the birds that breed in Colorado. Each entry is an article on the nesting habits and requirements of each species. A great re-source for those who wish to go beyond bird watching.

Colorado Birds, A Reference to Their Distribution and Habitat, by Robert Andrews and Robert Righter, Denver Museum of Natural History. Known in Colo-rado birding circles as the "Two-Bobs" book, it gives the history of sightings for each species seen in Colorado, detailing where the birds were seen and the dates. Another valuable resource.

Bird Recordings

Bird Songs of the Rocky Mountain States and Provinces, by Robert Righter and Geoffrey Keller, Cornell Laboratory of Ornithology. With a more restricted territory to cover, this set has longer clips of each bird and more variations in the songs. A great choice for RMNP birding.

Peterson Field Guides Western Bird Songs, edited by Roger Tory Peterson, Cornell Laboratory of Ornithology/Houghton Mifflin. Covers the birds of the west-ern United States. Keyed to Peterson's bird guide. If you're traveling farther afield in the West, you'll need the extended coverage.

Other Guides

Rocky Mountain Tree Finder, by Tom Watts, Nature Study Guild. A keyed guide to trees that's easy and fun to use. Knowing the trees will help you find birds, too. Inexpensive and small enough for a shirt pocket.

A Field Guide to Western Butterflies, by Paul Opler and Amy Wright, Houghton Mifflin. An excellent guide for the butterflies of RMNP. Paul Opler gives workshops in the Park and lives in Colorado. Illustrations and supplemental photos. Butterflies are the next frontier.

Butterflies through Binoculars, The West, by Jeffrey Glassberg, Oxford. Another great guide to butterflies you'll find while birding in RMNP. This one uses only photos, which are generally excellent. As with the bird books above, you'll need to look at both and decide which you prefer.

Dragonflies through Binoculars, by Sidney Dunkle, Oxford. The only dragonfly field guide. Photographs of all North American species. And you thought birds were tough!

Guide to Colorado Wildflowers, by G. K. Guennel, Westcliffe. Two volumes, one for the plains and foothills and one for the mountains, but you'll need both if you're serious about flower identification. A great guide for the novice who doesn't want to plow through scientific terms. Illustrations and photographs.

Plants of Rocky Mountain National Park, by Linda and Richard Beidleman and Beatrice Willard, Falcon. Addresses all the plant life, not just flowers, but it's specific to RMNP. With scientific keys and photographs.

Rocky Mountain National Park Dayhiker's Guide, by Jerome Malitz, Johnson Books. A scenic guide to hikes in the Park with color pictures throughout. A good supplement to this text for the birder who enjoys hiking.

Land Above the Trees: A Guide to American Alpine Tundra, by Ann H. Zwinger and Beatrice E. Willard, Johnson Books. Describes the alpine regions of the U.S., including their plants, animals, climate, geology, land forms, and human history.

Other Books

Rocky Mountain Splendor, A Mile-by-Mile Guide for Rocky Mountain National Park, by Doris Osterwald, Western Guideways, Ltd. Learn history and geology and lots of other information about RMNP as you drive along its roads. Now out of print, unfortunately. If you can find a used copy, buy it.

Index

Hummingbird, cont.
  Magnificent, 167
  Rufous, 115, 118, 119, 167
    best locations for, 115, 118
  hummingbird feeders, *see* feeders,
    hummingbird
  hypothermia, hazards of, 145

Ibis, White-faced, 5, 36, 112, 124, 125,
    132, 155
insect problems, 146–147

Jaeger, Pomarine, 162
Jay, Blue, 172
  Gray, 12, 38, 51, 59, 97, 99, 100,
    102, 172
    best locations for, 99
    birding tips for, 99
  Pinyon, 172
  Steller's, 10, 12, 19, 38, 45, 51, 75,
    83, 99, 102, 105, 171
  Western Scrub-, *see* Scrub-jay, Western
Junco, Dark-eyed, 41, 45, 51, 72, 74,
    104, 105, 118, 119, 187, 188

Kaufman, Kenn, 23, 170
Kawuneeche Valley, 61
Kawuneeche Visitor Center, 62
Kestrel, American, 80, 158
Killdeer, 5, 11, 130, 161
Kingbird, Eastern, 30, 127, 170
  Western, 30, 127, 171
Kingfisher, Belted, 11, 104, 117, 131,
    167
Kinglet, Golden-crowned, 12, 13, 14,
    18, 29, 100, 101, 178
    best locations for, 12
  Ruby-crowned, 10, 12, 14, 15, 18, 23,
    25, 41, 42, 61, 62, 70, 74, 93,
    99, 102, 105, 117, 178
Kittiwake, Black-legged, 163
Kleinschnitz, F.C., 153, 158
krummholz, 15, 52, 53

Lake Estes, 11, 109, 121, 137, 140, 141
  directions to, 123
Lake Irene, 59, 61
Lark, Horned, 15, 52, 55, 56, 58, 111,
    174

Lava Cliffs, 55–56, 59
Lawn Lake, 5, 8, 9, 52
Lawn Lake flood, 9, 52
lightning, hazards of, 145
Lily Lake, 33, 34, 35–37
  directions to, 34
Little Horseshoe Park, 5, 16–17
Loch Vale, 100, 101
Longs Peak, 33, 37, 38
Longspur, Smith's, 188
Loon, Common, 123, 154
  Pacific, 154
Lumpy Ridge, 77, 79, 82
  directions to, 77
  weather warning for, 80

MacGregor Falls, 84, 85
MacGregor Ranch, 78, 79, 83
MacGregor Ranch Museum, 78, 111
Magpie, Black-billed, 9, 10, 23, 27, 30,
    38, 69, 73, 80, 89, 105, 112,
    114, 172
Mallard, 5, 11, 25, 35, 41, 42, 61, 88,
    102, 121, 124, 127, 155
Many Parks Curve, 51
maps, recommended, xvi
Martin, Purple, 174
Mary's Lake, 109, 115, 141
Mary's Lake Road, 34
Matthews-Reeser Bird Sanctuary, *see*
    Bird Sanctuary, Matthews-Reeser
McGraw Ranch, 87
Meadowlark, Western, 30, 111, 188
medical care, contact information for,
    151
Medicine Bow Curve, 15, 50, 53, 56,
    59
Meeker Park Lodge, 38
Merganser, Common, 115, 124, 156
  Hooded, 121, 123, 141, 156
  Red-breasted, 156
Merlin, 158
Mills, Enos, 38
Milner Pass, 59
Mockingbird, Northern, 180
Moorhen, Common, 160
moose, 61, 149
  hazards of, 149
Moraine Avenue, 34

SCOTT ROEDERER, a Colorado native, has birded Rocky Mountain National Park for over 30 years and has lived in Estes Park, gateway to the Park, since 1983. He and his wife, Julie, served as local guides and trip planners for a National Audubon convention in Estes Park and a national American Birding Association convention in Ft. Collins, scouting and co-leading trips in Rocky Mountain National Park for Kenn Kaufman, John Dunn, and other nationally known birders. He is a member of the American Birding Association and the Estes Park Bird Club and is the compiler of the Rocky Mountain National Park Christmas Bird Count. He is a book editor, flyfishing and birding guide, and high school guidance counselor. A LeConte's Sparrow, seen at Lake Estes in 1998, was his 600th life bird. This is his third book.